# CHINA LAW READER

中国法律读本

# CHINA LAW READER

中国法律读本

LAWRENCE FOSTER, TIFFANY YAJIMA, YAN LIN

Long River Press
San Francisco

China Law Reader

Published in the United States of America by
Sinomedia International Group
Long River Press
360 Swift Avenue, Suite 48
South San Francisco, CA 94080
www.longriverpress.com

Distributed by

Sinomedia International Group
China Books (www.chinabooks.com)

10 9 8 7 6 5 4 3 2 1

Printed in China

ISBN 10: 1-59265-151-8

ISBN 13: 978-1-59265-151-1

Editor: Jing Yang
Cover design: Tiffany Cha

Library of Congress Cataloging-in-Publication Data
China law reader / edited by Lawrence Foster, Tiffany Yajima, Yan Lin.
    pages cm
 ISBN 978-1-59265-151-1 (pbk.)
 1. Law--China. I. Foster, Lawrence, editor II. Yajima, Tiffany, editor.
III. Lin, Yan, (professor) editor.
 KNQ440.C47 2013
 349.51--dc23
                          2013019263

# Acknowledgements

We gratefully acknowledge the early and ongoing support of the University of Hawaii's National Resource Center for East Asia, in particular Drs. Robert Huey and Gay Satsuma. Their excitement about the value of this project kept us going through the long days and dark nights of drafting, editing, and revising.

We acknowledge the work of two research assistants at the William S. Richardson School of Law, Dr. Brian MacKintosh and Thomas Moriarty, Esq. They both did the initial work on the two law cases and Brian worked on English edits of the CLR.

Finally, Dr. Foster would like to thank the students in his Readings in Chinese Law course in 2008, 2009, 2010 who suggested ways to improve on drafts of the CLR.

# Authors of Introductions to the Readings

**Ronald C. Brown,** *Introduction to China's Labor Contract Law.* Mr. Brown is a Professor of Law at the University of Hawaii, William S. Richardson School of Law.

**Lawrence C. Foster,** *Introduction to the Constitution of the People's Republic of China.* Mr. Foster is a Professor of Law at the University of Hawaii, William S. Richardson School of Law and is a co-author of the *China Law Reader*.

**Luckie Hong,** *Introduction to China's Intellectual Property Law System.* Mr. Hong is a Registered Foreign Lawyer (PRC) with Jones Day, Hong Kong, SAR.

**Lin Yan,** *A Brief Legal History of Modern China and Introduction to the Legislation Law.* Dr. Lin is an Associate Professor of Law at Ko Guan Law School, Jiaotong University in Shanghai, China. Dr Lin is co-author of the *China Law Reader*.

**Mana Moriarty,** *Introduction to Case Law in China.* Mr. Moriarty has lived in China and overseas for more than a decade. His areas of interest include civil litigation, immigration, and discrimination law.

**Keiko Okuhara,** *Introduction to Chinese Legal Research.* Ms. Okuhara is Bibliographic Services/Systems Librarian at the William S. Richardson School of Law at the University of Hawaii.

**Wang Kai,** *Introduction to China's Property Law System.* Ms. Wang is of counsel at DLA Piper in Beijing.

**Wang Zhizhou,** *Introduction to Contract Law in the PRC and Introduction to the Law on Corporations in the PRC.* Mr. Wang is an LLM-LI candidate at the University of Wisconsin-Madison Law School and has an LLM from Shanghai Jiaotong University Law School.

**Xue Yi,** *Introduction to China's Anti-Monopoly Law System.* Mr. Xue is a Partner at Zhong Lun Law Firm in Beijing, PRC.

**Tiffany Yajima,** *Introduction to China's Environmental Laws.* Ms. Yajima is a licensed attorney who has lived and worked in mainland China for more than a decade. She is co-author of the *China Law Reader*.

**Yang Wantao,** *Introduction to China's Banking Law System.* Mr. Yang is a Partner at Zhong Lun Law Firm in Shanghai, PRC.

# China Law Reader
## Table of Contents

# Introduction to the *China Law Reader*

# 中国　　法律　　读本

Zhōngguó　　Fǎlǜ　　Dúběn

Welcome to the *China Law Reader* (CLR)!

The primary purpose of the CLR is to introduce you to the language of Chinese law. The ideal user is someone who has completed at least two years of Chinese language study and is now ready to read actual law-related Chinese language texts in order to learn the specialized language of Chinese law. A side benefit of the CLR is to provide a broad introduction to the nature and substance of Chinese law.

The selections may be read in any order. Each selection has a complete, independent vocabulary section. As you read through several selections, you will begin to see some repetition in vocabulary and grammar patterns. These patterns and vocabulary, together with the vocabulary specific to each area of law, represent the language of Chinese law.

Few of the selections are complete texts. This is because the primary purpose of the CLR is to introduce the reader to the language of Chinese law, not Chinese law itself. Thus, we opted for breadth rather than depth in order to expose the reader to a wide variety of legal documents and areas of law. Each text was selected based on several objective and subjective criteria including importance of the material, "hot topic" issues and the personal preferences of the authors.

Where applicable, each selection includes a URL for the original text. In selecting readings, we discovered that there are many corrupted versions of the original texts available on line, even on Chinese government websites. This adds to the complexity of researching Chinese law, a topic which will be touched on in a separate section of the CLR.

Related, we chose not to provide citations to English language translations of the readings. In preparing the text, we reviewed a number of these translations and often found wide variation among translations of the same text. We felt many of these translations were less than ideal which further justified our continued work on the CLR.

The selections range from the Constitution to laws to interpretations of those laws by a variety of government agencies, and from regulations to a variety of documents drafted by Chinese lawyers including law office e-mail.

Each section of the CLR is preceded by a brief introduction to the area of law in that section. These introductions are written by the authors and a variety of practitioners and professors with special expertise in those areas.

In each text, bolding is used to indicate a vocabulary item. Italicizes are used to help the reader navigate through a complex sentence and also indicates two or more words which go together, e.g. the subject, verb, and object of a complicated sentence.

In the vocabulary sections, we include a variety of comments to help the reader better understand the text. These are called Law Practice Tips and Background Tips. Law Practice Tips provide information on how the law works in real life. Background Tips provide background information on such topics as legal English, grammar, culture and political terminology.

Finally, there is a brief section at the end of the CLR that provides the reader with basic information about how to research Chinese law and refers the reader to the gurus of Chinese legal research such as Professor Luo Wei at Washington University Law School whose web page http://law.wustl.edu/Chinalaw/ and text *Chinese Law and Legal Research*, are tremendous aids to those interested in researching Chinese law in English or Chinese.

In the vocabulary sections, some translations use general English translations. In the particular context, the word might have a slightly different or more appropriate English meaning. It is assumed that the reader will be able to come up with that more appropriate meaning on their own. In the case of specific legal terms, the most commonly used English translation is provided. For example, the term 检察院 is translated as "procuratorate" rather than its more literal translation of "office of [government] investigation." Moreover, in part because there is no official translation of Chinese laws, there is no official translation of any of the terms of art found in Chinese legal documents. The lack of an official translation can make it difficult to do electronic research in English on Chinese law. Even the names of Chinese laws may have two or more English translations. For example, the name of the Chinese law, 律师法(Lùshīfǎ), has at least two translations: Law on Lawyers and Lawyers Law.

When necessary, we primarily consulted two dictionaries in providing translations in the vocabulary sections. The first is John DeFrancis (ed.), *ABC Chinese-English Dictionary*, 1996, University of Hawaii Press. The second is 叙述华 and 文嘉 eds., 新汉英法学词典, 4th ed. 2005, 法律出版社. We also consulted the Chinese internet search engine Baidu (百度) http://www.baidu.com/.

In each vocabulary section, we have included

pīnyīn (romanization) for each character. The pīnyīn follows the rules set forth in the DeFrancis dictionary. For example, in instances where a tone changes due to the nature of the following tone (known as "tone sandhi"), the original tone is provided and it is assumed the reader will know the basic conventions on how tones change. For example, when there are two third tones in a row, the first third tone shifts to a second tone when pronounced. In the CLR, both tones will be shown as third tones. Thus, the pīnyīn for the two characters 很好 would be hěnhǎo, but pronounced hénhǎo.

We are indebted for the pioneering work of Chi Wenshun whose language texts published by the University of California Press in the 1960s and 1970s first introduced Chinese language students in the West to PRC legal materials: *Readings in Chinese Communist Ideology*, *Readings in Chinese Communist Documents*, and *Readings in the Chinese Communist Cultural Revolution*. Those familiar with the format of those texts will recognize the similar format used in this text.

For those of you interested in a formal linguistic approach to the language of legal Chinese, see the pioneering work by Professor Deborah Cao of Griffiths University in Australia, such as her 2004 book *Chinese Law: a Language Perspective*.

For those interested in using the CLR in an educational setting, Professor Foster found in-class group reading and translation works best. The in-class format is meant to encourage rough translation because it reveals students' understanding (or misunderstanding) of the grammar and language of the text. For many of the readings, polished translations are widely available on the Internet for reference. Students can and do use those translations but the practice should be discouraged because the in-class focus should be on comprehension, not polish.

The famous Chinese translator, Yan Fu (严复 1854-1921), had three goals for translations: 1) faithfulness to the original text (信 xìn), 2) clarity and coherence (达 dá), and 3) elegance (雅 yǎ). The CLR focuses on the first two of these three goals. This focus betrays the bias of a lawyer. The normal primary goal of legal writing is accuracy and clear communication.

A brief word about the authors. Lawrence C. Foster earned a Ph.D. in Chinese Language and Literature in 1974 from the University of Washington and spent five years teaching Chinese language before he entered law school. He currently is a Professor of Law at the William S. Richardson School of Law at the University of Hawaii. He recently spent over two years working as Senior Counsel at a major international Chinese law firm in Shanghai.

Lin Yan (林严) is Assistant Professor of Law and former Associate Dean at Shanghai Jiao Tong University's Ko Guan Law School where he specializes in Chinese constitutional law, comparative constitutional law, as well as legislation. He received his LLM from East China University of Politics and Law in Shanghai and an SJD from the University of Wisconsin.

Tiffany Yajima (陆妙兰) is a graduate of the William S. Richardson School of Law at the University of Hawaii. She served as extern to a federal judge in the U.S. District Court for the District of Hawaii, was elected President of the law school's Pacific-Asian Legal Studies Organization, and served as Editor and Managing Editor of the Asian Pacific Law & Policy Journal. Prior to law school, she was senior researcher at a major U.S. international law firm in Shanghai. She now resides in Honolulu where she consults for think tanks and organizations focused on Asia-pacific-related issues.

## I. The Language of Chinese Law

### A. The Importance of Language and Law

Law is all about language. Law makers communicate the law through language and lawyers spend a good deal of their time communicating about the law (i.e. interpreting the law) to clients, other lawyers, and decision makers. It is of great importance to have appropriate language to fulfill the intention of the drafter. In the U.S., law and the language of law are often vague and, at times, ambiguous. Legal Chinese is no different in this respect. Two primary skills of the lawyer are to know how to understand, i.e. interpret the law, and then communicate that understanding to others. Therefore, this book can aid in facilitating an understanding of the language of Chinese law and thus make a contribution to foreign understanding of Chinese law and Chinese legal documents.

### B. Four Common Characteristics of Legal Chinese

There are four common characteristics of legal Chinese, the use of: legal terms of art, literary Chinese, commonly used phrases and grammar patterns, and complex sentences. These characteristics, other than the use of legal terms of art, are not exclusive to legal Chinese.

### 1. Legal Terms of Art

The commonly used terms of art are in the vocabulary section of each reading. Because most readings come from different areas of law, many of the terms of art are not repeated from reading to reading. Some more general legal terms of art, such as 法律 (fǎlù law) and 法院 (fǎyuàn court), are found throughout the readings.

### 2. Use of Literary Chinese

Literary Chinese words such as 其 (modern 他/它(们)的), 者 (modern 的人), 及 and 与 (modern 跟 or 和), and 本 (modern 这个) are commonly used in legal Chinese.

### 3. Commonly used words and grammar patterns

经 (jīng) literally means "to go through" or "experience." In translation, it marks a passive verb as in the phrase 经相关机构的批准 to be approved by the relevant agency. The full Chinese term would be the compound 经过 (jīngguò).

由 (yóu by) as in the phrase 由共产党领导的老百姓 the people, who are lead by the CCP, is also used in the sense of "it is up to x to do y."

与 (yǔ together with) as in the phrase 与职工协商 to consult with the staff and workers

Z 所称 (suǒchēng) x 是指 (shìzhǐ) y the term x as it is referred to in z means y

但 (dàn)……除外 (chúwài) except for ...

上／下列 (shàng ／ xiàliè) referred to above/below...

以下简称 (yǐ xià jiǎn chēng) referred to below as...

向 (xiàng) and 对 (duì). These two terms are sometimes translated the same in English (e.g. "to" or "towards") but are actually quite different in Chinese.

向 is used when you do something to or with a person or an entity, e.g. file a report with x, apply to x to do y, register with/at x, report to x, file a lawsuit with the court and disclose to x. Here are some of the verbs it is commonly used with: 报告, 辞职, 登记, 递交, 发出, 发放, 进行, 起诉, 上诉, 设施, 申报, 申请, 提出, 提供, 投资, 泄漏, 支付, 执行, 转售, and 追偿.

对 usually means "with regard to", "with", and "for" (introduces an object or a subject) e.g. to not comply with x, to bear responsibility for x, to act as guarantor for x, to object to x, and to be binding on x. Occasionally, it is used together with 于 (yú), i.e. 对于. Here are some of the verbs it is commonly used with: 不服, 承担责任, 成立, 采取, 担保, 调查, 负责, 给予, 进行, 决定, 免除, 适用, 实加, 实施, 实行, 提供, 享有, 限制, 有异议, 有约束力, 予以, 约定, 造成, 追认, 支付, and 作出.

A lesser used cousin of 对 (duì) in this respect is 就 (jiù). In the selections in this text, it is only used a couple of times.

### 4. Complex Sentences

Legal Chinese tends to be more complex than everyday Chinese. This complexity is perhaps one reason why Chinese book stores offer so many books designed to explain the laws to the Chinese lay person. A good example is the series of publications explaining individual laws prepared by the China Legal Publishing House (中国法制出版社), an organization directly under the State Council's Legal Affairs Office (国务院法制办公室). Their 2008 book, *The Labor Contract Law of the PRC Annotated* (《中华人民共和国劳动合同法：注解与配套》) lists a total of sixty related publications.

For most of the selections in the CLR, the primary challenge will be the vocabulary. In each selection, however, there will be several complex sentences. In some cases, these complex sentences are marked by their length; in some cases, they are marked by their complex modification; and, in a few cases, they are marked by both their length and their complex modification. Below are two sentences which exemplify the complexity of legal Chinese. A goal of the CLR is to get the reader to a stage where they are comfortable in reading complex sentences.

This sentence from Article 2 of the Contract Law is an example of a short, but complicated sentence (see that section of the CLR for the vocabulary used in this sentence).

本法所称**合同**是平等主体的自然人、法人、其他组织之间设立、变更、终止民事权利义务关系的**协议**。

The first thing to notice about the sentence is that it uses the dùnhào (顿号), a punctuation mark unique to Chinese. The dùnhào is very similar to the comma in that it marks a series of verb phrases or noun phrases. The first series of dùnhào in this sentence is used to mark three kinds of actors: natural persons (自然人 zìránrén), legal persons (法人 fǎrén), and other entities (其他组织 qítā zǔzhǐ). The terms "natural and legal persons" are legal terms explained in a Law Practice Tip comment in the vocabulary section.

The second series of dùnhào is used to mark the three kinds of actions by these actors: formation (设立 shèlì), amendment (变更 biàngēng), and termination (终止 zhōngzhī). The subject of the sentence is contract (合同 hétong), marked in bold font above. The word "contract" is modified by the first four characters of the sentence: "(the term x) as it is referred to in this law" (本法所称 x běnfǎ suǒchēng x).

The verb of the sentence is "is" (是 shì), and is bolded and italicized above. The object of the sentence is the last two characters of the sentence, "agreement" (**协议** xiéyì), bolded and underlined above. Thus, the core sentence is: "The term 'contract' as it is referred to in this law is an agreement."

When working with complex sentences, it is often best to begin with identifying the basic components of the sentence, e.g. the subject, verb, and object. Then address the modifiers of those components.

For example, in the sample sentence above, the characters between "is" and "agreement" form three clauses which modify "agreement." The first modification is the actors listed above. The second modification is the kind of actions taken by these actors. The final modification actually modifies the three kinds of actions: what kinds of actions, actions affecting the civil rights and duties and the relationships between (之间 zhījiān) the three actors.

The term "civil rights" is a civil law term which may not be understood by a common law lawyer. The meaning of this term is explained in a Law Practice Tip in the vocabulary section of this text.

The next complicated sentence, from Article 4 of the 2008 Labor Contract Law (see that section of the CLR for the vocabulary used in this sentence), is a good example of how long and complicated legal Chinese can be and thus is the perfect example to demonstrate how to work your way through this kind of sentence.

用人单位**在**制定、修改或者决定有关劳动报酬、工作时间、休息休假、劳动安全卫生、保险福利、职工培训、劳动纪律以及劳动定额管理等直接涉及劳动者切身利益的规章制度或者重大事项**时**，应当经职工代表大会或者全体职工讨论，提出方案和意见，与工会或者职工代表平等协商确定。

The subject of the sentence is "employer" (用

人单位 yòngrén dānwèi which translates literally as "the employing entity"), followed by a temporal clause with three verb phrases with multiple objects. Thus, the first part of the sentence through the end of the temporal clause would read something like "Employers, when doing x, y, and z...." The next word is "shall/must" (应当 yīngdāng). The text following 应当 elaborates on the process employers must follow when doing x, y, and z. The main verb in the sentence is "determine" (确定 quèrèn) and it is at the very end of the sentence. The text between 应当 and 确定 describes the three things the employer must do in the process leading to the ultimate determination by the employer. Each of those three things (clauses) is separated by a comma.

Note the use of the grammar pattern 在⋯⋯时, marked in **bold and enlarged font**. This pattern is used in the sense of "when" (lit. "at the time when") and it is generally used to mark a temporal clause. The temporal clause in this sentence is **bolded and underlined**.

The next thing to notice about the sentence is the now familiar use of the dùnhào. In this sentence, the first dùnhào is used to mark a series of verb phrases: enacting (制定 zhìdìng), amending (修改 xiūgǎi), and deciding (决定 juédìng).

The next series of dùnhào are used to mark a series of noun phrases which are the objects of the three verb phrases: workers' compensation (劳动报酬 láodòng bàochóu), work hours (工作时间 gōngzuò shíjiān), rest times and vacations (休息休假 xiūxīxiūjià), work health and safety (劳动

安全卫生 láodòng ānquán wèishēng), social insurance benefits (保险福利 bǎoxiǎn fúlì), training for the staff and workers (职工培训 zhígōng péixùn), work discipline (劳动纪律 láodòng jìlǜ), management of work quotas (劳动定额管理 láodòng dìng'é guǎnlǐ), and rule systems (规章制度 guīzhāng zhìdù) or major matters (重大事项 zhòngdà shìxiàng).

The term "major matters" is not defined in the statute but arguably includes such matters as large-scale layoffs or closures. The use of vague phrases is common in most, if not all, legal systems and is the reason why most statutes and regulations require the legal research and analytical skills of a lawyer to interpret them correctly.

When used alone at the end of several nouns, 等 (děng) means "etc." In this sentence, 等 is best translated as "and other kinds of." The text following 等 lists the final two objects: "any other kind of rule system or major matter which would directly impact the personal benefits of the employees." Note the complex modification of "rule system" and "major matter" **bolded, italicized, and underlined**, in the text. Complex modification is another marker of legal Chinese. Also note that, in Chinese, the comma is not used in front of the word "etc." 等 as it is in modern legal English.

The first thing the employer must do is have a "discussion" (讨论 tǎolùn) with either the representative assembly of the staff and workers or all of the staff and workers. Note the use of the term 经 (jīng). This term is commonly used in legal Chinese. It literally means "to go through" or "experience." It often makes the following verb passive. In this sentence, it applies to each of the three verbs which follow it: "discuss" (讨论 tǎolùn), "put forward" (提出 tíchū) and "consult" (协商 xiéshāng).

During the course of that讨论, the employer must put forward a plan and have the employees offer their opinions. Finally, the employer must consult on the basis of equality "together with" (与 yǔ) the union or the representative assembly of the staff and workers. Once the process is complete, the employer may make the determination.

As an example of the complexity of this sentence, when this law was first enacted, there was a good deal of discussion as to who made the ultimate determination, the employer or the employer in consultation together with the staff and workers. The text is ambiguous, but the current interpretation is that the ultimate determination is made by the employer.

In sum, when you come across a complex legal Chinese sentence begin by identifying the subject/verb/object of the sentence. Then, look for: patterns such as temporal markers; words such as 经 (jīng), 与 (yǔ), or 由 (yóu); the use of dùnhào and/or commas; and the use of complex modification.

Finally, while the modern school of legal English prefers short sentences, there are still many, many examples of long sentences in legal English. The sentence above from the Labor Contract Law is a good example of a long sentence in legal Chinese. Many legal Chinese sentences, when translated, can be transformed into a series of short sentences, particularly when a comma or a semi-colon marks the end of a stand-alone clause.

### C. Mandatory Terms in Legal Chinese

Any discussion of the use of mandatory phrases in Chinese must begin with a discussion of three of those terms in English: shall, should, and may. In modern legal English, there is a movement away from using "shall" and "should" in legal documents other than legislation because these two terms are ambiguous terms. (Mary Barnard Ray and Jill J. Ramsfield, *Legal Writing: Getting it Right and Getting it Written,* 2010. ) The courts in the U.S. have held that "shall" as it is used in contracts could mean "will," "may," or "must." Thus, the general rule in modern legal English is to only use "shall" in legislation. In this context, the use of "shall" tends to be limited to the meaning of "must." Likewise, the term "should" could mean "must," "may," or "ought" and thus should be avoided so as to reduce the possibility of ambiguity.

In modern legal English, when the parties to a contract want to use a mandatory term, the terms "should" and "shall" are replaced with "must" and with such terms as "the parties agree that...."

Three of the more commonly used mandatory phrases used in modern legal Chinese are 应当 (yīngdāng shall/must), 必须 (bìxū shall/must), and 不得 (bùdé shall/must/may not – in the sense of a prohibition). As is apparent from a July 2010 discussion on the Chinese law e-mail list (CHINALAW@

HERMES.GWU.EDU) and the literature, there is some confusion in modern legal Chinese about the precise meaning of these terms, thus when translated into English, the confusion is doubled.

One view is that, in contemporary legal Chinese legislative materials, 应当 and 必须 are functionally equivalent and both mean "shall/must", while 应当 in colloquial usage can also mean "should" or "ought to." (Deborah Cao, *Chinese Law: A Language Perspective,* 2004, pp. 56-67). Another view is that 必须 is the stronger of the two and always means "shall/must", while 应当 is weaker and could, even in some legislative contexts, mean "should" or "ought to." (Claudia Ross and Lester Ross, "Language and Law: Sources of Systemic Vagueness and Ambiguous Authority in Chinese Statutory Language," in Karen Turner, James Feinerman, and Kent Guy, eds. *The Limits of the Rule of Law in China*, 2000, pp. 224-240.)

For lawyers, who generally try to be as precise as possible in their use of language, these mandatory terms in English or Chinese can be very difficult to use and translate.

As Professor Cao notes "contemporary Chinese law and its legal language are still very much in a state of flux."( Id. at p. 60. )The authors of the *China Law Reader* suggest following modern legal English for English language texts (other than legislation, in which case, use the term "shall") and agree with Professor Cao in translating both 应当 and 必须 as "shall" (in the sense of "must") when they occur in legislative material.

In modern legal English, "may" is often confused with a related term, "can." "May" is used to denote permission from an authority, while "can" denotes capacity or ability. It is not uncommon to see the following phrase in an English language contract "The purchaser can pay the full amount of the purchase price at any time." In this sentence, the drafter should have used the term "may" to indicate that the purchaser has the permission of the seller to pay the full amount at any time. As written, the sentence merely acknowledges that the purchaser has the wherewithal to make the payment; it does not grant the purchaser permission to pay off the debt early.

Other related Chinese terms include 可以 (kěyǐ may), 禁止 (jìnzhǐ it is prohibited to x), 严禁 (yánèjìn it is strictly prohibited to x), and 不准 or 不许 (bùzhǔn or bùxǔ not allowed/permitted).

## II.  Sources of Law

Where one must go to find or interpret the law? In the U.S., statutes, rules, and regulations make up the law. In addition, case law is a source of law because the U.S. is a common law jurisdiction. China is more like a civil law jurisdiction with regards to judicial opinions. Thus, one major difference between U.S. and Chinese sources of law is that, in China, rather than using written appellate opinions to interpret the law, the Supreme People's Court and various administrative agencies will directly issue formal interpretations of the law. In the U.S., judicial interpretation is only done when there is an actual case before the court.

In the U.S., this kind of clarification through interpretation would be typically be done by the judges at the appellate courts through their written opinions dealing with cases which have come before them on appeal. In the U.S., there is the principle of "case in controversy" which means that judges generally may only address factual and legal issues which have come before them in an actual case that is still pending before them.

As you will see in the introduction to Chapter XI - Court Decisions, case law is beginning to play a more important role in Chinese law. However, currently, case law is not authoritative (binding). At best, case law might have some persuasive value.

In the CLR, there are two good examples of the use of official interpretations. One example is the 2009 judicial interpretation issued by the Supreme People's Court on the Contract Law. The second example is the series of interpretations (1998, 2004, 2007) jointly issued by the Supreme People's Court and the Supreme People's Procuratorate on Article 217 of the Criminal Law. Judicial interpretations usually come from a committee within the Supreme People's Court which meets regularly to discuss interpretation issues that have arisen at the trial court level.

For example, the interpretations remove some elements of ambiguity from the Criminal Law.

When specifying the threshold for a violation of Article 217, the Criminal Law—as it does in many other articles of the Criminal Law—uses vague terms like 较大 "relatively large" and 巨大 "enormous" when it refers to the threshold for a key element of the article, 违法所得数额 (wéifǎ suǒde shù'é meaning the "amount illegally obtained"). The 1998 Interpretation states that for individuals and entities, the term "relatively large" means RMB 50,000 and RMB 20,000 respectively. The 2004 Interpretation lowers this amount to RMB 30,000 (apparently for both individuals and entities, but this is not explicitly stated in the interpretation).

The 1998 Interpretation also clarifies that the term used in the statute, 印发 (yìnfā "copy distribute"), means "either copy or distribute." The 2004 Interpretation sets a volume threshold of 1,000 illegal copies and the 2007 Interpretation lowers this threshold to 500 illegal copies. The interpretations also spend some time clarifying the term "amount illegally obtained."

### III. Conclusion

We hope that the CLR will be of some use to future generations of foreigners interested in learning the language of Chinese law and will contribute to a better understanding of Chinese law. We welcome any suggestion you might have on how to improve on this book.

# A Brief Legal History of Modern China

By *Lin Yan*, Professor of Law

Modern China's legal system began to function after the fall of the "Gang of Four" in 1976. The collapse of the "Gang of Four" demonstrated the Chinese Communist Party's determination to end the turmoil of lawlessness and embrace the notion of "rule of law". In order to have a legal basis on which to punish the members of the "Gang of Four", the National People's Congress ("NPC") enacted both the Criminal Law and the Criminal Procedure Law. In 1980, the People's Supreme Court tried the "Gang of Four" and rendered sentences based on those two statutes. Although both the law-making process and the trial seemed retrospective, it was the first time in the history of the People's Republic of China that the ruling party resolved an internal power struggle through law. The other reason for adopting "rule of law" was that the country needed a sustainable and predictable legal system to attract foreign investments. Therefore, one of seven statutes passed by NPC in 1979 was the Law on Chinese-Foreign Equity Joint Ventures.

From then on, three major themes have become dominant in the construction of the Chinese legal system:

### 1. Adopting the New Constitution, but Still Struggling between the Planned Economy and the Market Economy (1982-1991)

In 1982, China adopted the current Constitution, which established the foundation for the contemporary legal system. The Constitution frames the basic governmental structure and affords people certain fundamental rights. The Constitution embraces the notion of "Democratic Centralization" as the guiding rule for distributing governmental powers. Under this principle, the legislative branch enjoys supremacy over the executive and the judiciary; and the Central Government is far more powerful than the provincial and local governments. The fundamental rights include both negative rights (political rights and personal liberties) and positive rights (welfare rights). However, the Constitution does not articulate any specific form of constitutional review.

In the early 1980s, both the Central Government and local governments launched a years-long anti-crime campaign in order to control the social unrest caused by the population movement from rural China to the cities. During the campaign, the government advocated the ideas of "speedy trial, harsher punishment", under which wrongful convictions and abuses were common. The government also used the Criminal Law to punish those individuals who engaged in business transactions without permission. (This type of transaction was termed "speculation").

In 1986, the NPC adopted the General Principles of Civil Law ("the General Principles") in order to address the needs of the "reform and opening-up" policy. The General Principles provides basic rules for daily dealings among citizens and organizations, such as contractual arrangements, tort liability, and so on. However, it also protects several indispensable elements of the planned economy. For instance, it prohibits people from "disturbing the national economic plan."

In the second half of the 1980s, the country was preoccupied with the mission to combat against inflation and corruption in order to ensure social stability. In 1989, the NPC passed the Administrative Litigation Law, authorizing the court to conduct judicial review of administrative agency decisions. This marked the beginning of the trend of restricting and formalizing the governmental power through law.

### 2. Providing the Legal Framework for the Market Economy (1992-2002)

After 1989, the government was struggling with the question of whether it should continue to implement the "reform and opening up" policy. During a two-year-long debate, the economy staggered.

In order to reenergize the economic engine, Deng Xiaoping, the ruling party's supreme leader, decided to travel to several southern cities in 1992 to vocally advocate his determined goal of directing China toward a market economy. After his Southern Tour, the theme of "market economy construction" was irreversibly unveiled and materialized. Thus, the legal system was guided to reflect this new theme.

From 1993, both the NPC and its Standing Committee accelerated the pace of market-economy-oriented legislations. As a result, the Anti-Unfair Competition Law, Consumer Rights Protection Law, Company Law, Labor Law, Guaranty Law, Insurance Law, Price Law, Securities Law, and Contract Law were all adopted. These statutes built a solid foundation for the market economy. The biggest shift of the substance of these legislations was minimizing or even eliminating the elements of the planned economy. For instance, the Contract Law of 1999 accurately reflected this shift by giving people the autonomy to initiate and complete business transactions.

From the early 1990s, Chinese legal scholars urged the government to emphasize the merit, rather than the form, of the legal system and human rights protection was a major concern. To address this concern, the NPC reframed the criminal system by adopting the 1997 Criminal Law and the 1998 Criminal Procedure Law. Both statutes significantly restrict the powers of the public security bureau, the procuratorate, and the court; and offer criminal suspects unprecedented protection against abuse.

From the late 1990s, the government devoted a good deal of energy in overhauling its regulatory mechanisms in order to realize its commitments as a member of the World Trade Organization. The main feature of that movement was reducing red-tape procedures and increasing the transparency of the governmental decision-making process.

### 3. Serving the Construction of a Harmonious Society (2003-present)

The two-decade-long economic development has generated various negative social impacts: the enlarging wealth gap among people; the growing disparity of development between rural China and its urban counterpart; the worsening environment; and widespread corruption. All these have made the country more unstable and posed a serious challenge to the government and the ruling party. In order to make China healthier, more stable, and prosperous, the current leadership, led by President Hu Jintao, began to promote the idea of "scientific development" to build a "harmonious" society.

Under this new theme, the focus of legal system construction has been switched from relying on the invisible hand to asking the government to play a more active role. Therefore, the Labor Contract Law was adopted to afford employees more protection; the Employment Promotion Law was enacted to require that the government offer assistance to citizens in job-hunting; various environment-related statutes were passed to control pollution, and so on. So far, the enforcement of these progressive statutes is both painful and far from a success.

### 4. A Brief Conclusion and Prediction

For sure, the ruling party will continue to use law to address new challenges and to achieve new goals. It is hard to deny that the three-decade-long engagement with law has made the government more accountable and the people safer. We have good cause to be optimistic about the future of the rule of law with Chinese characteristics.

# Chapter 1
# Constitutional Law

# 宪 法

Xiàn    Fǎ

# A. Introduction to the Constitution of the People's Republic of China

By *Lawrence C. Foster*, Professor of Law

The PRC's provisional constitution was the General Program, enacted in 1948. The first formal constitution was enacted in 1978. New constitutions were enacted in 1975, 1978, and again in 1982. As you will see in the following reading, the 1982 Constitution is still in force, but it has been amended four times, most recently in 2004. All of the new constitutions and the post-1982 amendments reflect significant changes to China's political scene. For example, the 1982 Constitution, as originally enacted in 1982, embodied Deng Xiaoping's core ideas for modernizing China. Good examples of later changes include the post-1982 additions to the 1982 Constitution of the concepts of socialist market economy, human rights, and rule of law as well as greater protection of property rights of the people.

The 1982 Constitution has been described alternatively as the "core law of China" and "the least important document in China's legal system." The latter description is perhaps due to the fact that, at present, unlike the constitutions of more developed legal systems around the world, the rights enshrined in the 1982 Constitution are not justiciable; i.e. alleged violations of "constitutional rights" by the government or individuals are not grounds for a lawsuit in China. However, in recent years, there have been increasing reports in the media of citizens claiming enforceable constitutional rights. It has been suggested by some scholars in the West that it is just a matter of time for these claims to be justiciable in the Chinese courts.

As you read the language of the Preamble to the 1982 Constitution, you will note that its language is different from the language found in most Chinese laws. In large part, this is because much of the language in the 1982 Constitution is political rhetoric, not normative pronouncements. The one law whose language comes closest is the General Principles section of the 2007 Property Law. The reason for this is simple: the ownership of property, and real property in particular, is a highly charged political issue in China.

# B. Text of Constitution of the People's Republic of China[1]

1982年12月4日第五届 全国人民代表大会第五次会议 通过1982年12月4日全国人民代表大会公告 公布 施行，*根据*1988年4月12日第七届全国人民代表大会第一次会议通过的《中华人民共和国宪法 修正 案》、1993年3月29日第八届全国人民代表大会第一次会议通过的《中华人民共和国宪法修正案》、1999年3月15日第九届全国人民代表大会第二次会议通过的《中华人民共和国宪法修正案》和2004年3月14日第十届全国人民代表大会第二次会议通过的《中华人民共和国宪法修正案》修正。

---

1 Source: Zhonghua Renmin Gongheguo xian fa [Constitution (P.R.C.)] (promulgated by the Nat'l People's Cong., Dec. 4, 1982) *available at* http://www.gov.cn/gongbao/content/2004/content_62714.htm (last visited May 30, 2011).

序言

中国是世界上历史最悠久的国家之一。中国各族人民共同 创造了光辉灿烂的文化，具有光荣的革命 传统。

一八四0年以后，封建的中国逐渐 变成 半殖民地、半封建的国家。中国人民为国家独立、民族解放和民主 自由 进行了前仆后继的英勇奋斗。

二十世纪，中国发生了翻天覆地的伟大历史变革。

一九一一年孙中山先生领导的辛亥革命，废除了封建帝制，创立了中华民国。但是，中国人民反对帝国 主义和封建主义的历史任务还没有完成。

一九四九年，*以* 毛泽东主席*为* 领袖的中国共产党领导中国各族人民，*在* 经历了长期的艰难 曲折的武装 斗争和其他形式的斗争*以后*，终于 推翻了帝国主义、封建主义和官僚资本主义的统治，取得了新民主主义革命的伟大胜利，建立了中华人民共和国。从此，中国人民掌握了国家的权力，成为国家的主人。

中华人民共和国成立以后，我国社会逐步实现了*由*新民主主义*到*社会主义的过渡。生产 资料 私有制的社会主义改造已经完成，人剥削人的制度已经消灭，社会主义制度已经确立。工人 阶级领导的、以工农 联盟为基础的人民民主专政，实质上 即 无产阶级专政，得到巩固和发展。中国人民和中国人民解放军战胜了帝国主义、霸权主义的侵略、破坏和武装挑衅，维护了国家的独立和安全，增强了国防。经济 建设 取得了重大的成就，独立的、比较完整的社会主义工业 体系已经基本形成，农业生产显著 提高。教育、科学、文化等事业有了很大的发展，社会主义思想教育取得了明显的成效。广大人民的生活有了较大的改善。

中国新民主主义革命的胜利和社会主义事业的成就，*是*中国共产党领导中国各族人民，*在* 马克思 列宁主义、毛泽东思想的指引*下*，坚持 真理，修正错误，战胜许多艰难险阻*而*取得*的*。我国将 长期 处于社会主义初级 阶段。国家的根本任务是，沿着中国特色社会主义道路，集中力量进行社会主义现代化建设。中国各族人民将继续在中国共产党领导下，在马克思列宁主义、毛泽东思想、邓小平 理论和"三个代表"重要思想指引下，坚持人民民主专政，坚持社会主义道路，坚持改革 开放，不断 完善社会主义的各项制度，发展社会主义市场经济，发展社会主义民主，健全社会主义法制，自力更生，艰苦奋斗，逐步实现工业、农业、国防和科学技术的现代化，推动 物质 文明、政治文明和精神文明协调发展，把我国建设成为**富强**、民主、文明的社会主义国家。

在我国，剥削阶级作为阶级已经消灭，但是阶级斗争还将在一定**范围**内长期**存在**。中国人民对**敌视**和破坏我国社会主义制度的国内外的**敌对**势力和敌对**分子**，**必须**进行斗争。

台湾是中华人民共和国的**神圣** 领土的一部分。完成**统一** 祖国的**大业**是包括台湾**同胞**在内的全中国人民的神圣**职责**。

社会主义的建设事业必须**依靠**工人、农民和**知识分子**，**团结** 一切可以团结的力量。在长期的革命和建设**过程**中，已经**结成** 由中国共产党领导的，有各民主**党派**和各人民**团体 参加**的，**包括 全体**社会主义**劳动** 者、社会主义事业的建设者、**拥护**社会主义的爱国者和拥护祖国统一的爱国者的**广泛**的爱国统一**战线**，这个统一战线将继续巩固和发展。中国**人民政治协商会议**是有广泛代表性的统一战线**组织**，过去**发挥**了重要的历史**作用**，今后在国家政治生活、社会生活和**对外** 友好活动中，在进行社会主义现代化建设、维护国家的统一和团结的斗争中，将**进一步发挥**它的重要作用。中国共产党领导的多党**合作**和政治协商制度将长期存在和发展。

中华人民共和国是全国各族人民共同**缔造**的统一的多民族国家。平等、团结、**互助**的社会主义民族**关系**已经确立，并将继续加强。

在维护民族团结的斗争中，要反对**大民族主义**，主要是**大汉族主义**，也要反对**地方民族主义**。国家尽一切**努力**，促进全国各民族的共同**繁荣**。

中国革命和建设的成就是*同*世界人民的支持*分不开*的。中国的**前途**是同世界的前途紧密地**联系**在一起的。中国坚持独立自主的对外**政策**，坚持互相**尊重** 主权和领土 完整、互不侵犯、互不干涉 **内政**、平等互利、和平共处的五项 **原则**，发展同各国的**外交**关系和经济、文化的**交流**；坚持反对帝国主义、霸权主义、殖民主义，加强同 世界各国人民的团结，支持被压迫民族和发展中国家**争取**和维护民族独立、发展民族经济的**正义**斗争，*为*维护世界和平和促进人类进步事业*而*努力。

本宪法以法律的形式**确认**了中国各族人民奋斗的**成果**，**规定**了国家的**根本制度**和**根本任务**，是国家的根本法，具有最高的法律**效力**。全国各族人民、一切国家机关 和武装力量、各**政党**和各社会团体、各**企业**事业组织，都必须以宪法为根本的活动**准则**，并且**负有**维护宪法**尊严**、**保证**宪法**实施**的职责。

**第三条** 中华人民共和国的国家机构实行民主集中**制**的原则。

全国人民代表大会和地方各级人民代表大会都*由*民主**选举** 产生，对人民**负责**，受人民**监督**。国家**行政**机关、**审判**机关、检察机关都由人民代表大会产生，对它负责，受它监督。中央和地方的国家机构**职权的划分，遵循**在中央的统一领导下，**充分**发挥地方的**主动性、积极性**的原则。

**第五条** 国家维护社会主义**法制**的统一和尊严。

一切法律、行政**法规**和地方性法规都不得同宪法**相抵触**。一切国家机关和武装力量、各政党和各社会团体、各企业事业组织都必须遵守宪法和法律。一切**违反**宪法和法律的**行为**，必须**予以 追究**。任何组织或者个人都不得有**超越**宪法和法律的**特权**。

**第六十七条** 全国人民代表大会常务委员会行使**下列**职权：

（一）**解释**宪法，监督宪法的实施；

（二）**制定**和修改**除**应当由全国人民代表大会制定的法律*以外*的其他法律；

（三）在全国人民代表大会**闭会**期间，对全国人民代表大会制定的法律进行部分**补充**和修改，但是不得同**该**法律的基本原则相抵

触；

（四）解释法律；

（六）监督国务院、中央军事委员会、最高人民法院和最高人民检察院的工作；

（七）**撤销**国务院制定的同宪法、法律相抵触的行政法规、**决定和命令**；

（八）撤销省、自治区、直辖市国家权力机关制定的同宪法、法律和行政法规相抵触的地方性法规和**决议**；

（十一）根据最高人民法院院长的**提请**，**任免**最高人民法院副院长、审判员、**审判委员会委员**和军事法院院长；

**第八十九条** 国务院行使下列职权：

（一）根据宪法和法律，规定行政**措施**，制定行政法规，**发布**决定和命令；

**第一百二十六条** 人民法院依照法律规定**独立**行使审判权，不受行政机关、社会团体和个人的干涉。

# C. Vocabulary of Constitution of the People's Republic of China

| Chinese | Pinyin | English |
| --- | --- | --- |
| 届 | Jiè | Session |
| 全国人民代表大会 | Quánguó Rénmín Dàibiǎo Dàhuì | National People's Congress (NPC) |
| 会议 | Huìyì | Meeting |
| 通过 | Tōngguò | Enact; pass |
| 公告 | Gōnggào | Public announcement |
| 公布 | Gōngbù | Promulgate |
| 施行 | Shīxíng | Come into force |
| 根据 | Gēnjù | Based on; according to |
| 宪法 | Xiànfǎ | Constitution |
| 修正 | Xiūzhèng | Revise; amend; correct |
| 案 | Àn | Draft |
| 目录 | Mùlù | Table of contents |
| 序言 | Xùyán | Preamble |
| 章 | Zhāng | Chapter |

| | | |
|---|---|---|
| 总纲 | Zǒnggāng | General principles |
| 基本 | Jīběn | Basic |
| 权利 | Quánlì | Rights |
| 义务 | Yìwù | Duty; obligation |
| 机构 | Jīgòu | Organization; structure |
| 节 | Jié | Section |
| 主席 | Zhǔxí | President |
| 国务院 | Guówùyuàn | State Council |
| 中央 | Zhōngyāng | Central |
| 军事 | Jūnshì | Military affairs |
| 委员会 | Wěiyuánhuì | Commission |
| 地方 | Dìfāng | Local |
| 各级 | Gèjí | All levels |
| 民族 | Mínzú | Ethnic minority; nationality |
| 自治 | Zìzhì | Autonomous |
| 机关 | Jīguān | Organ (administrative; government) |
| 法院 | Fǎyuàn | Court |
| 检察院 | Jiǎncháyuàn | Procuratorate (prosecutor) |
| 旗 | Qí | Flag |
| 徽 | Huī | Emblem; seal |
| 悠久 | Yōujiǔ | Long |
| 族 | Zú | Race; nationality |

| | | |
|---|---|---|
| 共同 | Gòngtóng | Together; jointly |
| 创造 | Chuàngzào | Create |
| 光辉 | Guānghuī | Brilliant |
| 灿烂 | Cànlàn | Magnificent; splendid |
| 具有 | Jùyǒu | Fully possess; have |
| 光荣 | Guāngróng | Glorious |
| 革命 | Gémìng | Revolution |
| 传统 | Chuántǒng | Tradition |
| 封建 | Fēngjiàn | Feudal |
| 逐渐 | Zhújiàn | Gradually |
| 变成 | Biànchéng | Become; change into |
| 半 | Bàn | One-half; semi- |
| 殖民地 | Zhímíndì | Colony |
| 为 | Wèi | For the sake of; in order to |
| 独立 | Dúlì | Independent |
| 解放 | Jiěfàng | Liberate |
| 民主 | Mínzhǔ | Democracy |
| 自由 | Zìyóu | Free; freedom |
| 进行 | Jìnxíng | Carry out; conduct |
| 前仆后继 | Qiánpūhòujì | Advance wave upon wave |
| 英勇 | Yīngyǒng | Heroic; brave |
| 奋斗 | Fèndòu | Fight; struggle |

| 世纪 | Shìjì | Century |
|---|---|---|
| 发生 | Fāshēng | Occur; happen |
| 翻天覆地 | Fāntiānfùdì | Earth shaking |
| 伟大 | Wěidà | Great |
| 变革 | Biàngé | Change |
| 孙中山 | Sūn Zhōngshān | Sun Yatsen |
| 领导 | Lǐngdǎo | Leadership |
| 辛亥革命 | Xīnhài Gémìng | Xinhai Revolution (1911) |
| 废除 | Fèichú | Abolish |
| 帝制 | Dìzhì | Imperial |
| 创立 | Chuànglì | Create |
| 帝国 | Dìguó | Imperialist |
| 主义 | Zhǔyì | -ism |
| 任务 | Rènwù | Duty |
| 完成 | Wánchéng | Complete |
| 以 x 为 y | Yǐ x wéi y | Take x as y |
| 毛泽东 | Máo Zédōng | Mao Zedong |
| 领袖 | Lǐngxiù | Leader |
| 共产党 | Gòngchǎndǎng | Chinese Communist Party (CCP) |
| 在 x 以后 | Zài x yǐhòu | After x |
| 经历 | Jīnglì | Experience |
| 艰难 | Jiānnán | Difficulties |

| | | |
|---|---|---|
| 曲折 | Qūzhé | Tortuous; winding |
| 武装 | Wǔzhuāng | Armed |
| 斗争 | Dòuzhēng | Struggle |
| 形式 | Xíngshì | Form |
| 终于 | Zhōngyú | In the end |
| 推翻 | Tuīfān | Overthrow |
| 官僚资本 | Guānliáozīběn | Bureaucratic capital |
| 统治 | Tǒngzhì | Control |
| 取得 | Qǔdé | Obtain; acquire |
| 伟大 | Wěidà | Great |
| 胜利 | Shènglì | Victory |
| 建立 | Jiànlì | Establish |
| 从此 | Cóngcǐ | From this time on |
| 掌握 | Zhǎngwò | Grasp |
| 权力 | Quánlì | Power |
| 成为 | Chéngwéi | Become |
| 主人 | Zhǔrén | Master |
| 成立 | Chénglì | Form; establish |
| 逐步 | Zhúbù | Gradually |
| 实现 | Shíxiàn | Realize; achieve; bring about |
| 由 x 到 y | Yóu x dào y | From x to y |
| 过渡 | Guòdù | Transition |

| | | |
|---|---|---|
| 生产 | Shēngchǎn | Produce; manufacture |
| 资料 | Zīliào | Means |
| 私有制 | Sīyǒuzhì | Private (ownership) system |
| 社会 | Shèhuì | Social; society |
| 改造 | Gǎizào | Transform; reform |
| 人剥削人 | Rén bōxuē rén | Exploitation of people by people |
| 制度 | Zhìdù | System (political or administrative) |
| 消灭 | Xiāomiè | Eliminate; expire; abolish; extinguish |
| 确立 | Quèlì | Establish |
| 工人 | Gōngrén | Worker |
| 阶级 | Jiējí | Class |
| 工农 | Gōngnóng | Workers and peasants |
| 联盟 | Liánmèng | Alliance |
| 基础 | Jīchǔ | Foundation |
| 专政 | Zhuānzhèng | Dictatorship |
| 实质上 | Shízhìshàng | In essence |
| 即 | Jí | Thus; which |
| 无产阶级 | Wúchǎnjiējí | Proletariat (lit. class without property) |
| 巩固 | Gǒnggù | Consolidate; strengthen |
| 发展 | Fāzhǎn | Development |
| 战胜 | Zhànshèng | Triumph over; vanquish |
| 霸权 | Bàquán | Hegemony |

| 侵略 | Qīnlüè | Invasion; aggression |
| 破坏 | Pòhuài | Destroy; violate (an agreement) |
| 挑衅 | Tiǎoxìn | Provocation |
| 维护 | Wéihù | Protect |
| 安全 | Ānquán | Safety; security |
| 增强 | Zēngqiáng | Strengthen; increase |
| 国防 | Guófáng | National defense |
| 经济 | Jīngjì | Economy |
| 建设 | Jiànshè | Construction |
| 取得 | Qǔdé | Obtain |
| 成就 | Chéngjiù | Accomplishment; achievement |
| 完整 | Wánzhěng | Complete |
| 工业 | Gōngyè | Industry |
| 体系 | Tǐxì | System |
| 基本 | Jīběn | Basic |
| 形成 | Xíngchéng | Take shape |
| 农业 | Nóngyè | Agriculture |
| 显著 | Xiǎnzhù | Notable; striking |
| 提高 | Tígāo | Raise; increase; improve |
| 事业 | Shìyè | Cause; undertaking |
| 明显 | Míngxiǎn | Obviously; clearly |
| 成效 | Chéngxiào | Effect; result |

| 广大 | Guǎngdà | Broad |
|---|---|---|
| 改善 | Gǎishàn | Improve |
| x 是 y 而 z 的 | x Shì y ér z de | x is z'd because of y |
| 在 x 下 | Zài x xià | Under x |
| 马克思 | Mǎkèsī | Marx |
| 列宁 | Lièníng | Lenin |
| 指引 | Zhǐyǐn | Guidance |
| 坚持 | Jiānchí | Unremitting; persist |
| 真理 | Zhēnlǐ | Truth |
| 错误 | Cuòwù | Mistake |
| 艰难险阻 | Jiānnán xiǎnzǔ | Dangers and difficulties |
| 将 | Jiāng | Will |
| 长期 | Chángqī | Long term; long lasting |
| 处于 | Chǔyú | Be located in; be in a certain condition |
| 初级 | Chūjí | Initial |
| 阶段 | Jiēduàn | Stage |
| 沿着 | Yánzhe | Following along |
| 特色 | Tèsè | Distinguishing feature; quality; feature |
| 力量 | Lìliàng | Strength |
| 继续 | Jìxù | Continue |
| 邓小平 | Dēng Xiǎopíng | Deng Xiaoping |
| 理论 | Lǐlùn | Theory |

| | | |
|---|---|---|
| 三个代表 | Sānge dàibiǎo | The Three Represents |
| 改革 | Gǎigé | Reform |
| 开放 | Kāifàng | Open |
| 不断 | Bùduàn | Continuously; constantly |
| 完善 | Wánshàn | Improve; perfect |
| 项 | Xiàng | Counter for 制度 |
| 市场 | Shìchǎng | Market |
| 健全 | Jiànquán | Strengthen; perfect |
| 法制 | Fǎzhì | Legal system |
| 自力更生 | Zìlìgēngshēng | Self reliance; literally change your life by your own efforts |
| 艰苦 | Jiānkǔ | Arduous; hard; tough |
| 技术 | Jìshù | Technology; skill |
| 推动 | Tuīdòng | Promote |
| 物质 | Wùzhì | Material |
| 文明 | Wénmíng | Civilization; culture |
| 政治 | Zhèngzhì | Political |
| 精神 | Jīngshén | Spiritual |
| 协调 | Xiétiáo | Coordinate |
| 富强 | Fùqiáng | Rich and strong |
| 范围 | Fànwéi | Scope |
| 存在 | Cúnzài | Exist |

| 敌视 | Díshì | Be hostile to… |
|------|-------|----------------|
| 敌对 | Díduì | Hostile |
| 分子 | Fènzǐ | Elements |
| 必须 | Bìxū | Shall; must |
| 神圣 | Shénshèng | Sacred; holy |
| 领土 | Lǐngtǔ | Territory |
| 统一 | Tǒngyī | Unify |
| 祖国 | Zǔguó | Motherland |
| 大业 | Dàyè | Great endeavor |
| 同胞 | Tóngbāo | Countrymen |
| 职责 | Zhízé | Duty; responsibility; obligation |
| 依靠 | Yīkào | Rely on |
| 知识 | Zhīshì | Intellectual |
| 团结 | Tuánjié | Unite; rally |
| 一切 | Yīqiè | All; every |
| 过程 | Guòchéng | Process; course |
| 结成 | Jiéchéng | Form |
| 由 x | Yóu x | By x |
| 党派 | Dǎngpài | Political parties and groups |
| 团体 | Tuántǐ | Group; organization |
| 参加 | Cānjiā | Join in; participate in |
| 包括 | Bāokuò | Include |

| | | |
|---|---|---|
| 全体 | Quántǐ | All (lit. entire body) |
| 劳动 | Láodòng | Labor |
| 者 | Zhě | 者 is literary Chinese and is used after an adjective or verb as a substitute for a person, entity, or thing. Here, it changes "work" into "worker" |
| 拥护 | Yǒnghù | Protect |
| 广泛 | Guǎngfàn | Broad |
| 战线 | Zhànxiàn | Battle front; front |
| 人民政治 | Rénmín Zhèngzhì | People's Political |
| 协商会议 | Xiéshāng Huìyì | Consultative Conference |
| 组织 | Zǔzhī | Organization |
| 发挥 | Fāhuī | Give free reign to; bring into play |
| 作用 | Zuòyòng | Function; use |
| 对外 | Duìwài | Foreign |
| 友好 | Yóuhǎo | Friendly |
| 维护 | Wéihù | Protect |
| 进一步 | Jìnyībù | Further |
| 合作 | Hézuò | Cooperate |
| 缔造 | Dìzào | Found; create |
| 平等 | Píngděng | Equal; equality |
| 互助 | Hùzhù | Mutual aid; assistance |

| 关系 | Guānxi | Guanxi; relationship |
|---|---|---|
| 大民族主义 | Dàmínzúzhǔyì | Majoritarianism |
| 大汉族主义 | Dàhànzúzhǔyì | Chauvinism by the Han race |
| 地方民族主义 | Dìfāngmínzúzhǔyì | Local chauvinism |
| 尽 | Jìn | All; utmost |
| 努力 | Nǔlì | Work hard |
| 繁荣 | Fánróng | Flourish |
| 同 x 分不开 | Tóng x fēnbùkāi | Inseparable from x |
| 前途 | Qiántú | Future |
| 紧密 | Jǐnmì | Close; intimate |
| 联系 | Liánxì | Contact; connection |
| 政策 | Zhèngcè | Government policy |
| 尊重 | Zūnzhòng | Respect; esteem |
| 主权 | Zhǔquán | Sovereign rights; sovereignty |
| 互 | Hù | Mutual |
| 干涉 | Gānshè | Interfere |
| 内政 | Nèizhèng | Internal politics |
| 利 | Lì | Benefit |
| 共处 | Gòngchǔ | Coexist |
| 项 | Xiàng | Counter for 原则 |
| 原则 | Yuánzé | Principle |
| 外交 | Wàijiāo | Foreign affairs |

| 交流 | Jiāoliú | Exchange |
|------|---------|----------|
| 压迫 | Yāpò | Oppression |
| 争取 | Zhēngqǔ | Strive for; fight for |
| 正义 | Zhèngyì | Just; righteous |
| 为 x 而 y | Wèi x ér y | Do y for the sake of x |
| 人类 | Rénlèi | Mankind |
| 确认 | Quèrèn | Affirm; confirm |
| 成果 | Chéngguǒ | Result |
| 规定 | Guīdìng | Stipulate; provide |
| 根本 | Gēnběn | Fundamental |
| 效力 | Xiàolì | Effectiveness; validity |
| 政党 | Zhèngdǎng | Political party |
| 企业 | Qǐyè | Enterprise |
| 准则 | Zhǔnzé | Norm; standard; criterion |
| 负有 | Fùyǒu | Bear; carry |
| 尊严 | Zūnyán | Dignity; honor; sanctity |
| 保证 | Bǎozhèng | Guarantee; ensure |
| 实施 | Shíshī | Put into effect; implement; carry out |
| 制（制度） | Zhì (Zhìdù) | System (political or administrative) |
| 由 x | Yóu x | By x; it is up to x to... |
| 选举 | Xuánjǔ | Elect; election |
| 产生 | Chǎnshēng | Cause; bring about |

| | | |
|---|---|---|
| 负责 | Fùzé | Bear responsibility |
| 监督 | Jiāndū | Control; supervise |
| 行政 | Xíngzhèng | Administrative |
| 审判 | Shěnpàn | Judicial adjudication; trial |
| 职权 | Zhíquán | Official powers; authority |
| 划分 | Huàfēn | Division; differentiation |
| 遵循 | Zūnxún | Follow; abide by; adhere to |
| 充分 | Chōngfèn | Fully |
| 主动 | Zhǔdòng | Initiative |
| 性 | Xìng | Suffix for -ness, -ity, -ive, -ize |
| 积极 | Jījí | Energetic; dynamic |
| 法制 | Fǎzhì | Legal system |
| 法规 | Fǎguī | Administrative laws and regulations |
| 相 | Xiāng | Mutually |
| 抵触 | Dǐchù | Conflict |
| 违反 | Wéifǎn | Violate (a law) |
| 行为 | Xíngwéi | Act; conduct; behavior |
| 予以 | Yǔyǐ | 予以 and 加以 both mean "to do x." In English, we would not translate either |
| 追究 (追究责任) | Zhuījiū (Zhuījiū zérèn) | Investigate and affix responsibility or liability |
| 任何 | Rènhé | Any |

| 个人 | Gèrén | Individual |
|---|---|---|
| 超越 | Chāoyuè | Exceed; transcend |
| 特权 | Tèquán | Privilege; prerogative |
| 下列 | Xiàliè | The following; set forth below |
| 解释 | Jiěshì | Interpret |
| 制定 | Zhìdìng | Formulate; enact |
| 除 x 以外 | Chú x yǐwài | Except for x |
| 闭会 | Bìhuì | Not in session |
| 补充 | Bǔchōng | Supplement |
| 该 | Gāi | That |
| 撤销 | Chèxiāo | Cancel; rescind; revoke |
| 决定 | Juédìng | Decide; decision |
| 命令 | Mìnglìng | Order |
| 决议 | Juéyì | Resolution |
| 提请 | Tíqǐng | Submit a request |
| 任免 | Rènmiǎn | Appoint and remove (or dismiss) someone |
| 审判委员会 | Shěnpàn Wěiyuánhuì | Judicial Adjudication Committee |
| 措施 | Cuòshī | Measures |
| 发布 | Fābù | Issue |
| 独立 | Dúlì | Independent |

# Chapter 2
# Legislation Law

# 立 法 法

Lì      Fǎ      Fǎ

# A. Introduction to the Legislation Law

By *Lin Yan*, Professor of Law

The Chinese Constitution only provides a fairly abstract and vague legislative system, providing little clear guidance on legislative jurisdiction or procedures. In wording, both the National People's Congress (NPC) and its Standing Committee monopolize legislative power. But in reality, the State Council has dominated the legislative process for decades. During the 1980s and 1990s, the NPC's Standing Committee diversified China's legislative system by authorizing greater legislative power in several coastal provinces and cities to facilitate "reform and opening up".

With the accumulation of legislation and rules, conflicts among these laws and rules became inevitable and more visible, and further affected the enforcement of the law. To achieve harmony among the various laws and rules, the NPC adopted the Legislation Law in 2000.

The Legislation Law has brought the following three major changes: First, it created a relatively consistent legislative hierarchy. Under the Law, there are four major types of legislation: laws (made by the NPC or its Standing Committee); administrative regulations (made by the State Council); local regulations (made by provincial, municipal people's congresses or their standing committee); and rules (made by ministries under the State Council, or provincial and municipal people's government). Laws are superior to administrative regulations and administrative regulations are superior to local regulations and rules. The Law reserves several subject matters to the NPC and its Standing Committee in order to defend the Central Government's supremacy and to better aid human rights protection (Article 8). At the same time, the Law unprecedentedly authorizes provincial and municipal people's congresses to legislate on "local affairs" (Article 64).

Second, the Law establishes the legislative

procedure in more detail. The most visible change is empowering the legal committee in various people's congresses to conduct a uniform review after the first reading of a bill. The main goal behind this mechanism is to guarantee consistency at various levels of legislation. The other important change is allowing and encouraging public participation during the legislative process, especially by requiring law makers to solicit opinions from the masses and welcome their comments.

Third, the Law sets up a kind of constitutional review system. To guarantee the supremacy of the Constitution and laws, the Law authorizes the NPC's Standing Committee to conduct a review of inferior rules. Citizens are also allowed to petition the Standing Committee to initiate such a review. Rights activists in China have relied on this mechanism to help abolish bad laws and regulations. It has become a useful weapon for human rights protection.

# B. Text of the Legislation Law[1]

# 中华人民共和国立法法

## （2000年3月15日第九届 全国人民代表大会第三次 会议 通过）

---

1 Source: Zhonghua Renmin Gongheguo li fa fa [Law on Legislation (P.R.C.)] (promulgated by the Nat'l People's Cong., March15, 2000) *available at* http://china. findlaw. cn/info/guojiafa/lifafajieshi/117270_10.html (last visited Sep. 9, 2012).

第一章 总则

第二条 法律、行政法规、地方性法规、自治条例和单行条例的制定、修改和废止，适用本法。

国务院 部门规章和地方政府规章的制定、修改和废止，依照本法的有关规定执行。

第二章 法律

第一节 立法权限

第七条 全国人民代表大会和全国人民代表大会常务委员会行使 国家立法权。

全国人民代表大会制定和修改刑事、民事、国家机构的和其他的基本 法律。

全国人民代表大会常务委员会制定和修改除 应当 由全国人民代表大会制定的法律以外的其他法律；在全国人民代表大会闭会期间，对全国人民代表大会制定的法律进行 部分 补充和修改，但是不得 同 该法律的基本原则 相抵触。

第八条 下列 事项只能制定法律：

(一) 国家主权的事项；

(二) 各级人民代表大会、人民政府、人民法院和人民检察院的产生、组织和职权；

(三) 民族 区域自治制度、特别 行政区制度、基层 群众自治制度；

(四) 犯罪和刑罚；

(五) 对公民 政治 权利的剥夺、限制 人身自由的强制 措施和处罚；

(六) 对非国有 财产的征收；

(七) 民事基本制度；

(八) 基本经济制度以及 财政、税收、海关、金融和 外贸的基本制度；

(九) 诉讼和仲裁制度；

(十) 必须由全国人民代表大会及 其常务委员会制定法律的其他事项。

第九条 本法第八条规定的事项尚未制定法律的，全国人民代表大会及其常务委员会有权作出决定，授权国务院可以根据 实际需要，对其中的部分事项先制定行政法规，但是有关犯罪和刑罚、对公民政治权利的剥夺和限制人身自由的强制措施和处罚、司法制度等事项除外。

第四十七条 全国人民代表大会常务委员会的法律解释同法律具有 同等 效力。

第三章 行政法规

第五十六条 国务院根据宪法和法律，制定行政法规。

行政法规可以就下列事项作出规定：

(一) 为执行法律的规定需要制定行政法规的事项；

(二) 宪法第八十九条规定的国务院行政管理 职权的事项。

应当由全国人民代表大会及其常务委员

会制定法律的事项，国务院根据全国人民代表大会及其常务委员会的授权决定先制定的行政法规，*经过实践检验*，制定法律的**条件成熟**时，国务院应当**及时 提请**全国人民代表大会及其常务委员会制定法律。

第四章 地方性法规、自治条例和单行条例、规章

第一节 地方性法规、自治条例和单行条例

第六十三条 省、**自治区**、**直辖市**的人民代表大会及其常务委员会根据本行政区域的具体情况和实际需要，在不*同*宪法、法律、行政法规*相抵触*的**前提下**，可以制定地方性法规。

**较大的市**的人民代表大会及其常务委员会根据本市的具体情况和实际需要，在不同宪法、法律、行政法规和本省、自治区的地方性法规相抵触的前提下，可以制定地方性法规，*报*省、自治区的人民代表大会常务委员会*批准*后施行。省、自治区的人民代表大会常务委员会对**报请**批准的地方性法规，应当对其**合法性**进行**审查**，同宪法、法律、行政法规和本省、自治区的地方性法规不抵触的，应当在四个月内**予以**批准。

省、自治区的人民代表大会常务委员会在对报请批准的较大的市的地方性法规进行审

查时，发现**其**同本省、自治区的人民政府的**规章相抵触**的，应当作出**处理**决定。

本法*所称*较大的市*是指*省、自治区的人民政府**所在地**的市，经济特区所在地的市和*经*国务院批准的较大的市。

第六十四条 地方性法规可以就下列事项作出规定：

（一）**为执行法律**、行政法规的规定，需要根据本行政区域的实际情况作具体规定的事项；

（二）**属于地方性事务**需要制定地方性法规的事项。

除本法第八条规定的事项外，其他事项国家尚未制定法律或者行政法规的，省、自治区、直辖市和较大的市根据本地方的具体情况和实际需要，可以先制定地方性法规。在国家制定的法律或者行政法规生效后，地方性法规同法律或者行政法规相抵触的规定**无效**，制定**机关**应当及时予以修改或者废止。

第六十六条 民族自治地方的人民代表大会有权**依照 当地**民族的政治、经济和文化的特点，制定自治条例和单行条例。自治区的自治条例和单行条例，报全国人民代表大会常务委员会批准后生效。自治州、自治县的自治条例和单行条例，报省、自治区、直辖市的人民代表大会常务委员会批准后**生效**。

自治条例和单行条例可以依照当地民族

的特点，对法律和行政法规的规定作出**变通**规定，但不得**违背**法律或者行政法规的基本原则，不得对宪法和民族区域自治法的规定以及其他有关法律、行政法规**专门**就民族自治地方所作的规定作出变通规定。

第二节 规章

第七十一条 国务院各部、委员会、中国人**民银行**、**审计署**和具有行政管理**职能**的**直属 机构**，可以根据法律和国务院的行政法规、**决定**、**命令**，在本部门的权限**范围**内，制定规章。

部门规章规定的事项应当属于执行法律或者国务院的行政法规、决定、命令的事项。

第五章 适用与备案

第七十八条 宪法具有最高的法律效力，一切法律、行政法规、地方性法规、自治条例和单行条例、规章都不得同宪法相抵触。

第七十九条 法律的效力**高于**行政法规、地方性法规、规章。

行政法规的效力高于地方性法规、规章。

第八十二条 部门规章之间、部门规章与地方政府规章之间具有同等效力，在**各自**的权限范围内施行。

第八十三条 同一机关制定的法律、行政法规、地方性法规、自治条例和单行条例、规章，**特别规定** **与** **一般规定**不**一致** 的，适用特别规定；新的规定与旧的规定不一致的，适用新的规定。

第八十四条 法律、行政法规、地方性法规、自治条例和单行条例、规章不**溯及既往**，但为了更好地**保护**公民、**法人**和其他组织的权利和**利益**而作的特别规定除外。

第八十五条 法律之间对同一事项的新的一般规定与旧的特别规定不一致，不能**确定如何适用**时，由全国人民代表大会常务委员会**裁决**。

行政法规之间对同一事项的新的一般规定与旧的特别规定不一致，不能确定如何适用时，由国务院裁决。

第八十七条 法律、行政法规、地方性法规、自治条例和单行条例、规章有下列情形之一的，由有关机关依照本法第八十八条规定的权限予以**改变**或者撤销：

(一) **超越**权限的；

(二) **下位法** **违反** **上位法**规定的；

(三) 规章之间对同一事项的规定不一致，经裁决应当改变或者撤销一**方**的规定的；

(四) 规章的规定被认为**不适当**，应当予以改变或者撤销的；

(五) 违背**法定程序**的。

第八十九条 行政法规、地方性法规、自治条例和单行条例、规章应当在公布后的三十日内依照下列规定*报*有关机关*备案*：

（一）行政法规报全国人民代表大会常务委员会备案；

（二）省、自治区、直辖市的人民代表大会及其常务委员会制定的地方性法规，报全国人民代表大会常务委员会和国务院备案；较大的市的人民代表大会及其常务委员会制定的地方性法规，由省、自治区的人民代表大会常务委员会报全国人民代表大会常务委员会和国务院备案；

（三）自治州、自治县制定的自治条例和单行条例，由省、自治区、直辖市的人民代表大会常务委员会报全国人民代表大会常务委员会和国务院备案；

（四）部门规章和地方政府规章报国务院备案；地方政府规章应当同时报本级人民代表大会常务委员会备案；

较大的市的人民政府制定的规章应当同时报省、自治区的人民代表大会常务委员会和人民政府备案；

（五）根据授权制定的法规应当报授权决定规定的机关备案。

第九十条 国务院、**中央军事委员会、最高人民法院**、最高人民检察院和各省、自治区、直辖市的人民代表大会常务委员会认为行政法规、地方性法规、自治条例和单行条例同宪法或者法律相抵触的，可以*向*全国人民代表大会常务委员会书面提出进行审查的要求，由常

务委员会**工作机构分送**有关的专门委员会进行审查、提出意见。

**前款**规定**以外**的其他国家机关和**社会 团体、企业 事业**组织以及公民认为行政法规、地方性法规、自治条例和单行条例同宪法或者法律相抵触的，可以向全国人民代表大会常务委员会**书面**提出进行审查的**建议**，由常务委员会工作机构进行研究，**必要**时，送有关的专门委员会进行审查、提出意见。

第九十一条 全国人民代表大会专门委员会在审查中认为行政法规、地方性法规、自治条例和单行条例同宪法或者法律相抵触的，可以向制定机关提出书面审查意见；也可以由法律委员会与有关的专门委员会**召开 联合**审查会议，要求制定机关**到会**说明情况，再向制定机关提出书面审查意见。制定机关应当在两个月内研究提出**是否**修改的意见，**并**向全国人民代表大会法律委员会和有关的专门委员会**反馈**。

全国人民代表大会法律委员会和有关的专门委员会审查认为行政法规、地方性法规、自治条例和单行条例同宪法或者法律相抵触**而**制定机关不予修改的，可以向委员长会议提出书面审查意见和予以撤销的**议案**，由委员长会议决定是否提请常务委员会会议审议决定。

第九十四条

本法自2000年7月1日起**施行**。

# C. Vocabulary of Legislation Law

| Chinese | Pinyin | English |
|---|---|---|
| 立法 | Lìfǎ | Legislation (lit. to legislate; set up laws) |
| 届 | Jiè | Session |
| 全国人民代表大会 | Quánguó Rénmín Dàibiǎo Dàhuì | National People's Congress (NPC) |
| 会议 | Huìyì | Meeting |
| 通过 | Tōngguò | Enact; pass |
| 目录 | Mùlù | Table of contents |
| 章 | Zhāng | Chapter[2] |
| 总则 | Zǒngzé | General principles |
| 法律 | Fǎlù | Law |

---

2 Law Practice Tip: Chinese laws and regulations typically consist of: parts (编), chapters (章), sections (节), and articles (条). There is no definitive English translation for these terms.

| 节 | Jié | Section[3] |
|---|---|---|
| 权限 | Quánxiàn | Authority; power |
| 程序 | Chéngxù | Procedure; process |
| 常务委员会 | Chángwù Wěiyuánhuì | Standing Committee (of the NPC) |
| 解释 | Jiěshì | Interpret; interpretation |
| 规定 | Guīdìng | Stipulation; provision |
| 行政 | Xíngzhèng | Administrative |
| 法规 | Fǎguī | Administrative laws and regulations[4] |
| 地方 | Dìfāng | Local |
| 性 | Xìng | Suffix for -ness, -ity, -ive, -ize |
| 自治条例 | Zìzhì tiáolì | Regulations on the exercise of autonomy[5] |
| 单行 | Dānxíng | Regulations enacted in autonomous areas[6] |
| 规章 | Guīzhāng | Rule; regulation |
| 适用 | Shìyòng | Apply |
| 备案 | Bèi'àn | Put on record; file |
| 附则 | Fùzé | Supplementary provisions |

---

3 Law Practice Tip: Chinese laws and regulations typically consist of: parts (编), chapters (章), sections (节), and articles (条). There is no definitive English translation for these terms.

4 Law Practice Tip: "行政法规" are regulations adopted by the State Council. They are the third level of legislation in China, only lower than the Constitution and Laws passed by National People's Congress or its Standing Committee.

5 Law Practice Tip: There is no standardized Chinese term or English translation for 条例. At the city level, it might be appropriate to call them ordinances rather than regulations.

6 Law Practice Tip: Literally meaning to "stand alone," these regulations often reflect the local culture, economy, etc.

| 条 | Tiáo | Article[7] |
|---|---|---|
| 制定 | Zhìdìng | Formulate; enact |
| 修改 | Xiūgǎi | Revise; modify; amend |
| 废止 | Fèizhǐ | Abolish; nullify |
| 本 | Běn | Literary Chinese for 这个 |
| 国务院 | Guówùyuàn | State Council |
| 部门 | Bùmén | Department; branch; section |
| 依照 | Yīzhào | In accordance with |
| 有关 | Yǒuguān | Relevant |
| 执行 | Zhíxíng | Carry out; implement |
| 行使 | Xíngshǐ | Exercise (a right) |
| 国家 | Guójiā | National |
| 权 | Quán | Authority; power; right |
| 刑事 | Xíngshì | Criminal |
| 民事 | Mínshì | Civil |
| 机构 | Jīgòu | Organization; structure |
| 基本 | Jīběn | Basic |
| 除 x 以外 | Chú x yǐwài | Except for x |
| 应当 | Yīngdāng | Shall; must[8] |

---

7 Law Practice Tip: In a statute, the term 条 (tiáo) is usually used for subsections of a Chapter and is usually translated as "article."

8 Law Practice Tip: In legal English, there is a difference between "must" and "shall." "Shall" has several meanings including "must" and "will." In modern legal English the trend is to avoid using "shall." When "shall" is used in the mandatory sense, then the word "must" is used.

| 由 x | Yóu x | By x |
|------|-------|------|
| 其他 | Qítā | Other |
| 闭会 | Bìhuì | Not in session |
| 对 | Duì | 对 and 向 combine with a number of different verbs to generally mean "to" or "for" |
| 进行 | Jìnxíng | Carry out; conduct |
| 部分 | Bùfen | Partial |
| 补充 | Bǔchōng | Supplement |
| 不得 | Bùdé | Must not; may not |
| 同 x 相抵触 | Tóng x xiāng dǐchù | Mutually conflict with x |
| 该 | Gāi | That[9] |
| 原则 | Yuánzé | Principle |
| 下列 | Xiàliè | The following; set forth below |
| 事项 | Shìxiàng | Item; matter |
| 主权 | Zhǔquán | Sovereign rights; sovereignty |
| 各级 | Gèjí | All levels |
| 法院 | Fǎyuàn | Court |
| 检察院 | Jiǎncháyuàn | Procuratorate (prosecutors) |
| 产生 | Chǎnshēng | Cause; bring about |

---

9 Law Practice Tip: In modern legal English, the term "that" is used. In older legal English, the term "said" is used.

| 组织 | Zǔzhī | Organization |
|------|-------|--------------|
| 职权 | Zhíquán | Official powers; authority |
| 民族 | Mínzú | Ethnic minority; nationality |
| 区域 | Qūyù | Area; region |
| 制度 | Zhìdù | System (political or administrative) |
| 特别 | Tèbié | Special |
| 基层 | Jīcéng | Grass roots; basic or primary level |
| 群众 | Qúnzhòng | Mass |
| 犯罪 | Fànzuì | Commit a crime |
| 刑罚 | Xíngfá | Criminal penalty or punishment |
| 公民 | Gōngmín | Citizen |
| 政治 | Zhèngzhì | Political |
| 权利 | Quánlì | Rights |
| 剥夺 | Bōduó | Deprive |
| 限制 | Xiànzhì | Restrict; limit |
| 人身 | Rénshēn | Personal |
| 自由 | Zìyóu | Free; freedom |
| 强制 | Qiángzhì | Mandatory; compulsory |
| 措施 | Cuòshī | Measures |
| 处罚 | Chǔfá | Penalty; punishment |
| 非国有 | Fēiguóyǒu | Non-government owned |
| 财产 | Cáichǎn | Property |

| 征收 | Zhēngshōu | Expropriate |
|------|-----------|-------------|
| 经济 | Jīngjì | Economy |
| 以及 | Yǐjí | As well as; and (literary Chinese meaning the same as 跟 and 和) |
| 财政 | Cáizhèng | Finance |
| 税收 | Shuìshōu | Tax revenue |
| 海关 | Hǎiguān | Customs |
| 金融 | Jīnróng | Banking |
| 外贸 | Wàimào | Foreign trade |
| 诉讼 | Sùsòng | Litigation |
| 仲裁 | Zhòngcái | Arbitration |
| 必须 | Bìxū | Shall; must |
| 及 | Jí | And; as well as (literary Chinese meaning the same as 跟 and 和) |
| 其 | Qí | Literary Chinese for 他的 |
| 尚未 | Shàngwèi | Literary Chinese for 还没 |
| 的 | De | 的 is often used without the term it modifies. Here the missing term could be 时候 (time, i.e. "when") or 情况 (circumstance) |
| 决定 | Juédìng | Decide |
| 授权 | Shòuquán | Authorize |

| | | |
|---|---|---|
| 根据 | Gēnjù | Based on; according to |
| 实际 | Shíjì | Actual; realistic; in practice |
| 但是 x 除外 | Dànshì x chúwài | With the exception of x |
| 司法 | Sīfǎ | Judicial |
| 具有 | Jùyǒu | Fully possess; have |
| 同等 | Tóngděng | Equivalent; equal |
| 效力 | Xiàolì | Effectiveness; validity |
| 宪法 | Xiànfǎ | Constitution |
| 就 | Jiù | With regard to; as for |
| 为 x | Wèi x | For the sake of; in order to |
| 管理 | Guǎnlǐ | Manage |
| 职权 | Zhíquán | Official powers; authority |
| 经过 | Jīngguò | Go through; be x'd |
| 实践 | Shíjiàn | Put into practice |
| 检验 | Jiǎnyàn | Inspect |
| 条件 | Tiáojiàn | Requirements; conditions |
| 成熟 | Chéngshú | Mature; ripen |
| 及时 | Jíshí | Timely; promptly |
| 提请 | Tíqǐng | Submit a request |
| 自治区 | Zìzhìqū | Autonomous region |
| 直辖市 | Zhíxiáshì | Municipalities directly under control of the Central government |

| 同 x 相抵触 | Tóng x xiāngdǐchù | Mutually conflict with x |
|---|---|---|
| 前提 | Qiántí | Premise; prerequisite |
| 较 | Jiào | 比较[10] |
| 报 x 批准 | Bào x pīzhǔn | Report to x for approval |
| 报请 | Bàoqǐng | Report to |
| 合法 | Héfǎ | Legal |
| 审查 | Shěnchá | Investigate; review |
| 予以 | Yǔyǐ | 予以 and 加以 both mean "to do x." In English, we would not translate either |
| 其 | Qí | Literary Chinese for 他 |
| 规章 | Guīzhāng | Rule; regulation |
| 处理 | Chǔlǐ | Handle; deal with |
| 所称 x 是指 y | Suǒchēng x shìzhǐ y | The term x refers to y |
| 所在地 | Suǒzàidì | Local (lit. the place where it is located) |
| 经 (经过) | Jīng (Jīngguò) | Go through; be x'd |
| 为 | Wèi | For the sake of |
| 属于 | Shǔyú | Belong to; fall within |
| 事务 | Shìwù | Affairs; matters (political or economic) |
| 无效 | Wúxiào | Invalid; void |

---

10 Law Practice Tip: The term "relatively large" is often used in Chinese law. In the Legislation Law, the term is defined later in the text of the law. In the Criminal Law, the term is typically defined by later interpretations by the Supreme People's Court.

| 机关 | Jīguān | Organ (administrative or government) |
|---|---|---|
| 依照 | Yīzhào | In accordance with |
| 当地 | Dāngdì | Local |
| 生效 | Shēngxiào | Go into effect; become effective |
| 变通 | Biàntōng | Flexible |
| 违背 | Wéibèi | Violate; go against |
| 专门 | Zhuānmén | Specialized |
| 银行 | Yínháng | Bank (People's Bank of China) |
| 审计署 | Shěnjìshǔ | Auditing Administration of the PRC |
| 职能 | Zhínéng | Function; role |
| 直属 | Zhíshǔ | Directly under |
| 机构 | Jīgoù | Organization; organ |
| 决定 | Juédìng | Decision |
| 命令 | Mìnglìng | Order |
| 范围 | Fànwéi | Scope |
| 高于 x | Gāoyú x | Higher than x |
| 各自 | Gèzì | Each one |
| 特别规定 | Tèbié guīdìng | Special provision |
| 与 | Yǔ | And; together with |
| 一般规定 | Yībān guīdìng | General provision |
| 一致 | Yīzhì | Identical (views or opinions); in agreement |

| 溯及既往 | Sùjíjìwǎng | Retroactive |
|---|---|---|
| 保护 | Bǎohù | Protect |
| 法人 | Fǎrén | Legal person (i.e. legally established entity) |
| 利益 | Lìyì | Interest; benefit |
| 确定 | Quèdìng | Define; fix; determine |
| 如何 | Rúhé | How |
| 裁决 | Cáijué | Decide |
| 之一 | Zhīyī | 的一个 |
| 改变 | Gǎibiàn | Change |
| 撤销 | Chèxiāo | Cancel; rescind; revoke |
| 超越 | Chāoyuè | Exceed; surpass |
| 下位法 | Xiàwèifǎ | Inferior law |
| 违反 | Wéifǎn | Violate (a law) |
| 上位法 | Shàngwèifǎ | Superior law |
| 一方 | Yīfāng | One party or side |
| 不适当 | Bùshìdàng | Inappropriate; improper |
| 法定 | Fǎdìng | Legally mandated |
| 报 x 备案 | Bào x bèi'àn | Report to x to put on record or file |
| 中央军事委员会 | Zhōngyāng Jūnshì Wěiyuánhuì | Central Military Commission |
| 最高人民法院 | Zuìgāo Rénmín Fǎyuàn | Supreme People's Court |
| 向 | Xiàng | 对 and 向 combine with a number of |

| | | different verbs to generally mean "to" or "for" |
|---|---|---|
| 工作 | Gōngzuò | Work |
| 分送 | Fēnsòng | Send or distribute (to the respective agency) |
| 前款 | Qiánkuǎn | Preceding clause; above provision |
| 以外 | Yǐwài | Except for |
| 社会 | Shèhuì | Social; society |
| 团体 | Tuántǐ | Group; organization |
| 企业 | Qǐyè | Enterprise |
| 事业 | Shìyè | Cause; undertaking |
| 书面 | Shūmiàn | Written |
| 建议 | Jiànyì | Suggestions |
| 必要 | Bìyào | Necessary |
| 召开 | Zhāokāi | Convene |
| 联合 | Liánhé | Joint |
| 到会 | Dàohuì | Attend (a meeting) |
| 是否 | Shìfǒu | Whether |
| 并 | Bìng | And; moreover |
| 反馈 | Fǎnkuì | Give feedback |
| 而 | Ér | And; and yet |
| 议案 | Yì'àn | Proposal; motion |
| 施行 | Shīxíng | Come into force |

# D. Text of Red-Titled Documents[11] (2010)

广东 拟 规定 "红头文件" 有效期最长5年

《广东省 行政 机关 规范 性文件管理规定》修订 征求意见

"红头文件" 不可设定 收费 项目老百姓可对 "红头文件" 说 "不"

大洋网讯（《广州日报》记者 练情情）广东省政府**法制办**近日公布《广东省行政机关规范性文件管理规定（修订征求意见**稿**）》（以下简称 "修订稿"），并公开征求公众意见。对修订稿有意见或**建议** *的*，可于2010年1月8日前*向*广东省政府法制办*反映*。

"红头文件" 三不准

*所谓*规范性文件，*是指 除*政府规章 *外*，各级行政机关制定的，对公民、法人或者其他组织 具有 普遍 约束力的、可以反复 适用的文件，一般是以 "规定"、**"决定"**、**"命令"**、"办法"、"通知"、"公告"、"规则"、"细

则"、"规范" 和 "通告" 等名称 出现，这些都被老百姓**通称** 为 "红头文件"。

为规范 "红头文件"，修订稿规定了 "三不准"。一、制定规范性文件，应当**符合 宪法、法律**、**法规**和规章的规定，不得**违反 上级**行政机关的命令、 决定，不得**超越** 本行政机关的**职权** 范围。

二、规范性文件不得设定下列 事项：（一）行政**处罚**；（二）行政**许可**；（三）行政**强制 措施**；（四）行政事业性收费项目，*但*省人民政府规范性文件*除外*；（五）其他应当*由*法律、法规、规章或者上级行政机关设定的事项。

三、没有法律、法规、规章作为**依据**，规

---

11 Source: Guang dong ni gui ding "hong tou wen jian" you xiao qi zui chang wu nian [Guangdong Proposes to Make "Red Titled Documents" Effective for a Maximum of Five Years] *available at* http://news.dayoo.com/guangzhou/200912/11/73437_11507915.htm (last visited Sep. 16, 2011).

范性文件不得作出限制公民、法人或者其他组织权利或者增加公民、法人或者其他组织义务的规定。

**有效期届满 "红头文件" 自动失效**

修订稿增加了对行政机关规范性文件的有效期规定,有效期届满,自动失效。修订稿规定,规范性文件有效期根据实际情况确定,自施行之日起最长不得超过5年。暂行或者试行的规范性文件有效期自施行之日最长不超过2年。安排 部署工作有时限 要求的规范性文件,有效期不得超过工作时限。

如果制定机关、起草部门或者实施机关认为有效期届满需要继续实行的,可以在规范性文件有效期届满前一年,对规范性文件的施行情况进行评估,根据评估情况重新修订。评估程序 参照《广东省政府规章立法后评估程序规定》执行。

**老百姓可对 "红头文件" 提审查建议**

2005年2月1日开始实施的《广东省行政机关规范性文件管理规定》首次规定了公民可对 "红头文件" 提审查建议。此次修订对提审查建议的程序和处理作了进一步明确规定,政府法制机构在收到审查建议后,应当在15个工作日内作出处理,决定是否 启动 监督程序,并将处理结果答复提出审查建议的公民、法人或者其他组织。

规范性文件审查建议人对政府法制机构的处理结果不满意的,还可以提请 上一级政府法制机构复核。

**制定 "红头文件" 也要征求公众意见**

修订稿规定,规范性文件起草部门应当通过 网络或者报刊等媒体向社会公布规范性文件草案,广泛征求公众意见。征求公众意见的时间不得少于30日。规范性文件涉及的领域有行业 协会、中介机构或者其他社会组织的,规范性文件起草部门应听取其意见。

行政机关制定规范性文件,实行统一的合法性审查制度。政府规范性文件,应当经本级政府法制机构审核。部门规范性文件,应当经本级政府法制机构审查后再行 发布。政府法制机构审查规范性文件草案,若发现存在可行性或者适当性问题时,可以向规范性文件起草部门提出建议。

对未经政府法制机构审查同意以及未经规定载体发布的部门规范性文件,政府法制机构可以向社会公示 该文件无效。对未经备案的规范性文件,政府法制机构可以提请本级人民政府责令 改正或者撤销。

http://www.dayoo.com 2009-12-11 09:50 来源:《广州日报》。

# E. Vocabulary of Red-Titled Documents (2010)

| Chinese | Pinyin | English |
| --- | --- | --- |
| 广东 | Guǎngdōng | Guangdong (Province) |
| 拟 | Nǐ | Intend; plan to |
| 规定 | Guīdìng | Stipulate; provide[12] |
| 有效期 | Yǒuxiàoqī | Term of effectiveness |
| 行政 | Xíngzhèng | Administrative |
| 机关 | Jīguān | Organ (administrative or government) |
| 规范 | Guīfàn | Standard; norm |
| 性 | Xìng | Suffix for -ness, -ity, -ive, -ize |
| 管理 | Guǎnlǐ | Manage |
| 修订 | Xiūdìng | Revise; amend |
| 征求 | Zhēngqiú | Solicit; seek[13] |

---

12 Law Practice Tip: In China, printed versions of laws, rules, and regulations are typically printed with the title of the new law, rule, or regulation printed in red. Red is also the most commonly used color for printed slogans and banners.

13 Law Practice Tip: The practice of seeing public input on pending legislation began at the national level in the mid-2000s but is still limited to major legislation. A few national and local-level agencies now seek public input on draft rules and regulations. There is no legal mandate to seek public input. The provincial government in Guangdong is among the first to make it legally mandated in certain areas.

| | | |
|---|---|---|
| 设定 | Shèdìng | Set up; establish |
| 收费 | Shōufèi | Fee; charge |
| 项目 | Xiàngmù | Project |
| 大洋网讯 | Dàyáng wǎng xùn | Dayang Web News (dayoo.com) |
| 练 | Liàn | A Chinese surname |
| 法制办 (法制办公室) | Fǎzhìbàn (Fǎzhì bàn'gōngshì) | Legal Affairs Office (lit. Legal System Office) |
| 稿 | Gǎo | Draft |
| 以下简称 x | Yǐxià jiǎnchēng x | Abbreviated below as x[14] |
| 并 | Bìng | And; moreover |
| 公众 | Gōngzhòng | Public |
| 建议 | Jiànyì | Suggestions |
| 的 | De | 的 is often used without the term it modifies. Here the missing term could be 时候 (time, i.e. "when') or 情况 (circumstance) |
| 于 | Yú | In; on |
| 向 | Xiàng | 对 and 向 combine with a number of different verbs to generally mean "to" or "for" |

14 Law Practice Tip: In modern legal English, the term would be "below." In older legal English, the term would be "hereinafter."

| | | |
|---|---|---|
| 反映 | Fǎnyìng | Report; make known |
| 准 | Zhǔn | Permit; allow |
| 所谓 x 是指 y | Suǒwèi x shìzhǐ y | The term x means y |
| 除 x 外 | Chú x wài | Except for x |
| 规章 | Guīzhāng | Rule; regulation |
| 各级 | Gèjí | All levels |
| 制定 | Zhìdìng | Formulate; enact |
| 对 (对于) | Duì (Duìyú) | As for; towards |
| 法人 | Fǎrén | Legal person (i.e. legally established entity)[15] |
| 组织 | Zǔzhī | Organization |
| 具有 | Jùyǒu | Fully possess; have |
| 普遍 | Pǔbiān | General; widespread |
| 约束力 | Yuèshùlì | Binding force |
| 反复 | Fǎnfù | Repeatedly; over and over again |
| 适用 | Shìyòng | Apply |
| 决定 | Juédìng | Decide |
| 命令 | Mìnglìng | Order |
| 办法 | Bànfǎ | Method |
| 通知 | Tōngzhī | Notice |

---

15 Law Practice Tip: This is a legal term of art. Natural persons are individuals. Legal persons are entities created by law (e.g. a corporation).

| 公告 | Gōnggào | Public announcement |
|------|---------|---------------------|
| 规则 | Guīzé | Rule; regulation |
| 细则 | Xìzé | Detailed provisions |
| 规范 | Guīfàn | Standardize; normalize |
| 通告 | Tōnggào | Announcement |
| 名称 | Míngchēng | Name (of an entity or object) |
| 出现 | Chūxiàn | Appear |
| 通称 | Tōngchēng | Commonly known as |
| 为 | Wéi | Take; treat as |
| 为 | Wèi | For the sake of; in order to |
| 符合 | Fúhé | Conform to; comply with |
| 宪法 | Xiànfǎ | Constitution |
| 法律 | Fǎlù | Law |
| 法规 | Fǎguī | Administrative laws and regulations[16] |
| 违反 | Wéifǎn | Violate (a law) |
| 上级 | Shàngjí | Higher, superior level |
| 超越 | Chāoyuè | Exceed; surpass |
| 本 | Běn | Literary Chinese for 这个 |
| 职权 | Zhíquán | Official powers; authority |

---

16 Law Practice Tip: "行政法规" are legislations adopted by the State Council. They are the third level of legislation in China, only lower than the Constitution and Laws passed by National People's Congress or its Standing Committee.

| | | |
|---|---|---|
| 范围 | Fànwéi | Scope |
| 下列 | Xiàliè | The following; set forth below |
| 事项 | Shìxiàng | Item; matter |
| 处罚 | Chǔfá | Penalize; punish |
| 许可 | Xǔkě | Approval; permission |
| 强制 | Qiángzhì | Mandatory; compulsory |
| 措施 | Cuòshī | Measures |
| 事业 | Shìyè | Cause; undertaking |
| 但 x 除外 | Dàn x chúwài | With the exception of x |
| 由 x | Yóu x | By x |
| 依据 | Yījù | Follow; act in accordance with |
| 权利 | Quánlì | Rights |
| 增加 | Zēngjiā | Increase |
| 义务 | Yìwù | Duty; obligation |
| 届满 | Jièmǎn | Expire |
| 失效 | Shīxiào | Become invalid |
| 确定 | Quèdìng | Define; fix; determine |
| 自 x 起 | Zì x qǐ | Beginning from x |
| 暂行 | Zànxíng | Temporary |
| 试行 | Shìxíng | Trial[17] |

---

17 Law Practice Tip: In China, it is common to issue new laws and rules in a "trial," i.e. temporary, version. Some trial or temporary regulations may be in force for a number of years before more permanent regulations are promulgated. Apparently, Guangzhou wants to be sure these kinds of regulations have a limited lifetime.

| 安排 | Ānpái | Arrange |
|---|---|---|
| 部署 | Bùshǔ | Delegate; arrange |
| 时限 | Shíxiàn | Time limit |
| 要求 | Yāoqiú | Demands; requirements |
| 起草 | Qǐcǎo | Draft; draw up |
| 实行 | Shíxíng | Implement; carry out |
| 施行 | Shīxíng | Come into force; take effect |
| 进行 | Jìnxíng | Carry out; conduct |
| 评估 | Pínggū | Evaluate; evaluation |
| 程序 | Chéngxù | Procedure; process |
| 参照 | Cānzhào | Refer to; consult |
| 审查 | Shěnchá | Investigate; review |
| 实施 | Shíshī | Put into effect; implement; carry out |
| 首次 | Shǒucì | For the first time |
| 此次 | Cǐcì | This time |
| 处理 | Chǔlì | Handle; deal with |
| 明确 | Míngquè | Make clear and definite; clarify |
| 是否 | Shìfǒu | Whether |
| 启动 | Qǐdòng | Start |
| 监督 | Jiāndū | Control; supervise |
| 将 | Jiāng | Literary Chinese for 把 |
| 答复 | Dáfù | Answer; reply |

| 满意 | Mǎnyì | Satisfied |
|---|---|---|
| 提请 | Tíqǐng | Submit a request |
| 上一级 | Shàngyījí | Next highest level |
| 复核 | Fùhé | Review; reexamination |
| 通过 | Tōngguò | Go through |
| 网络 | Wǎngluò | Network |
| 报刊 | Bàokān | Periodical publication |
| 媒体 | Méitǐ | Media |
| 广泛 | Guǎngfàn | Broad |
| 少于 | Shǎoyú | Less; fewer than |
| 涉及 | Shèjí | Involve; concern |
| 领域 | Lǐngyù | Area |
| 行业 | Hángyè | Trade; profession; industry |
| 协会 | Xiéhuì | Associations |
| 中介 | Zhōngjiè | Intermediary |
| 听取 | Tīngqǔ | Listen to; hear (a report) |
| 统一 | Tǒngyī | Unified |
| 合法 | Héfǎ | Legal |
| 制度 | Zhìdù | System (political or administrative) |
| 经 (经过) | Jīng (Jīngguò) | Go through; be x'd |
| 再行 | Zàixíng | Once again |
| 发布 | Fābù | Issue |

| 若 | Ruò | Literary Chinese for 如果 |
| 存在 | Cúnzài | Exist |
| 可行 | Kěxíng | Can be done or carried out |
| 以及 | Yǐjí | As well as; and; too (literary Chinese meaning the same as 跟 and 和) |
| 公示 | Gōngshì | Public notice |
| 该 | Gāi | That[18] |
| 备案 | Bèi'àn | Put on record; file |
| 责令 | Zélìng | Order; instruction |
| 改正 | Gǎizhèng | Correct; amend |
| 撤销 | Chèxiāo | Cancel; rescind; revoke |
| 来源 | Láiyuán | Source |
| 发表 | Fābiǎo | Publish |
| 评论 | Pínglùn | Comment |

18 Law Practice Tip: In modern legal English the term "that" is used. In older legal English, the term "said" is used.

# Chapter 3
# **Contract Law**
# 合同法

Hé    Tóng    Fǎ

# A. Introduction to Contract Law in the PRC

By *Wang Zhizhou*, LLM

Traditionally in China, civil transactions among individuals were conducted without formal, written contracts. Beginning in 1949, contract law was mainly used to regulate contractual relationship between governmental bodies, state-owned enterprises (SOEs), and cooperatives.

The reform and open policy which prevailed in the late 1970s marked a new era for the development of China's economy and, along with it, contract law. The landmark of the building process of a new contract law system in China was the passage of the Law of the PRC on Economic Contracts in 1981. Two other laws on contracts were passed in 1985 and 1987, respectively addressing foreign-related contracts and technology contracts. This tripartite system largely formed the legal system of contracts for more than a decade before the new Contract Law of the PRC superseded them in 1999.

The 1999 law consists of 428 clauses divided into three parts, making it China's longest piece of civil legislation when it was released. The first part contains general principles for contracts and fundamental provisions dealing with such basic contract law issues as formation, termination, and liability for breach. The second part, by contrast, specifically deals with several kinds of contracts. The final part provides rules on how the new law applies to disputes that arose before it took effect.

The drafters of the new law learned from the experiences of and borrowed ideas from various countries' laws (particularly Germany, Japan, France, and Italy) as well as international treaties. The following new features make the 1999 Contract Law fundamentally different from its predecessors. First, the new law has a positive attitude in encouraging transactions. Ideas like freedom of contracting have been introduced and recognized by this law, a court's power to void a contract is much more limited, concluding a contract is much easier, and, with limited exceptions, the court is urged to abide by the parties' true intentions instead of focusing too much on the form of the agreement. Second, civil contracts among individuals and commercial contracts between business organizations all come under this new law. Therefore, the new contract law finally functions as a vehicle generally regulating contractual relationships among all equal private parties. Third, relativity of contracts is greatly honored under this law, which will accordingly shield the contractual relationship from any third party's intervention. Fourth, good faith in contracting and no contradiction against public policy and social order are explicitly stated as fundamental principles.

The remarkable achievement of the 1999 Contract Law goes hand in hand with the reality of and the demand from the changing Chinese society since the early 1980s. The reform and open policy initiated by the government from the late 1970s paved the way for the rapid growth of a market economy and therefore individual productivity was encouraged and further inspired. On the one hand, the concept of freedom of contracting closely matches this trend and activated individual enthusiasm for joining in business activities; on the other hand, the reality that more and more transactions are conducted based on contracts will demand a legal system that will recognize the formation of a contract and its enforceability. However, the principle of good faith in contracting and compliance with public policy and social order allow the courts to exercise their discretion in redressing inequity and unfairness due to fraud or an unacceptable imbalance of bargaining power.

Following the new law, the Supreme Court of the PRC released two judicial interpretations (the most recent in 2009) which, from a practical point of view, have strengthened the basic principles and embodied the framework established by the 1999 Contract Law. Particularly, the provisions in the 2009 interpretations which adopted an even more lenient approach in judging the validity of a contract and the requirements for the formation of a contract, and a new rule allowing clausula rebus sic stantibus (termination of a contract if unforeseen circumstances arise) have given a new signal of the government's determination to encourage more private transactions and enforce more contracts after the 2008 global financial crisis.

Although it may be difficult to summarize the whole history of the law on contracts in China in just a few short words, it is not too early to conclude that the development of this system has well reflected the government's attitude towards a market economy and the freedom of individuals to enter into contracts. With more confidence gained by China for its remarkable economic achievement and the irreversible process of openness, optimists cannot be too wrong in predicting the appearance of a further improved and liberal legal system of contract in China.

# B. Text of Contract Law[1]

## 中华人民共和国合同 法

**1999年3月15日第九届 全国人民代表大会第二次会议 通过**

**1999年3月1 5日中华人民共和国主席 令第十五号公布**

**自1999年1 0月1日起 施行**

---

1 Source: Zhonghua Renmin Gongheguo Zhongguo he tong fa [Contract Law (P.R.C.)] (promulgated by the Nat'l People's Cong., Mar. 15, 1999, effective Oct. 1, 1999) *available at* http://www.gov.cn/banshi/2005-07/11/content_13695.htm (last visited May 31, 2011).

总则

**第一章　一般规定**

第一条　为了**保护**合同当事人的合法 权益,维护 社会 经济 秩序,促进社会主义 现代化建设,**制定** 本法。

第二条　本法*所称*合同是 平等 主体 *的* 自然人、法人、其他**组织**之间**设立**、变更、终止民事权利义务关系的**协议**。

**婚姻**、**收养**、**监护**等有关 身份关系的协议,**适用**其他**法律**的规定。

第三条　合同当事人的法律**地位**平等,一方 **不得 将**自己的意志 强加给另一方。

第四条　当事人依法 **享有 自愿**订立合同的权利,**任何** 单位和个人不得非法 **干预**。

第五条　当事人应当 **遵循 公平 原则 确定**各方的权利和义务。

第六条　当事人**行使**权利、履行义务应当遵循**诚实 信用**原则。

第七条　当事人订立、履行合同,应当遵守法律、**行政 法规**,尊重社会公德,不得**扰乱**社会经济秩序,**损害社会公共 利益**。

第八条　依法**成立**的合同,对当事人**具有法律约束力**。当事人应当**按照 约定**履行自己的义务,不得**擅自**变更或者解除合同。

依法成立的合同,受法律保护。

第二章　合同的订立

第九条　当事人订立合同,应当具有**相应**的民事权利 能力和民事行为能力。

当事人依法可以委托**代理人**订立合同。

第十条　当事人订立合同,有**书面 形式**、口头形式和其他形式。

法律、行政法规规定**采用**书面形式**的**,应当采用书面形式。当事人约定采用书面形式的,应当采用书面形式。

第十一条　书面形式**是**指合同书、信件和**数据 电文（包括 电报**、电传、传真、电子数据交换和电子邮件）等可以**有形地表现**所**载内容**的形式。

第十二条　合同的内容*由*当事人约定,一般包括以下条款:

（一）当事人的名称或者姓名和**住所**;

（二）**标的**;

（三）**数量**;

（四）**质量**；

（五）**价款**或者**报酬**；

（六）履行**期限**、地点和**方式**；

（七）违约责任；

（八）**解决 争议**的方法。

当事人可以**参照 各类**合同的**示范 文本**订立合同。

第十三条　当事人订立合同，采取 **要约**、**承诺**方式。

第十四条　要约是希望和他人订立合同的**意思表示**，该意思表示应当**符合 下列**规定：

（一）内容**具体确定**；

（二）**表明 经 受要约人**承诺，**要约人 即**受该意思表示约束。

第十五条　要约**邀请**是希望他人向自己发出要约的意思表示。**寄送的价目表**、**拍卖 公告**、**招标**公告、**招股**说明书、**商业 广告**等为要约邀请。

商业广告的内容符合要约规定的，**视为**要约。

第三章　合同的效力

第四十四条　依法成立的合同，*自* 成立 *时* **生效**。

法律、行政法规规定应当**办理 批准**、**登记**等**手续**生效的，依照**其**规定。

第四十五条　当事人对合同的效力可以约定**附 条件**。附生效条件的合同，自条件**成就**时生效。附解除条件的合同，自条件成就时**失效**。

当事人为自己的利益不**正当地阻止**条件成就的，视为条件已成就；不正当地**促成**条件成就的，视为条件不成就。

第四十六条　当事人对合同的效力可以约定附期限。附生效期限的合同，自期限**届至**时生效。附终止期限的合同，自期限**届满**时失效。

第四十七条　**限制**民事行为能力人订立的合同，经法定代理人**追认**后，该合同有效，**但 纯获利益**的合同或者**与**其**年龄**、**智力**、**精神 健康 状况 相 适应** *而* 订立的合同，不必经法定代理人追认。

**相对人**可以**催告**法定代理人在一个月内**予以追认**。法定代理人未作表示的，**视为拒绝追认**。合同被追认之前，**善意**相对人有**撤销**的权利。撤销应当以**通知**的方式作出。

附则

第四百二十八条　本法自１９９９年１０月１日起施行，《中华人民共和国经济合同法》、《中华人民共和国**涉外**经济合同法》、《中华人民共和国技术合同法》同时**废止**。

# C. Vocabulary of Contract Law

| Chinese | Pinyin | English |
|---------|--------|---------|
| 合同 | Hétóng | Contract |
| 法 | Fǎ | Law |
| 届 | Jiè | Session |
| 全国人民代表大会 | Quánguó Rénmín Dàibiǎo Dàhuì | National People's Congress (NPC) |
| 会议 | Huìyì | Meeting |
| 通过 | Tōngguò | Enact; pass |
| 主席 | Zhǔxí | Chairman |
| 令 | Lìng | Decree |
| 公布 | Gōngbù | Promulgate |
| 自 x 起 | Zì x qǐ | Beginning from x |
| 施行 | Shīxíng | Come into force |
| 章 | Zhāng | Chapter[2] |

---

2 Law Practice Tip: There is no standard English translation for this term and related terms such as 条 tiáo (Article). In part this is because their usage in Chinese is not standardized.

| 一般 | Yībān | General |
|------|-------|---------|
| 规定 | Guīdìng | Stipulations; provisions |
| 订立 | Dìnglì | Enter into (a contract) |
| 效力 | Xiàolì | Effectiveness; validity |
| 履行 | Lǚxíng | Perform; fulfill; carry out |
| 变更 | Biàngēng | Change; amend |
| 转让 | Zhuǎnràng | Transfer possession |
| 权利 | Quánlì | Rights |
| 义务 | Yìwù | Duty; obligation |
| 终止 | Zhōngzhǐ | Termination (at end of contract term) |
| 违约 | Wéiyuē | Breach; violate (a contract) |
| 责任 | Zérèn | Responsibility; liability |
| 供用 | Gōngyòng | Supply for use |
| 气 | Qì | Gas |
| 热力 | Rèlì | Heat |
| 赠与 | Zèngyǔ | Give; gift |
| 借款 | Jièkuǎn | Loan |
| 租赁 | Zūlìn | Rent |
| 融资 | Róngzī | Financial |
| 承揽 | Chénglǎn | Contractor; to do a job |
| 建设 | Jiànshè | Construction |
| 工程 | Gōngchéng | Engineering |

| 运输 | Yùnshū | Transportation; freight |
| 技术 | Jìshù | Technology; skill |
| 保管 (保护管理) | Bǎoguǎn (Bǎohù guǎnlǐ) | Depositary |
| 仓储 | Cāngchǔ | Storage |
| 委托 | Wěituō | Entrust; delegate; consign |
| 行纪 | Hángjì | Brokerage |
| 居间 | Jūjiān | Middleman; intermediary |
| 附则 | Fùzé | Supplementary provisions |
| 总则 | Zǒngzé | General principles |
| 条 | Tiáo | Article[3] |
| 保护 | Bǎohù | Protect |
| 当事人 | Dāngshìrén | Parties |
| 合法 | Héfǎ | Legal |
| 权益 | Quányì | Rights and interests |
| 维护 | Wéihù | Protect |
| 社会 | Shèhuì | Social; society |
| 经济 | Jīngjì | Economy; economic |
| 秩序 | Zhìxù | Order |
| 促进 | Cùjìn | Promote; advance |

---

3 Law Practice Tip: Chinese laws and regulations typically consist of: parts (编), chapters (章), sections (节), and articles (条). There is no definitive English translation for these terms.

| 主义 | Zhǔyì | -ism |
|---|---|---|
| 现代 | Xiàndài | Modern |
| 化 | Huà | -ize (lit. change to x) |
| 制定 | Zhìdìng | Formulate; enact |
| 本 | Běn | Literary Chinese for 这个 |
| 所称 y 是 z 的 a | Suǒchēng y shì z de a | The term y means a which are z |
| 平等 | Píngděng | Equal |
| 主体 | Zhǔtǐ | Subject[4] |
| 自然人 | Zìrán rén | Natural person[5] |
| 法人 | Fǎrén | Legal person |
| 组织 | Zǔzhī | Organization |
| 设立 | Shèlì | Establish; set up |
| 民事 | Mínshì | Civil |
| 协议 | Xiéyì | Agreement |
| 婚姻 | Hūnyīn | Marriage |
| 收养 | Shōuyǎng | Adoption (lit. receive and raise) |
| 监护 | Jiānhù | Guardianship |
| 有关 | Yǒuguān | Relevant |
| 身份 | Shēnfèn | Status; capacity; identity |

---

4 Law Practice Tip: A generic civil law term encompassing natural persons and legal persons.

5 Law Practice Tip: This and the next term are legal terms of art. Natural persons are individuals. Legal persons are entities created by law (e.g. a corporation or a partnership).

| 适用 | Shìyòng | Apply |
|------|---------|-------|
| 法律 | Fǎlù | Law |
| 地位 | Dìwèi | Status; position |
| 一方 | Yīfāng | One party or side |
| 不得 | Bùdé | Must not; may not |
| 将 | Jiāng | Literary Chinese for 把 |
| 意志 | Yìzhì | Will |
| 强加 | Qiángjiā | Impose; force |
| 另 | Lìng | The other; 另外的 |
| 依法 | Yīfǎ | Legally; in accordance with the law |
| 享有 | Xiǎngyǒu | Have; enjoy (rights; benefits prestige; etc.) |
| 自愿 | Zìyuàn | Voluntarily |
| 任何 | Rènhé | Any |
| 单位 | Dānwèi | Entity[6] |
| 非法 | Feīfǎ | Illegal |
| 干预 | Gānyù | Intervene; interfere |
| 应当 | Yīngdāng | Shall; must[7] |
| 遵循 | Zūnxún | Follow; abide by; adhere to |

6 Law Practice Tip: Dānwèi is used to describe the organization to which you belong, e.g. your employer. In the past, when there was no private economy, the Dānwèi played a much more significant role in the lives of its workers. It provided housing, schools, hospitals, cafeterias, etc. In modern Chinese is it often best translated as "entity."

7 Law Practice Tip: In legal English, there is a difference between "must" and "shall." "Shall" has several meanings including "must" and "will." In modern legal English the trend is to avoid using "shall." When "shall" is used in the mandatory sense, then the word "must" is used.

| 公平 | Gōngpíng | Fair |
|------|----------|------|
| 原则 | Yuánzé | Principle |
| 确定 | Quèdìng | Define; fix; determine |
| 行使 | Xíngshǐ | Exercise (a right) |
| 诚实信用 | Chéngshí xìnyòng | Good faith |
| 行政法规 | Xíngzhèng fǎguī | Administrative laws and regulations[8] |
| 尊重 | Zūnzhòng | Respect; esteem |
| 公德 | Gōngdé | Social ethics; morality |
| 扰乱 | Rǎoluàn | Disturb; harass |
| 损害 | Sǔnhài | Harm; damage |
| 公共 | Gōnggòng | Public |
| 利益 | Lìyì | Interest; benefit |
| 成立 | Chénglì | Form; establish |
| 具有 | Jùyǒu | Fully possess; have |
| 约束力 | Yuēshùlì | Binding force |
| 按照 | Ànzhào | In accordance with |
| 约定 | Yuēdìng | Agreed upon |
| 擅自 | Shànzì | Do something without authorization; unwarranted; at will |

---

8 Law Practice Tip: "行政法规" are legislations adopted by the State Council. They are the third level of legislation in China, only lower than the Constitution and Laws passed by National People's Congress or its Standing Committee.

| | | |
|---|---|---|
| 解除 | Jiěchú | Terminate (before end of contract term) |
| 相应 | Xiāngyìng | Corresponding |
| 民事权利 | Mínshì quánlì | Civil rights[9] |
| 能力 | Nénglì | Ability; capability; capacity |
| 民事行为 | Mínshì xíngwéi | Civil acts |
| 代理人 | Dàilǐrén | Agent |
| 书面 | Shūmiàn | Written |
| 形式 | Xíngshì | Form |
| 口头 | Kǒutóu | Oral |
| 采用 | Cǎiyòng | Select; use; adopt |
| 的 | De | 的 is often used without the term it modifies. Here the missing term could be 时候 (time, i.e. "when") or 情况 (circumstance) |
| 是指 | Shìzhǐ | This refers to; means |
| 信件 | Xìnjiàn | Letter |
| 数据 | Shùjù | Data |
| 电文 | Diànwén | Electronic text |
| 包括 | Bāokuò | Include |

---

9 Law Practice Tip: Literally, rights under civil law. This and Civil Acts (below) are civil law concepts. Natural persons and legal persons come into the world with innate capacity, called Civil Rights capacity. The law then puts limits on this innate capacity resulting in Civil Acts capacity, e.g. age limitations for natural persons and other limitations for legal persons.

| 电报 | Diànbào | Telegram; cable |
|---|---|---|
| 电传 | Diànchuán | Teletype; telex |
| 传真 | Chuánzhēn | Facsimile |
| 电子数据交换 | Diànzǐ shùjù jiāohuàn | Electronic data interchange system (EDI) |
| 电子邮件 | Diànzǐ yóujiàn | E-mail |
| 有形 | Yǒuxíng | Tangible |
| 表现 | Biǎoxiàn | Show; display; manifest |
| 载 | Zǎi | Record; put in writing |
| 内容 | Nèiróng | Content |
| 由 x | Yóu x | By x |
| 条款 | Tiáokuǎn | Provision; clause |
| 住所 | Zhùsuǒ | Residence; domicile |
| 标的 | Biāodì | Subject matter |
| 数量 | Shùliàng | Quantity; amount |
| 质量 | Zhìliàng | Quality |
| 价款 | Jiàkuǎn | Price |
| 报酬 | Bàochóu | Compensation; pay |
| 期限 | Qīxiàn | Time limit; term |
| 方式 | Fāngshì | Way; manner; method |
| 解决 | Jiějué | Resolve |
| 争议 | Zhēngyì | Dispute |
| 参照 | Cānzhào | Refer to; consult |

| 各类 | Gèlèi | All kinds of |
|---|---|---|
| 示范 | Shìfàn | Model; form |
| 文本 | Wénběn | Text |
| 采取 | Cǎiqǔ | Take; adopt |
| 要约 | Yāoyuē | Offer |
| 承诺 | Chéngnuò | Promise to do something; acceptance |
| 意思表示 | Yìsī biǎoshì | Expression of intent or interest |
| 该 | Gāi | That[10] |
| 符合 | Fúhé | Conform to; comply with |
| 下列 | Xiàliè | The following; set forth below |
| 具体 | Jùtǐ | Concrete; specific |
| 表明 | Biǎomíng | Mark; indicate |
| 经 (经过) | Jīng (Jīngguò) | Go through; be x'd |
| 受要约人 | Shòuyāoyuērén | Offeree |
| 要约人 | Yāoyuērén | Offeror |
| 即 | Jí | Promptly; as soon as |
| 邀请 | Yāoqǐng | Invite (to make an offer) |
| 寄送 | Jìsòng | Send |
| 价目表 | Jiàmùbiǎo | Price list |
| 拍卖 | Pāimài | Auction |

---

10 Law Practice Tip: In modern legal English the term "that" is used. In older legal English, the term "said" is used.

| 公告 | Gōnggào | Public announcement |
|------|---------|---------------------|
| 招标 | Zhāobiāo | Invite bids; public tender |
| 招股 | Zhāogǔ | Raise capital by floating shares |
| 商业 | Shāngyè | Commercial |
| 广告 | Guǎnggào | Advertisements |
| 视为 | Shìwéi | Considered as; seen as |
| 自 x 时 | Zì x shí | Beginning from x |
| 生效 | Shēngxiào | Go into effect; become effective; valid |
| 办理 | Bànlǐ | Handle; take care of |
| 批准 | Pīzhǔn | Approve; approval |
| 登记 | Dēngjì | Registration |
| 手续 | Shǒuxù | Process; procedures |
| 其 | Qí | Literary Chinese for 他 (们) 的 |
| 附 | Fù | Attached; supplementary |
| 条件 | Tiáojiàn | Requirement; condition |
| 成就 | Chéngjiù | Achieve; meet; fulfill |
| 失效 | Shīxiào | Become invalid |
| 正当 | Zhèngdàng | Proper; legitimate |
| 阻止 | Zǔzhǐ | Hinder |
| 促成 | Cùchéng | Facilitate; bring about |
| 届至 | Jièzhì | Fall due |
| 届满 | Jièmǎn | Expire |

| 限制 | Xiànzhì | Restrict; limit |
|------|---------|-----------------|
| 追认 | Zhuīrèn | Recognize retroactively |
| 但 | Dàn | 但是; 可是 |
| 纯获 | Chúnhuò | Purely obtain |
| 与 x 而 y | Yǔ x ér y | Together with x do y |
| 年龄 | Niánlíng | Age |
| 智力 | Zhìlì | Intelligence |
| 精神健康 | Jīngshén jiànkāng | Mental health |
| 状况 | Zhuàngkuàng | Condition; state; situation |
| 相 | Xiāng | Mutual |
| 适应 | Shìyìng | Suit; fit |
| 相对人 | Xiāngduìrén | Opposite party |
| 催告 | Cuīgào | Demand |
| 予以 | Yǔyǐ | 予以 and 加以 both mean "to do x." In English, we would not translate either |
| 拒绝 | Jùjué | Refuse |
| 善意 | Shànyì | Good faith |
| 撤销 | Chèxiāo | Cancel; rescind; revoke |
| 通知 | Tōngzhī | Notify |
| 涉外 | Shèwài | Foreign |
| 废止 | Fèizhǐ | Abolish; nullify |

# D. Text of the Contract Law Supreme Court Interpretations (May 2009)[11]

【发布 单位】最高人民法院

【发布文号】法释〔2009〕5号

【发布日期】2009-04-24

【生效日期】2009-05-13

【失效日期】——

【所属 类别】国家法律 法规

【文件 来源】人民法院报

最高人民法院关于**适用**《中华人民共和国合同法》**若干问题**的**解释**（二）

(法释〔2009〕5号, 2009年2月9日最高人民法院**审判** 委员会第1462次会议 通过）

## 中华人民共和国最高人民法院公告

《最高人民法院关于适用〈中华人民共和国合同法〉若干问题的解释（二)》已 于2009年2月9日**由**最高人民法院审判委员会第1462次会议通过, **现** 予公布, **自**2009年5月13日**起** 施行。

二〇〇九年四月二十四日

---

11 Source: Zui gao ren min fa yuan guan yu shi yong <Zhonghua Renmin Gongheguo he tong fa> ruo gan wen ti de jie shi (er) [Supreme People's Court Interpretation on Several Issues Concerning Application of the Contract Law II (P.R.C.)] (promulgated by the Sup. People's Ct, Feb. 9, 2009, effective May 13, 2009) *available at* http://www.law-lib.com/law/law_view.asp?id=486 (last visited May 31, 2011).

为了 正确 审理合同纠纷 案件，根据《中华人民共和国合同法》的规定，对人民法院适用合同法的有关问题作出如下解释：

一、合同的订立

第一条　当事人对合同是否 成立 *存在* 争议，人民法院能够确定当事人名称或者姓名、标的和数量 的，一般应当认定合同成立。*但*法律另有规定或者当事人另有约定的*除外*。

对合同欠缺的前款规定以外的其他 内容，当事人达不成协议的，人民法院依照合同法第六十一条、第六十二条、第一百二十五条等有关规定予以确定。

第二条　当事人未以书面 形式或者口头形式订立合同，但从双方 从事的民事 行为能够推定双方有订立合同意愿的，人民法院可以认定是以合同法第十条第一款中的"其他形式"订立的合同。但法律另有规定的除外。

第三条　悬赏人以公开 方式 声明对完成一定行为的人支付 报酬，完成特定行为的人请求悬赏人支付报酬的，人民法院依法予以支持。但悬赏有合同法第五十二条规定情形的除外。

第四条　采用书面形式订立合同，合同约定的签订地与 实际签字或者盖章地点不符的，人民法院应当认定约定的签订地为合同签订地；合同没有约定签订地，双方当事人签字或者盖章不在同一地点的，人民法院应当认定最后签字或者盖章的地点为合同签订地。

第五条　当事人采用合同书形式订立合同的，应当签字或者盖章。当事人在合同书上摁 手印的，人民法院应当认定其 具有与签字或者盖章同等的法律效力。

第六条　提供 格式条款的一方对格式条款中免除或者限制其责任的内容，在合同订立时采用足以 引起对方注意的文字、符号、字体等特别标识，并 按照对方的要求对该格式条款予以说明的，人民法院应当认定符合合同法第三十九条所称"采取 合理的方式"。

提供格式条款一方*对*已尽合理提示 及说明义务 *承担* 举证 *责任*。

第七条　下列情形，不违反法律、行政法规强制 性规定的，人民法院可以认定为合同法所称"交易 习惯"：

（一）在交易行为当地或者某一 领域、某一行业 通常采用并为交易对方订立合同时所知道或者应当知道的做法；

（二）当事人双方经常 使用的习惯做法。

对于交易习惯，由提出 主张的一方当事人承担举证责任。

第八条　依照法律、行政法规的规定经批准或者登记才能生效的合同成立后，有义务办理 申请批准或者申请登记等手续的一方当事人未按照法律规定或者合同约定办理申请批 准或者未申请登记的，属于合同法第四十二条第（三）项规定的"其他违背 诚实 信用 原则的行为"，人民法院可以根据案件的具体 情况和相对人的请求，判决相对人 自己办理有关手续；对方当事人对由此 产生的费用和给相对人造成的实际损失，应当承担损害赔偿责任。

二、合同的效力

第九条　提供格式条款的一方当事人违反合同法第三十九条第一款关于提示和说明义务的规定，导致对方没有注意免除或者限制其责任的条款，对方当事人申请撤销该格式条款的，人民法院应当支持。

第十条　提供格式条款的一方当事人违反合同法第三十九条第一款的规定，并具有合同法第四十条规定的情形之一的，人民法院应当认定该格式条款无效。

第十一条　根据合同法第四十七条、第四十八条的规定，追认的意思表示自 到达相对人时生效，合同自订立时起生效。

第十二条　无权 代理人以被代理人的名义订立合同，被代理人已经开始履行合同义务的，视为对合同的追认。

第十三条　被代理人依 照合同法第四十九条的规定承担有效代理行为所产生的

责任后，可以向无权代理人追偿 因代理行为而 遭受的损失。

第十四条　合同法第五十二条第（五）项规定的"强制性规定"，是指效力性强制性规定。

第十五条　出卖人 就同一标的物订立多重 买卖合同，合同均不具有合同法第五十二条规定的无效情形，买受人因不能按照合同约定取得标的物所有权，请求追究出卖人违约责任的，人民法院应予支持。

三、合同的履行

第十六条　人民法院根据具体案情可以将合同法第六十四条、第六十五条规定的第三人 列为 无 独立 请求权的第三人，但不得依职权将其列为该合同诉讼案件的被告或者有独立请求权的第三人。

第十七条　债权人 以 境外当事人为被告提起的代位权 诉讼，人民法院根据《中华人民共和国民事诉讼法》第二百四十一条的规定确定管辖。

第十八条　债务人 放弃其未到期的债权或者放弃债权担保，或者恶意延长到期债权的履行期，对债权人造成损害，债权人依照合同法第七十四条的规定提起撤销权诉讼的，人民法院应当支持。

第十九条　对于合同法第七十四条规定

的"**明显不合理的低价**",人民法院应当以交易当地一般**经营者**的判断,并**参考**交易当时交易地的**物价部门指导价**或者市场交易价,结合其他相关**因素综合考虑**予以确认。

**转让价格达不到**交易时交易地的指导价或者市场交易价百分之七十的,一般可以视为明显不合理的低价;对转让价格**高于**当地指导价或者市场交易价百分之三十的,一般可以视为明显不合理的高价。

债务人以明显不合理的高价**收购他人财产**,人民法院可以根据债权人的申请,**参照**合同法第七十四条的规定予以撤销。

**第二十条** 债务人的**给付**不足以**清偿**其对同一债权人所**负**的**数笔**相同**种类**的全部债务,应当**优先抵充**已到期的债务;**几项**债务均到期的,优先抵充对债权人**缺乏**担保或者担保**数**额最少的债务;担保数额相同的,优先抵充债务**负担**较重的债务;负担相同的,按照债务到期的**先后顺序抵充**;到期时间相同的,**按比例抵充**。但是,债权人与债务人对清偿的债务或者清偿抵充顺序有约定的除外。

**第二十一条** 债务人**除主债务之外**还应当支付**利息和费用,当**其给付不足以清偿全部**债务时**,并且当事人没有约定的,人民法院应当按照下列顺序抵充:

(一)**实现债权的有关费用;**

(二)利息;

(三)主债务。

四、合同的权利义务终止

**第二十二条** 当事人一方违反合同法第九十二条规定的义务,给对方当事人造成损失,对方当事人请求赔偿实际损失的,人民法院应当支持。

**第二十三条** 对于依照合同法第九十九条的规定可以**抵销**的到期债权,当事人约定不得抵销的,人民法院可以认定该约定有效。

**第二十四条** 当事人对合同法第九十六条、第九十九条规定的合同**解除**或者债务抵销虽有**异议**,但在约定的异议期限**届满**后才提出异议并向人民法院**起诉**的,人民法院不予支持;当事人没有约定异议期间,在解除合同或者债务抵销通知到达之**日起**三个月以后才向人民法院起诉的,人民法院不予支持。

**第二十五条** 依照合同法第一百零一条的规定,债务人将合同标的物或者标的物**拍卖、变卖所得价款交付提存**部门时,人民法院应当认定提存成立。

提存成立的,视为债务人在其提存**范围**内已经履行债务。

**第二十六条** 合同成立以后**客观情况**发生了当事人在订立合同时**无法预见的、非不可抗力**造成的不属于**商业风险**的重大**变化**,继续履行合同对于一方当事人明显不公平或者不能实现合同**目的**，当事人请求人民法院**变更**或者解除合同的，人民法院应当根据公平原则，并结合案件的实际情况确定是否变更或者解除。

五、违约责任

第二十七条　当事人通过**反诉**或者**抗辩**的方式，请求人民法院依照合同法第一百一十四条第二款的规定**调整 违约金**的，人民法院应予支持。

第二十八条　当事人依照合同法第一百一十四条第二款的规定，请求人民法院**增加**违约金的，增加后的违约金数额以**不超过**实际**损失额**为限。增加违约金以后，当事人又请求对方赔偿损失的，人民法院不予支持。

第二十九条　当事人主张约定的违约金**过高**请求予以**适当 减少**的，人民法院应当以

实际损失为**基础**，兼顾合同的履行情况、当事人的**过错 程度**以及**预期 利益**等综合因素，根据公平原则和诚实信用原则予以**衡量**，并作出**裁决**。

当事人约定的违约金超过造成损失的百分之三十的，一般可以认定为合同法第一百一十四条第二款规定的"**过分**高于造成的损失"。

六、附则

第三十条　合同法施行后成立的合同发生纠纷的案件，本解释施行后已**尚未 终审**的，适用本解释；本解释施行前已经终审，当事人申请再审或者照审判**监督 程序**决定再审的，不适用本解释。

# E. Vocabulary of Contract Law Supreme Court Interpretations (May 2009)

| Chinese | Pinyin | English |
|---------|--------|---------|
| 发布 | Fābù | Issue |
| 单位 | Dānwèi | Entity[12] |
| 法院 | Fǎyuàn | Court |
| 释 | Shì | Interpretation |
| 日期 | Rìqī | Date |
| 生效 | Shēngxiào | Go into effect; become effective |
| 失效 | Shīxiào | Become invalid |
| 所属 | Suǒshǔ | Those which fall under x (belong to x) |
| 类别 | Lèibié | Category |
| 法律 | Fǎlù | Law |
| 法规 | Fǎguī | Administrative laws and regulations[13] |

---

12 Law Practice Tip: Dānwèi is used to describe the organization to which you belong, e.g. your employer. In the past, when there was no private economy, the Dānwèi played a much more significant role in the lives of its workers. It provided housing, schools, hospitals, cafeterias, etc.

13 Law Practice Tip: "行政法规" are legislations adopted by the State Council. They are the third level of legislation in China, only lower than the Constitution and Laws passed by National People's Congress or its Standing Committee.

| 文件 | Wénjiàn | Document |
|------|---------|----------|
| 来源 | Láiyuán | Source |
| 适用 | Shìyòng | Apply |
| 合同 | Hétóng | Contract |
| 若干 | Ruògān | Several |
| 解释 | Jiěshì | Interpretation |
| 审判 | Shěnpàn | Judicial adjudication; trial |
| 委员会 | Wěiyuánhuì | Committee[14] |
| 会议 | Huìyì | Meeting |
| 通过 | Tōngguò | Enact; pass |
| 公告 | Gōnggào | Public announcement |
| 已 | Yǐ | 已经 |
| 于 | Yú | In; on |
| 由 x | Yóu x | By x |
| 现 | Xiàn | 现在 |
| 予 | Yǔ | Give (literary Chinese) |
| 自 x 起 | Zì x qǐ | Beginning from x |
| 施行 | Shīxíng | Come into force; take effect |
| 为了 | Wèile | In order to; for the sake of |

---

14 Law Practice Tip: In China, every court has a judicial adjudication committee that consists of high ranking leaders of the court. Even though they don't review cases as a judge, they play a dominant role in framing important judicial policies, as well as handling complicated cases. It has been hotly debated whether an internal organ like this harms the independence of the judges.

| 正确 | Zhèngquè | Correctly; properly |
| 审理 | Shěnlǐ | Try; hear (a case) |
| 纠纷 | Jiūfēn | Dispute |
| 案件 | Ànjiàn | Case |
| 根据 | Gēnjù | Based on; according to |
| 规定 | Guīdìng | Stipulation |
| 有关 | Yǒuguān | Relevant |
| 如下 | Rúxià | As set forth below |
| 订立 | Dìnglì | Enter into (a contract) |
| 条 | Tiáo | Article[15] |
| 当事人 | Dāngshìrén | Parties |
| 是否 | Shìfǒu | Whether |
| 成立 | Chénglì | Form; establish |
| 存在 | Cúnzài | Existing; actual |
| 争议 | Zhēngyì | Dispute |
| 确定 | Quèdìng | Define; fix; determine |
| 标的 | Biāodì | Subject matter |
| 数量 | Shùliàng | Quantity; amount |

---

15 Law Practice Tip: Chinese laws and regulations typically consist of: parts (编), chapters (章), sections (节), and articles (条). There is no definitive English translation for these terms.

| 的 | De | 的 is often used without the term it modifies. Here, the omitted term is probably 时候 (when) or 情况 (circumstances) |
| 一般 | Yībān | Generally |
| 认定 | Rèndìng | Determine; establish; confirm |
| 但 x 除外 | Dàn x chúwài | With the exception of x |
| 另有 | Lìngyǒu | Other; additional; otherwise |
| 约定 | Yuēdìng | Agree upon |
| 欠缺 | Qiànquē | Lack; be deficient |
| 前款 | Qiánkuǎn | Preceding clause; above provision |
| 其他 | Qítā | Other |
| 内容 | Nèiróng | Content |
| 协议 | Xiéyì | Agreement |
| 依照 | Yīzhào | In accordance with |
| 予以 | Yǔyǐ | 予以 and 加以 both mean "to do x." In English, we would not translate either |
| 未 | Wèi | Literary Chinese for 还没 |
| 书面 | Shūmiàn | Written |
| 形式 | Xíngshì | Form |
| 口头 | Kǒutóu | Oral |
| 但 | Dàn | 但是; 可是 |
| 双方 | Shuāngfāng | Both sides |

| 从事 | Cóngshì | Engage in |
|------|---------|-----------|
| 民事 | Mínshì | Civil |
| 行为 | Xíngwéi | Act; conduct; behavior |
| 推定 | Tuīdìng | Infer; deduce; presume |
| 意愿 | Yìyuàn | Intention; wish |
| 以 | Yǐ | Same meaning as 把 and 用 |
| 悬赏 | Xuánshǎng | Offer a reward |
| 公开 | Gōngkāi | Open; public |
| 方式 | Fāngshì | Way; manner; method |
| 声明 | Shēngmíng | State; announce; make clear |
| 完成 | Wánchéng | Complete |
| 支付 | Zhīfù | Pay (money) |
| 报酬 | Bàochóu | Compensation; pay |
| 特定 | Tèdìng | Specific; specified; specifically designated |
| 请求 | Qǐngqíu | Request; ask |
| 支持 | Zhīchí | Support |
| 情形 | Qíngxíng | Circumstances; situation |
| 采用 | Cǎiyòng | Select; use; adopt |
| 签订 | Qiāndìng | Sign (a contract, agreement) |
| 与 | Yǔ | And; together with |
| 实际 | Shíjì | Actual; realistic; in practice |

| 盖章 | Gàizhāng | Chop; affix seal; stamp (v.)[16] |
| 符 (符合) | Fú (Fúhé) | Conform to; match |
| 为 | Wéi | Take; treat as |
| 摁 | Èn | Press (with finger) |
| 手印 | Shǒuyìn | Thumb print (lit. hand print) |
| 其 | Qí | Literary Chinese for 他 |
| 具有 | Jùyǒu | Fully possess; have |
| 同等 | Tóngděng | Same class, rank, or status |
| 效力 | Xiàolì | Effective; valid |
| 提供 | Tígōng | Provide; offer |
| 格式 | Géshì | Form; formulaic |
| 免除 | Miǎnchú | Prevent; avoid |
| 限制 | Xiànzhì | Restrict; limit |
| 责任 | Zérèn | Responsibility; liability |
| 足以 | Zúyǐ | Sufficient; enough to |
| 引起 | Yǐnqǐ | Give rise to; lead to |
| 符号 | Fúhào | Symbol; mark |
| 字体 | Zìtǐ | Font |
| 标识 | Biāoshì | Identifier; mark |

---

16 Law Practice Tip: In China, companies have a single official chop (stamp) which is used to "sign" documents and authorize bank transactions. They use a red ink pad. A common tactic in a partnership dispute is to abscond with the company chop. This chop has the same effect as a corporate seal in the U.S., but is used to "sign" all manner of official documents. The English word "chop" is used in China as both a noun and a verb, e.g. "take the chop and chop the invoice."

| 并 | Bìng | And; moreover |
|---|---|---|
| 按照 | Ànzhào | In accordance with |
| 该 | Gāi | That[17] |
| 符合 | Fúhé | Conform to; comply with |
| 所称 | Suǒchēng | Refers to |
| 采取 | Cǎiqǔ | Take; adopt |
| 合理 | Hélǐ | Reasonable |
| 对 x 承担······责任 | Duì x chéngdān······zérèn | Bear liability (lit. responsibility) for x |
| 尽 | Jìn | All; utmost |
| 提示 | Tíshì | Point out; call attention to |
| 及 | Jí | And; as well as (literary Chinese meaning the same as 跟 and 和) |
| 义务 | Yìwù | Duty; obligation |
| 举证 | Jǔzhèng | Produce proof |
| 下列 | Xiàliè | The following; set forth below |
| 违反 | Wéifǎn | Violate (a law) |
| 行政 | Xíngzhèng | Administrative |
| 强制 | Qiángzhì | Mandatory; compulsory |
| 性 | Xìng | Suffix for -ness, -ity, -ive, -ize |
| 交易 | Jiāoyì | Trade |

---

17 Law Practice Tip: In modern legal English the term "that" is used. In older legal English, the term "said" is used.

| | | |
|---|---|---|
| 习惯 | Xíguàn | Custom |
| 某一 | Mǒuyī | A certain |
| 领域 | Lǐngyù | Area |
| 行业 | Hángyè | Trade; profession; industry |
| 通常 | Tōngcháng | Normal |
| 所 | Suǒ | Which |
| 做法 | Zuòfǎ | Way of doing |
| 经常 | Jīngcháng | Regularly; daily |
| 使用 | Shǐyòng | Use |
| 对于 | Duìyú | As for; toward |
| 提出 | Tíchū | Raise; propose (an idea) |
| 主张 | Zhǔzhāng | Claim; argument |
| 经 (经过) | Jīng (Jīngguò) | Go through; be x'd |
| 批准 | Pīzhǔn | Approval |
| 登记 | Dēngjì | Registration |
| 办理 | Bànlǐ | Handle; take care of |
| 申请 | Shēnqǐng | Apply for |
| 手续 | Shǒuxù | Process; procedure |
| 属于 | Shǔyú | Belong to; fall within |
| 项 | Xiàng | Counter for article; clause |
| 违背 | Wéibèi | Violate; go against |
| 诚实信用 | Chéngshí xìnyòng | Good faith |

| | | |
|---|---|---|
| 原则 | Yuánzé | Principle[18] |
| 具体 | Jùtǐ | Concrete; specific |
| 情况 | Qíngkuàng | Circumstance; situation |
| 相对人 | Xiāngduìrén | Opposite party |
| 判决 | Pànjué | Judgment |
| 对方 | Duìfāng | Other party |
| 由此 | Yóucǐ | From this |
| 产生 | Chǎnshēng | Cause; bring about |
| 费用 | Fèiyòng | Expenses |
| 造成 | Zàochéng | Cause; bring about |
| 损失 | Sǔnshī | Losses (financial, economic, etc.) |
| 损害 | Sǔnhài | Harm; damages |
| 赔偿 | Péicháng | Compensate |
| 导致 | Dǎozhì | Lead to |
| 撤销 | Chèxiāo | Cancel; rescind; revoke |
| 无效 | Wúxiào | Invalid; void |
| 追认 | Zhuīrèn | Recognize retroactively |
| 意思表示 | Yìsī biǎoshì | Expression of interest or intent |
| 自 x 时 | Zì x shí | Beginning from x |
| 到达 | Dàodá | Reach; arrive |

---

18 Law Practice Tip: The principle of good faith is an important principle in China's civil code.

| | | |
|---|---|---|
| 无权 | Wúquán | Unauthorized |
| 代理人 | Dàilǐrén | Agent |
| 被代理人 | Bèidàilǐrén | Principal |
| 名义 | Míngyì | Titular; in the name of; as a pretext |
| 履行 | Lǚxíng | Perform; fulfill; carry out |
| 视为 | Shìwéi | Considered as; seen as |
| 向 | Xiàng | 向 and 对 combine with a number of different verbs to generally mean "to" or "for" |
| 追偿 | Zhuīcháng | Recovery; recourse |
| 因 x 而 y | Yīn x ér y | To y because of x |
| 遭受 | Zāoshòu | Suffer |
| 是指 | Shìzhǐ | This refers to; means |
| 出卖人 | Chūmàirén | Seller |
| 就 | Jiù | With regards to; as for |
| 标的物 | Biāodìwù | Subject matter |
| 多重 | Duōchóng | Multiple |
| 买卖 | Mǎimài | Sales |
| 均 | Jūn | All; completely; 都 |
| 买受人 | Mǎishòurén | Buyer |
| 取得 | Qǔdé | Obtain; acquire |
| 所有权 | Suǒyǒuquán | Ownership; title (lit. right of ownership) |
| 追究 (追究责任) | Zhuījiū (Zhuījiū zérèn) | Investigate and affix responsibility or liability |

| 违约 | Wéiyuē | Breach; violate (a contract) |
|---|---|---|
| 案情 | Ànqíng | Details of a case; facts of a case |
| 将 | Jiāng | Literary Chinese for 把 |
| 第三人 | Dìsānrén | Third party |
| 列为 | Lièwéi | Be classified as |
| 无 | Wú | Literary Chinese for 没有 |
| 独立 | Dúlì | Independent |
| 请求权 | Qǐngqiúquán | Right of claim (lit. right to request) |
| 无独立请求权 的第三人 | Wúdúlì qǐngqiúquán de dìsānrén | Third party intervenor with no independent right of claim |
| 不得 | Bùdé | Must not; may not |
| 职权 | Zhíquán | Official powers; authority |
| 诉讼案件 | Sùsòng ànjiàn | Lawsuit (lit. litigation case) |
| 被告 | Bèigào | Defendant |
| 债权人 | Zhàiquánrén | Creditor |
| 以 x 为 y | Yǐ x wéi y | Take x as y |
| 境外 | Jìngwài | Foreign (lit. outside the border) |
| 提起 | Tíqǐ | Bring (an action) |
| 代位权 | Dàiwèiquán | Right of subrogation |
| 诉讼 | Sùsòng | Litigation; lawsuit |
| 管辖 | Guǎnxiá | Jurisdiction |
| 债务人 | Zhàiwùrén | Debtor |

| 放弃 | Fàngqì | Abandon; give up |
|------|--------|------------------|
| 到期 | Dàoqī | Come to term; mature |
| 债权 | Zhàiquán | Creditor's claim |
| 担保 | Dānbǎo | Guarantee |
| 恶意 | È'yì | Bad faith; malice |
| 延长 | Yáncháng | Prolong; extend |
| 撤销权 | Chèxiāoquán | Right of rescission |
| 明显 | Míngxiǎn | Obviously; clearly |
| 低价 | Dījià | Low price |
| 经营 | Jīngyíng | Engage in or run a business |
| 者 | Zhě | 者 is literary Chinese and is used after an adjective or verb as a substitute for a person, entity, or thing[19] |
| 判断 | Pànduàn | Decide; determine (by a lay person) |
| 参考 | Cānkǎo | Consult; refer to |
| 物价 | Wùjià | Commodity price; price |
| 部门 | Bùmén | Department; branch; section |
| 指导价 | Zhǐdǎojià | Guiding price |
| 结合 | Jiéhé | Combine; integrate |
| 因素 | Yīnsù | Factors; elements |

---

19 Law Practice Tip: In modern legal Chinese, 者 is often used, as it is here, to indicate both natural and legal persons.

| 综合 | Zōnghé | Aggregated; in the aggregate |
|---|---|---|
| 考虑 | Kǎolù | Think over; consider |
| 确认 | Quèrèn | Affirm; confirm |
| 转让 | Zhuǎnràng | Transfer possession |
| 达不到 | Dábùdào | Does not reach |
| 高于 x | Gāoyú x | Higher than x |
| 收购 | Shōugòu | Purchase; buy |
| 他人 | Tārén | Other people |
| 财产 | Cáichǎn | Property |
| 参照 | Cānzhào | Refer to; consult |
| 给付 | Gěifù | Payment |
| 清偿 | Qīngcháng | Pay off debts |
| 负 | Fù | Bear (e.g. legal responsibility) |
| 数 | Shù | Several |
| 笔 | Bǐ | Counter for sums of money, e.g. debts |
| 种类 | Zhǒnglèi | Kind; type; variety |
| 优先 | Yōuxiān | Have priority |
| 抵充 | Dǐchōng | Offset |
| 几 | Jǐ | Multiple; several |
| 项 | Xiàng | Counter for debt |
| 缺乏 | Quēfá | Be short of; lack |
| 数额 | Shù'é | Amount |

| 负担 | Fùdān | Bear (a burden) |
|---|---|---|
| 先后 | Xiānhòu | Successively; in order |
| 顺序 | Xùnxù | In sequence |
| 按 (按照) | Àn (Ànzhào) | Based on; in accordance with |
| 比例 | Bǐlì | Proportional |
| 除 x 之外 | Chú x zhīwài | Except for x |
| 主债权 | Zhǔzhàiquán | Principal creditor's rights |
| 利息 | Lìxí | Interest |
| 当 x 时 | Dāng x shí | While (lit. at the time of x) |
| 实现 | Shíxiàn | Realize; achieve; bring about |
| 终止 | Zhōngzhǐ | Termination (at end of contract term) |
| 抵销 | Dǐxiāo | Cancel out; set off |
| 解除 | Jiěchú | Terminate (before end of contract term) |
| 异议 | Yìyì | Objection |
| 届满 | Jièmǎn | Expire |
| 起诉 | Qǐsù | Sue; start a lawsuit |
| 在 x 之日起 | Zài x zhīrì qǐ | Beginning from the day of x (之 is literary Chinese for 的) |
| 拍卖 | Pāimài | Auction |
| 变卖 | Biànmài | Sell off |
| 所得 | Suǒdé | What you have obtained |
| 价款 | Jiàkuǎn | Price |

| | | |
|---|---|---|
| 交付 | Jiāofù | Handover; deliver |
| 提存 | Tícún | Escrow |
| 范围 | Fànwéi | Scope |
| 客观 | Kèguān | Objective |
| 无法 | Wúfǎ | Unable to; cannot |
| 预见 | Yùjiàn | Foresee; predict |
| 非 | Fēi | Non-; un- |
| 不可抗力 | Bùkě kànglì | Force majeure |
| 商业 | Shāngyè | Commercial |
| 风险 | Fēngxiǎn | Risk |
| 变化 | Biànhuà | Change |
| 继续 | Jìxù | Continually |
| 目的 | Mùdì | Purpose |
| 变更 | Biàngēng | Change; amend |
| 反诉 | Fǎnsù | Counterclaim |
| 抗辩 | Kàngbiàn | Defense |
| 调整 | Tiáozhěng | Adjust; regulate; revise |
| 违约金 | Wéiyuējīn | Damages for breach |
| 增加 | Zēngjiā | Increase |
| 超过 | Chāoguò | Exceed |
| 损失额 | Sǔnshī'é | Amount of damages (losses) |
| 限 | Xiàn | Limit; restrict |

| 过高 | Guògāo | Too high |
| 适当 | Shìdàng | Suitable; appropriate |
| 减少 | Jiǎnshǎo | Reduce |
| 基础 | Jīchǔ | Foundation; basis |
| 兼顾 | Jiān'gù | Consider or deal with two or more things at the same time |
| 过错 | Guòcuò | Fault; wrong |
| 程度 | Chéngdù | Degree (level or extent) |
| 预期 | Yùqī | Anticipated; expected |
| 利益 | Lìyì | Interest; benefit |
| 衡量 | Héngliàng | Balance; weigh |
| 裁决 | Cáijué | Decision; verdict |
| 过分 | Guòfèn | Excessive |
| 附则 | Fùzé | Supplementary provisions |
| 尚未 | Shàngwèi | Literary Chinese for 还没 |
| 终审 | Zhōngshěn | Final judgment |
| 监督 | Jiāndū | Control; supervise |
| 程序 | Chéngxù | Procedure; process |

# Chapter 4
# Labor Contract Law
# 劳动合同法
Láo    Dòng    Hé    Tóng    Fǎ

# A. Introduction to China's Labor Contract Law

By *Ronald C. Brown*, Professor of Law, University of Hawaii

Unlike earlier times in China, foreign and domestic employers must now pay close attention to the labor and employment laws in China. Since the first Labor Law became effective in 1995, which included the original law dealing with labor contracts, the labor and employment laws have become very much more sophisticated. Likewise, the enforcement has become more consistent and statutory penalties are being used in ways which have come to induce employer compliance.

In 2008, the new Labor Contract Law became effective and confirmed earlier regulations and added new provisions, which caused employers in some quarters a certain level of concern, especially those operating on the margins of labor law compliance. The Law requires certain formalities and content in the formation of individual labor contracts. It requires mutual obligations regarding terms and performance and carefully lays out the requirements of termination. The termination provisions tie into other elements of the law requiring severance pay and other laws entirely, determining, for example, eligibility under the unemployment law. The Labor Contract Law further imposes legal liabilities for non-compliance with its provisions.

There are also provisions covering and protecting collective negotiations, including the role of the union, the negotiating parties and their obligations, as well as the formalities and administration of the agreement and the parties' relationship. It reiterates the principle that the collective contract supersedes the individual labor contract on any inconsistent provisions.

Lastly, new provisions clarify employer obligations regarding the use of restrictive covenants to protect the employer's confidential information and trade secrets. Labor disputes are channeled into mediation and arbitration. The Labor Contract Law is further developed by the Labor Mediation and Arbitration law which also provides new rights and duties for employers and employees. With these new laws, the caseload of arbitrations contesting violations of the Labor Contract Law and other labor laws has risen dramatically.

# B. Text of Labor Contract Law[1]

# 劳动 合同法

**自2008年1月1日起 施行**

第一章 总 则

第一条 *为了* 完善劳动合同制度, 明确劳动合同双方当事人的权利和义务, 保护劳动者的合法 权益, 构建和发展和谐 稳定的劳动关系, *制定* 本法。

第二条 中华人民共和国境内的企业、个体经济 组织、民办 非企业单位等组织 (以下称 用人单位) 与劳动者建立劳动关系, 订立、履行、变更、解除或者终止劳动合同, 适用本法。

第四条 用人单位应当 依法建立和完善劳动规章制度, 保障劳动者享有劳动权利、履行劳动义务。

用人单位*在*制定、修改或者决定 有关劳动报酬、工作时间、休息 休假、劳动安全 卫生、保险 福利、职工 培训、劳动纪律以及劳动定额管理等*直接* 涉及劳动者切身 利益的规章制度或者重大 事项 *时*, 应当经职工代表大会或者*全体职工*讨论, 提出方案和意见, 与工会或者职工代表平等协商 确定。

在规章制度和重大事项决定**实施** 过程中, 工会或者职工认为**不适当的**, 有权 向用人单位提出, **通过**协商予以修改完善。

用人单位应当***将***直接涉及劳动者切身利益的规章制度和重大事项决定公示, 或者告

---

1 Source: Zhonghua Renmin Gongheguo lao dong he tong fa [Labor Contract Law (P.R.C.)] (promulgated by the Standing Comm. Nat'l People's Cong., June 29, 2007, effective Jan. 1, 2008) *available at* http://npc.people.com.cn/GB/28320/60798/60801/5958797.html (last visited May 31, 2011).

知劳动者。

第五条 **县 级**以上人民政府劳动**行政 部门 会同**工会和企业方面代表，建立**健全 协调**劳动关系三方 **机制**，共同研究解决有关劳动关系的重大问题。

第六条 工会应当帮助、**指导**劳动者与用人单位依法订立和履行劳动合同，**并**与用人单位建立**集体**协商机制，**维护**劳动者的合法权益。

第二章 劳动合同的订立

第七条 用人单位自**用工** 之日起即与劳动者建立劳动关系。用人单位应当建立职工**名册 备查**。

第十条 建立劳动关系，应当订立**书面劳**动合同。

已建立劳动关系，**未 同时**订立书面劳动合同的，应当自用工之日起一个月内订立书面劳动合同。

用人单位与劳动者*在*用工*前*订立劳动合同的，劳动关系自用工之日起建立。

第十六条 劳动合同*由*用人单位与劳动者协商一致，并经用人单位与劳动者在劳动合同**文本上签字**或者**盖章** *生效*。

劳动合同文本由用人单位和劳动者各执一份。

第十九 条劳动合同期限三个月以上**不满**一年的，**试用期 不得 超过**一个月；劳动合同期限一年以上不满三年的，试用期不得超过二个月；三年以上**固定期限**和无固定期限的劳动合同，试用期不得超过六个月。

同一用人单位与同一劳动者只能**约定**一次试用期。

试用期**包含**在劳动合同期限内。劳动合同**仅**约定试用期的，试用期不**成立**，**该**期限为劳动合同期限。

第二十三条 用人单位与劳动者可以在劳动合同中约定**保守**用人单位的**商业秘密**和与**知识产权 相关**的**保密**事项。

**对 负**有保密义务的劳动者，用人单位可以在劳动合同或者保密**协议**中与劳动者约定**竞业 限制 条款**，并约定*在*解除或者终止劳动合同后，*在*竞业限制期限内**按月 给予**劳动者经济补偿。劳动者**违反**竞业限制约定的，应当**按**照约定向用人单位**支付 违约金**。

第二十四条 竞业限制的**人员 限于**用人单位的**高级**管理人员、高级**技术**人员和其他负有保密义务的人员。竞业限制的**范围**、**地域**、期限由用人单位与劳动者约定，竞业限制的约定不得违反**法律**、**法规**的**规定**。

在解除或者终止劳动合同后，**前款**规定的人员到与本单位**生产**或者**经营 同类产品**、从事同类业务的有竞争关系的其他用人单位，或者自己**开业**生产或者经营同类产品、从事同类业务的竞业限制期限，不得超过二年。

# C. Vocabulary of Labor Contract Law

| Chinese | Pinyin | English |
| --- | --- | --- |
| 劳动 | Láodòng | Labor |
| 合同 | Hétóng | Contract |
| 公布 | Gōngbù | Promulgate |
| 自 x 起 | Zì x qǐ | Beginning from x |
| 施行 | Shīxíng | Come into force |
| 章 | Zhāng | Chapter[2] |
| 总则 | Zǒngzé | General principles |
| 条 | Tiáo | Article[3] |
| 为了 | Wèile | In order to; for the sake of |
| 完善 | Wánshàn | Improve; perfect |
| 制度 | Zhìdù | System (political or administrative) |

---

2 Law Practice Tip: Chinese laws and regulations typically consist of: parts (编), chapters (章), sections (节), and articles (条). There is no definitive English translation for these terms.

3 Law Practice Tip: Chinese laws and regulations typically consist of: parts (编), chapters (章), sections (节), and articles (条). There is no definitive English translation for these terms.

| 明确 | Míngquè | Make clear and definite; clarify |
|---|---|---|
| 当事人 | Dāngshìrén | Party |
| 权利 | Quánlì | Rights |
| 义务 | Yìwù | Duty; obligation |
| 保护 | Bǎohù | Protect |
| 者 | Zhě | 者 is literary Chinese and is used after an adjective or verb as a substitute for a person, entity, or thing[4] |
| 合法 | Héfǎ | Legal |
| 权益 | Quányì | Rights and interests |
| 构建 | Gòujiàn | Form; establish; construct |
| 和谐 | Héxié | Harmonious |
| 稳定 | Wěndìng | Stable |
| 制定 | Zhìdìng | Formulate; enact |
| 本 | Běn | Literary Chinese for 这个 |
| 境内 | Jìngnèi | Domestic (lit. within the borders) |
| 企业 | Qǐyè | Enterprise |
| 个体 | Gètǐ | Individual |
| 经济 | Jīngjì | Economic |
| 组织 | Zǔzhī | Organization |

---

4 Law Practice Tip: In modern legal Chinese, it is often used to indicate both natural and legal persons as it is here.

| 民办 | Mínbàn | Community (run) |
|---|---|---|
| 非 | Fēi | Non-; un- |
| 单位 | Dānwèi | Entity[5] |
| 等 | Děng | Etc. |
| 以下 | Yǐxià | Below[6] |
| 称 | Chēng | Referred to as… (i.e. referred to below as…) |
| 用人 (用人单位) | Yòngrén (Yòngrén dānwèi) | Employers (lit. the entity that employs a person) |
| 与 | Yǔ | And; together with |
| 建立 | Jiànlì | Establish |
| 订立 | Dìnglì | Enter into (a contract) |
| 履行 | Lǚxíng | Perform; fulfill; carry out |
| 变更 | Biàngēng | Change; amend |
| 解除 | Jiěchú | Terminate (before the end of a contract) |
| 终止 | Zhōngzhǐ | Termination (at the end of the contract term) |
| 适用 | Shìyòng | Apply |
| 应当 | Yīngdāng | Shall; must[7] |

---

5 Law Practice Tip: Dānwèi is used to describe the organization to which you belong, e.g. your employer. In the past, when there was no private economy, the Dānwèi played a much more significant role in the lives of its workers. It provided housing, schools, hospitals, cafeterias, etc. In modern Chinese is it often best translated as "entity."

6 Law Practice Tip: In modern legal English, the term "below" would be used. In older legal English, the term would be "hereinafter."

7 Law Practice Tip: In legal English, there is a difference between "must" and "shall." "Shall" has several meanings including "must" and "will." In modern legal English the trend is to avoid using "shall." When "shall" is used in the mandatory sense, then the word "must" is used.

| | | |
|---|---|---|
| 依法 | Yīfǎ | Legally; in accordance with the law |
| 规章 | Guīzhāng | Rule; regulation[8] |
| 保障 | Bǎozhàng | Ensure; guarantee; safeguard |
| 享有 | Xiǎngyǒu | Have; enjoy (rights, benefits, prestige, etc.) |
| 在 x 时 | Zài x shí | When (at the time of) |
| 修改 | Xiūgǎi | Revise; modify; amend |
| 决定 | Juédìng | Decide |
| 有关 | Yǒuguān | Relevant |
| 报酬 | Bàochóu | Compensation; pay |
| 休息 | Xiūxi | Rest breaks |
| 休假 | Xiūjià | Vacation; holiday |
| 安全 | Ānquán | Safety; security |
| 卫生 | Wèishēng | Health; hygiene; sanitation |
| 保险 | Bǎoxiǎn | Insurance[9] |
| 福利 | Fúlì | Benefits; welfare |
| 职工 | Zhígōng | Staff and workers |
| 培训 | Péixùn | Training |
| 劳动纪律 | Láodòng jìlù | Work discipline |
| 定额 | Dìng'é | Quota; fixed amount |

8 Law Practice Tip: This system of rules for employees is sometimes found in the Employee Handbook.

9 Law Practice Tip: Social Security in China includes: pensions, unemployment, medical, disability, maternity, and childcare.

| 直接 | Zhíjiē | Directly |
|---|---|---|
| 涉及 | Shèjí | Involve; concern |
| 切身 | Qièshēn | Personal |
| 利益 | Lìyì | Interests; benefits |
| 重大 | Zhòngdà | Major; material |
| 事项 | Shìxiàng | Items; matters |
| 经 (经过) | Jīng (Jīngguò) | Go through; be x'd |
| 代表大会 | Dàibiǎo dàhuì | Representative assembly |
| 全体 | Quántǐ | All (lit. entire body) |
| 讨论 | Tǎolùn | Discussion |
| 方案 | Fāng'àn | Plan; scheme |
| 工会 | Gōnghuì | Union |
| 平等协商 | Píngděng xíeshāng | Consultation or negotiation on the basis of equality |
| 确定 | Quèdìng | Define; fix; determine |
| 实施 | Shíshī | Put into effect; implement; carry out |
| 过程 | Guòchéng | Process; course |
| 不适当 | Bùshìdàng | Inappropriate; improper |
| 的 | De | 的 is often used without the term it modifies. Here the term omitted is probably 时候 (when) or 情况 (circumstance) |
| 权 | Quán | Authority; power; right |

| | | |
|---|---|---|
| 向 | Xiàng | 对 and 向 combine with a number of different verbs to generally mean "to" or "for" |
| 通过 | Tōngguò | Go through |
| 予以 | Yǔyǐ | 予以 and 加以 both mean "to do x." In English, we would not translate either |
| 将 | Jiāng | Literary Chinese for 把 |
| 公示 | Gōngshì | Public notice |
| 告知 | Gàozhī | Inform; notify |
| 县 | Xiàn | County |
| 级 | Jí | Level |
| 行政 | Xíngzhèng | Administrative |
| 部门 | Bùmén | Department; branch; section |
| 会同 | Huìtóng | Handle jointly with |
| 健全 | Jiànquán | Strengthen; perfect |
| 协调 | Xiétiáo | Coordinate |
| 三方 | Sānfāng | Tri-partite |
| 机制 | Jīzhì | Mechanism |
| 指导 | Zhǐdǎo | Guide; direct |
| 并 | Bìng | And; moreover |
| 集体 | Jítǐ | Collective |
| 维护 | Wéihù | Protect |

| 用工 | Yònggōng | To use (a worker); to begin work |
| 之 | Zhī | Literary Chinese. The modern character would be 的 |
| 即 | Jí | Promptly; as soon as |
| 名册 | Míngcè | Register (n.) |
| 备查 | Bèichá | For future reference |
| 书面 | Shūmiàn | Written |
| 已 | Yǐ | 已经 |
| 未 | Wèi | Literary Chinese for 还没 |
| 同时 | Tóngshí | Same time |
| 在 x 前 | Zài x qián | Before x |
| 由 | Yóu | From the time when… |
| 一致 | Yízhì | Identical (views or opinions); in agreement |
| 文本 | Wénběn | Text |
| 签字 | Qiānzì | Signing; signature |
| 盖章 | Gàizhāng | Chop; affix seal; stamp (v.)[10] |
| 生效 | Shēngxiào | Go into effect; become effective |
| 执 | Zhí | Hold |

---

10 Law Practice Tip: In China, companies have a single official chop (stamp) which is used to "sign" documents and authorize bank transactions. They use a red ink pad. A common tactic in a partnership dispute is to abscond with the company chop. This chop has the same effect as a corporate seal in the U.S., but is used to "sign" all manner of official documents. The English word "chop" is used in China as both a noun and a verb, e.g. "take the chop and chop the invoice."

| 份 | Fèn | Measure word for a written document[11] |
|---|---|---|
| 满 | Mǎn | Complete; reach |
| 试用期 | Shìyòngqī | Probationary period |
| 不得 | Bùdé | Must not; may not |
| 超过 | Chāoguò | Exceed |
| 期限 | Qīxiàn | Time limit; term |
| 固定 | Gùdìng | Fixed; set |
| 无 | Wú | Literary Chinese for 没有 |
| 同一 | Tóngyī | The same |
| 约定 | Yuēdìng | Agree upon |
| 包含 | Bāohán | Include; contain |
| 仅 | Jǐn | Only |
| 成立 | Chénglì | Form; establish |
| 该 | Gāi | That[12] |
| 为 | Wéi | Take; treat as |
| 保守 | Bǎoshǒu | Guard; keep |
| 商业秘密 | Shāngyè mìmì | Trade secret |
| 知识产权 | Zhīshí chǎnquán | Intellectual property rights |

---

11 Law Practice Tip: This is one of the major changes in the law. In the past, a company simply had a master contract covering all employees. It was easy then for an employer to keep two sets of books regarding employees. This allowed them to save money on paying social insurance costs to the government or to deny that an individual was an employee when there was an industrial accident.

12 Law Practice Tip: In modern legal English the term "that" is used. In older legal English, the term "said" is used.

| 相关 | Xiāngguān | Related |
|---|---|---|
| 保密 | Bǎomì | Keep something a secret; confidential |
| 对 (对于) | Duì (Duìyú) | As for; towards |
| 负 | Fù | Bear (e.g. responsibility) |
| 协议 | Xiéyì | Agreement |
| 竞业 | Jìngyè | Competing industry |
| 限制 | Xiànzhì | Restrict; limit |
| 竞业限制 | Jìngyè xiànzhì | Anti-competition; non-compete |
| 条款 | Tiáokuǎn | Provision; clause |
| 在 x 后 | Zài x hòu | Once x; after x |
| 按月 | Ànyuè | Monthly |
| 给予 | Jǐyǔ | Give |
| 补偿 | Bǔcháng | Compensation |
| 违反 | Wéifǎn | Violate (a law) |
| 按照 | Ànzhào | In accordance with |
| 支付 | Zhīfù | Pay (money) |
| 违约金 | Wéiyuējīn | Damages (for breach) |
| 人员 | Rényuán | Personnel |
| 限于 | Xiànyú | Limited to |
| 高级 | Gāojí | High level; senior |
| 技术 | Jìshù | Technical; skilled |
| 范围 | Fànwéi | Scope |

| 地域 | Dìyù | Region; area |
| 法律 | Fǎlù | Laws |
| 法规 | Fǎguī | Administrative laws and regulations[13] |
| 规定 | Guīdìng | Stipulation; provision |
| 前款 | Qiánkuǎn | Preceding clause; above provision |
| 生产 | Shēngchǎn | Produce; manufacture |
| 经营 | Jīngyíng | Engage in or run a business |
| 同类 | Tónglèi | Same kind |
| 从事 | Cóngshì | Engage in |
| 开业 | Kāiyè | Start a business |

---

13 Law Practice Tip: "行政法规" are legislations adopted by the State Council. They are the third level of legislation in China, only lower than the Constitution and Laws passed by National People's Congress or its Standing Committee.

# D. Text of Standard Labor Contract

编号：

# 劳 动 合 同

（2008版）

上海市对外服务有限公司 印制

2008年1月1日

# 劳动合同

（2008版）

甲　方：上海市对外服务有限公司
（以下简称"甲方"）

住所：_____

法定代表人：_____

乙方：_____（以下简称"乙方"）

住址：_____

邮政编码：_____

身份证号码：_____

户口所在地地址：_____

鉴于用工单位需要使用乙方，委托甲方办理录用手续，现根据《中华人民共和国劳动法》、《中华人民共和国劳动合同法》与《上海市劳动合同条例》等有关法律、法规和规章的规定，本着平等、自愿的原则，经乙方确认已知晓《劳动合同法》中规定应由用人单位告知乙方的各项事项。现经甲、乙双方协商一致，特签订本劳动合同（以下简称"本合同"）。

第一条 工作内容和工作地点

1.1 根据工作需要，乙方到用工单位工作，具体单位将根据《派遣协议书》确定。

1.2 乙方理解并同意：乙方在用工单位的具体工作岗位、工作内容和工作地点，由乙方与用工单位自行约定。

1.3 乙方应履行用工单位制定的岗位职责，按时、按质、按量完成其本职工作。

1.4 乙方理解并承诺：愿服从用工单位根据其经营需要、乙方工作能力及其表现而安排或者调动的工作岗位、工作内容、劳动定额等。

第二条 合同期限和派遣期限

2.1 本合同为固定期限劳动合同，期限自[ ]年[ ]月[ ]日起至[ ]年[ ]月[ ]日止。其中[ ]年[ ]月[ ]日至[ ]年[ ]月[ ]日为试用期。

2.2 本合同期满即行终止；但期满时，乙方根据《派遣协议书》的约定，正在派遣期限内的，且甲、乙双方和用工单位均无异议的，本合同的终止可自动续延[ ]年，并依此类推。

第三条 劳动纪律

3.1 乙方应**自觉** 遵守国家的法律、法规和**社会** 公德、**职业** 道德,自觉**维护**甲方的**声誉**和**利益**。

3.2 乙方应**严格**遵守甲方制定和**修改**的各项**规章制度**、劳动纪律。

3.3 乙方理解并同意:在用工单位工作期间应严格遵守用工单位制定和修改的各项规章制度、工作**程序**、劳动纪律。

第四条 工作时间和**休息 休假**

4.1 甲方**实行**每天8小时、每周40小时、每周5天的工作制,但乙方理解并同意:在用工单位,具体**工时**制度由用工单位按国家有关规定**执行**;用工单位如果经劳动**行政 管理** 部门 **批准**实行**不定时工作**制或综合 **工时制***的*,乙方承诺愿意服从用工单位工作时间上的安排。

4.2 乙方理解并同意,在用工单位工作期间:用工单位可以根据国家规定按工作需要安排乙方**加班**;乙方加班必须**征得**用工单位**书面**同意。

4.3 乙方有**享受**各类国家规定的休息休假的**权利**,具体由用工单位按国家有关规定执行。

第五条 劳动**报酬**

5.1 在本合同期内,乙方在用工单位工作期间,具体劳动报酬和**支付 方式**根据《派遣协议书》确定。

5.2 乙方理解并同意:用工单位可以***根据***乙方工作岗位的**变更** *而* 相应地提高或**降低**乙方在用工单位的劳动报酬**待遇**,乙方理解并承诺愿服从用工单位的决定。

5.3 在本合同期内当乙方无用工单位工作期间,甲方依《中华人民共和国劳动合同法》规定执行**工资 标准**为所在地政府每年规定的最低工资标准,并根据当地人民政府的**调整**而调整,直至劳动合同**解除**或终止。

第六条 劳动**保护**、劳动**条件**和职业**危害**防护

6.1 乙方**享有**用工单位**提供**的相应的劳动保护和劳动条件。

6.2 乙方享有用工单位执行的国家劳动标准和用工单位提供的职业危害防护。

第七条 社会**保险**和**其他**

7.1 甲方**按照**国家有关规定,为乙方参加(社会保险/**小城镇**社会保险),或按上海市政府的规定参加**综合**保险,具体由用工单位根据本市规定确定在《派遣协议书》。

7.2 甲方按照国家和上海市的有关规定,为乙方参加**住房 公积金**,具体由用工单位根据本市规定确定。

7.3 乙方因病或非因工**负伤**期间,享有上海市规定的**医疗**期和**疾病**休假待遇,具体由用工单位根据本市规定执行。

**7.4 符合 计划生育**的乙方(女**职工**)享有本市规定的**产假**和其他**特殊**待遇,具体由用工

单位根据本市规定执行。

7.5 在被派遣期间, 甲方根据用工单位与甲方确定的**保障计划项目**, 在用工单位正常付费的情况下, 提供乙方保障服务。乙方理解并同意, **前述**保障服务在乙方被**退回**（或**撤回**）期间不享受。

第八条 **教育**与**培训**

8.1 用工单位可以根据工作需要**定期**或不定期地对乙方**进行**所必需的培训。

8.2 甲方或者用工单位可经常对乙方进行法律、法规和纪律教育。

第九条 **保密**约定

9.1 本合同期内**以及本合同终止或解除后, 未经**用工单位书面同意, 乙方不得向任何第三方（**包括但不限于甲方**）**泄漏**用工单位的**商业秘密**或利用该商业秘密**获利**。

9.2 本合同期内以及本合同终止或解除后, 未经甲方书面同意, 乙方不得向任何第三方（包括但不限于用工单位）泄漏甲方的商业秘密或利用该商业秘密获利。

第十条 **利益冲突**的约定

10.1 本合同期内, 乙方不得**从事**任何与用工单位利益相冲突的活动。

10.2 本合同期内, 乙方不得从事任何与甲方利益相冲突的活动。

10.3 "利益相冲突的活动"包括但不限于**投资 创业**, 帮助第三方创业, 被第三方**雇用**等。

第十一条 乙方的**保证**

11.1 乙方保证应根据用工单位的要求, **如实**说明了与劳动合同和用工单位的使用**直接相关**的基本情况。

11.2 乙方保证其与原用人单位已**依法解**除劳动合同或劳动关系, **并且不存在任何**与用工单位（或甲方）有关的**竞业** 限制。

11.3 乙方保证其将**及时**向甲方**递交**办理社会保险和住房公积金等的**有效 凭证**, 如**因**乙方**迟延递交而 造成**的任何**后果**, 乙方应承担相应责任。

11.4 乙方保证其向甲方提供的所有**信息、资料、证明**等均**属**真实、有效, 并承担相应之责任, 乙方同时保证个人信息有变化时及时通知甲方, 如未及时通知造成的后果由乙方承担责任。

11.5 乙方理解并同意, **诚信是重要的原则。**因此乙方保证, 不会作出任何不诚信的**行为**。

11.6 乙方保证在用工单位工作时, 以及**需**离开用工单位时, 会根据用工单位的要求进行工作和**财物**上的**移交**。

第十二条 乙方有下列情形之一的, 甲方可以解除本合同; 甲、乙双方依法办理解除劳动合同和**退工**手续。

12.1 乙方因在试用期内被用工单位证明不符合其用人标准或录用条件, 被用工单位退回的。

12.2 乙方**严重 违反**用工单位劳动纪律或规章制度, 被用工单位退回的。**其中严重违纪**的行为包括但不限于以下情形:

12.2.1 乙方因**卖淫嫖娼**被**收容教育**的;

12.2.2 乙方受公安 **治安 拘留 处罚**或者**被劳动教养**的;

12.2.3 乙方被**查实**在**应聘**时向甲方或用工单位提供的其个人资料是**虚假**的。

12.3 乙方理解并同意, 违反本合同第九、十、十一条约定的, 无论**情节轻重**, 均**视**为严重违反规章制度, 甲方可以**立即**解除本合同。

12.4 乙方严重**失职**、**营私舞弊**给用工单位利益造成重大**损害**, 被用工单位退回的。

12.5 乙方同时与其他用人单位建立劳动关系, 对完成用工单位的工作**任务**造成严重影响, 或者经用工单位提出, **拒不改正**, 被用工单位退回的。

12.6 乙方被依法**追究 刑事**责任。

12.7 乙方**患病**或者非因工负伤, 在规定的医疗期满后不能从事原工作, 也不能从事用工单位**另行**安排的工作, 被用工单位退回的。

12.8 乙方不能**胜任**工作, 经过培训或者调整工作岗位**仍**不能胜任工作, 被用工单位退回的。

12.9 其他国家规定可以解除劳动合同的情形。

第十三条 撤回

13.1 甲、乙双方协商一致, 派遣期限内, 因任何原因用工单位与甲方**之间**的劳务合同解除或终止的(包括但不限于用工单位**拖欠甲方管理费**被甲方通知解除双方劳务合同的), 甲方有权撤回乙方。

13.2 乙方理解并同意, 其被撤回期间的劳动报酬按本合同5.3的约定执行。

第十四条 凡有下列情形之一的, 乙方可以解除本合同; 甲、乙双方依法办理解除劳动合同和退工手续。

14.1 乙方**提前**三十日以书面**形式**通知甲方和用工单位的。

14.2 乙方在试用期内提前三日通知甲方和用工单位的。

14.3 法律、行政法规规定的其他情形。

甲、乙双方理解并同意, **即使乙方仅**通知了用工单位, **亦**应视作乙方已向甲方**辞职**。

第十五条 **违约责任**

任何一方违反本合同均应承担相应之一切责任, 包括但不限于**赔偿**给对方造成的经济**损失**。

第十六条 其他约定和说明

16.1 **释义**:

16.1.1 本合同中**所称**"法律、法规、规章", 若未作特殊说明, **系指**中华人民共和国的法律、法规、规章。

16.1.2 本合同中所称第三方, **若**未作特殊说明，系指**除**甲方、乙方和用工单位**之外**的第三方。

**16.1.3** 本合同中所称《派遣协议书》系本合同**附件**，是本合同**必要**的补充。

**16.2** 其他可能发生的**事宜**：

**16.2.1** 甲方可以为符合法定条件的乙方办理**公证**事宜的相关证明，但所发生的**费用**由乙方**自理**。

**16.2.2** 甲方可以为乙方**申办**出国（境）护照及**边防 通行证**等提供**便利**，但所发生的费用由乙方自理。

**16.2.3** 甲方可以为符合有关规定与**资格**的乙方**申报**和**评定 专业 技术 职称**提供便利，但所发生的费用由乙方自理。

**16.3** 本合同未尽事宜，双方另有约定的**从约定**；双方没有约定的，从相关法律、法规、规章；法律、法规、规章没有规定的，双方应**遵循**平等自愿、协商一致的原则，另行签订协议**作为**本合同的补充协议。本合同如与国家法律、法规不一致，**应以法律法规为准**。

**16.4** 乙方可以与用工单位另行签订协议，但甲方不承担该协议任何一方的**连带责任**。前述协议如与本合同相冲突，应以本合同为准。

**16.5 争议**的解决：本合同的签订地和履行地均为上海，双方在履行本合同中发生的争议，应**提交**上海市对外服务有限公司劳动争议**调解 委员会**调解；调解不成的**向**上海市**黄浦**区劳动争议**仲裁委员会 申请**仲裁；**对**仲裁**不服**的**向**上海市黄浦区人民**法院 起诉**；对**判决**不服的可**向**上海市第二中级人民法院**上诉**，上海市**第二中级**人民法院的判决**为终审**判决。

**16.6** 甲方与用工单位所签协议的内容，凡与乙方有关的（包括但不限于岗位、期限、劳动报酬和社会保险等），均与本合同和《派遣协议书》中约定一致；乙方已全部**知悉**。

**16.7** 乙方确认甲、乙双方之间的任何文件（包括但不限于本合同）经由甲方**送达**以下地址即为送达乙方，在以下地址需要变更时乙方应以书面形式或其他甲方**认可**的方式通知甲方，**否则乙方理解并同意甲方送达以下地址即为送达乙方**: [          ]邮编: [    ]

**16.8** 甲、乙双方理解并同意：如果国家和/或上海市**就**《劳动合同法》有**规范 性**文件**实施**的，本合同和附件应根据前述规范性文件变更。

**16.9** 本合同一式二份，均应由甲方**盖章**、乙方签字后**生效**；乙方一经签订本合同，即视为甲方已经视为送达本合同**文本**。

**16.10** 本合同甲、乙双方各**持**一份为凭，具有同等法律**效力**。

甲方：上海市对外服务有限公司

乙方：

**经办人**：

签订日期：[  ]年[  ]月[  ]日

签订地点：上海

# E. Vocabulary of Standard Labor Contract

| Chinese | Pinyin | English |
|---------|--------|---------|
| 编号 | Biānhào | Number; serial number |
| 劳动 | Láodòng | Labor |
| 合同 | Hétóng | Contract |
| 版 | Bǎn | Edition; version |
| 对外 | Duìwài | Foreign |
| 服务 | Fúwù | Service |
| 有限公司 | Yǒuxiàn gōngsī | Ltd.[14] |
| 印制 | Yìnzhì | Printed |
| 甲 | Jiǎ | A (The Chinese use the names of the "Ten Heavenly Stems" in order in a sequence of examples involving "A" ,"B" ,"C", etc.)[15] |

---

14 Background Tip: The Company referred to in this contract, 上海市对外服务有限公司, is commonly known as the Foreign Enterprise Service Corporation (FESCO). FESCO is a state-owned company that provides employment services for foreign companies in China. In the past, all foreign companies were required to use FESCO. It is now voluntary.

15 Law Practice Tip: In China, it is very common to use terms like Party A, Party B, etc. In the West, A, B, C, etc. is more commonly used, or, in some cases, "the party of the first part." In modern legal English the trend is to use an abbreviation of the party's name or a descriptive term such as "Seller" or "Employer" in order to make the document more understandable.

| | | |
|---|---|---|
| 方 | Fāng | Party |
| 以下简称 x | Yǐxià jiǎnchēng x | Abbreviated below as x[16] |
| 住所 | Zhùsuǒ | Residence; domicile |
| 法定 | Fǎdìng | Legal |
| 代表人 | Dàibiǎorén | Representative[17] |
| 乙 | Yǐ | B[18] |
| 住址 | Zhùzhǐ | Residential address |
| 邮政编码 | Yóuzhèng biānmǎ | Zip Code (lit. postal code) |
| 身份证 | Shēnfènzhèng | Identification card[19] |
| 号码 | Hàoma | Number |
| 户口 | Hùkǒu | Registered permanent residence[20] |
| 所在地 | Suǒzàidì | Local (lit. where x is located) |
| 地址 | Dìzhǐ | Address |
| 鉴于 | Jiànyú | In light of; whereas |
| 用工单位 | Yònggōng dānwèi | Employer; literally employing entity[21] |
| 委托 | Wěituō | Entrust; delegate; consign |

---

16 Law Practice Tip: In modern legal English, we would say "below." In older legal English, the term would be "hereinafter."

17 Law Practice Tip: In China, every entity must designate an individual to serve as its Legal Representative.

18 Background Tip: In China, the names of the "Ten Heavenly Stems" are used to sequence examples involving "A", "B", "C", etc.

19 Background Tip: Every Chinese citizen in China has a national Identification Card.

20 Background Tip: The hùkǒu system is used to restrict migration within China. For example, one cannot get a job in Shanghai unless he or she has a Shanghai hùkǒu. Most, if not all social benefits (pension, health insurance, etc.) are also based on one's hùkǒu.

21 Law Practice Tip: Dānwèi is used to describe the organization to which you belong, e.g. your employer. In the past, when there was no private economy, the Dānwèi played a much more significant role in the lives of its workers. It provided housing, schools, hospitals, cafeterias, etc.

| 办理 | Bànlǐ | Handle; take care of |
|---|---|---|
| 录用 | Lùyòng | Employ |
| 手续 | Shǒuxù | Process; procedure |
| 根据 | Gēnjù | Based on; according to |
| 条例 | Tiáolì | Regulation; rule[22] |
| 等 | Děng | Etc. |
| 有关 | Yǒuguān | Relevant |
| 法律 | Fǎlù | Law[23] |
| 法规 | Fǎguī | Administrative laws and regulations |
| 规章 | Guīzhāng | Rule; regulation |
| 规定 | Guīdìng | Stipulation; provision |
| 本着 | Běnzhe | Based on; in conformance with |
| 平等 | Píngděng | Equal; equality |
| 自愿 | Zìyuàn | Voluntary |
| 原则 | Yuánzé | Principle |
| 经 (经过) | Jīng (Jīngguò) | Go through; be x'd |
| 确认 | Quèrèn | Affirm; confirm |
| 知晓 | Zhīxiǎo | Understand |

---

22 Law Practice Tip: There is no standardized Chinese term or English translation for this. Because these are at the city level, in the U.S., they would be called ordinances rather than regulations.

23 Law Practice Tip: "行政法规" are legislations adopted by the State Council. They are the third level of legislation in China, only lower than the Constitution and Laws passed by National People's Congress or its Standing Committee.

| 由 x | Yóu x | By x |
|---|---|---|
| 用人单位 | Yòngrén dānwèi | Employer (lit. the entity that chooses a person for a job) |
| 告知 | Gàozhī | Inform; notify |
| 各项 | Gèxiàng | Each; 各 means each and 项 is the counter for 事项 |
| 事项 | Shìxiàng | Item; matter |
| 双方 | Shuāngfāng | Both sides |
| 协商 | Xiéshāng | Consult; discuss |
| 一致 | Yīzhì | Identical (views or opinions) |
| 特 | Tè | Specific (-ally) |
| 签订 | Qiāndìng | Sign (a document, etc.) |
| 条 | Tiáo | Article[24] |
| 内容 | Nèiróng | Content |
| 地点 | Dìdiǎn | Place; site; location |
| 具体 | Jùtǐ | Concrete; specific |
| 派遣 | Pàiqiǎn | Send |
| 协议 | Xiéyì | Agreement |
| 确定 | Quèdìng | Define; fix; determine |

---

24 Law Practice Tip: Chinese laws and regulations typically consist of: parts (编), chapters (章), sections (节), and articles (条). There is no definitive English translation for these terms.

| 理解 | Lǐjiě | Understand |
|------|-------|------------|
| 岗位 | Gǎngwèi | Post; station; position |
| 与 | Yǔ | And; together with |
| 自行 | Zìxíng | By oneself |
| 约定 | Yuēdìng | Agree upon |
| 履行 | Lǚxíng | Perform; fulfill; carry out |
| 制定 | Zhìdìng | Formulate; enact |
| 职责 | Zhízé | Duty; responsibility; obligation |
| 按时 | Ànshí | Timely |
| 质 | Zhì | Quality |
| 量 | Liàng | Quantity |
| 本职 | Běnzhí | This job's (position) |
| 工作 | Gōngzuò | Work |
| 承诺 | Chéngnuò | Promise to do something; acceptance |
| 服从 | Fúcóng | Obey (an order) |
| 经营 | Jīngyíng | Engage in or run a business |
| 能力 | Nénglì | Ability; capability; capacity |
| 及 | Jí | And; as well as (literary Chinese meaning 和 and 跟) |
| 表现 | Biǎoxiàn | Performance |
| 安排 | Ānpái | To arrange |
| 调动 | Diàodòng | Transfer |

| | | |
|---|---|---|
| 定额 | Dìng'é | Quota; fixed amount |
| 期限 | Qīxiàn | Time limit; term |
| 为 | Wèi | For the sake of; in order to |
| 固定 | Gùdìng | Fixed; set |
| 自 x 起 | Zì x qǐ | Beginning from x |
| 至……止 | Zhì zhǐ | Until... (lit. until x ends) |
| 试用期 | Shìyòngqī | Probationary period |
| 期满 | Qīmǎn | Expire; run out |
| 即行 | Jíxíng | Carry out or implement promptly or immediately |
| 终止 | Zhōngzhǐ | Terminate (at end of a contract term) |
| 且 | Qiě | Moreover |
| 均 | Jūn | All; completely; 都 |
| 无 | Wú | Literary Chinese for 没有 |
| 异议 | Yìyì | Objection; opposition |
| 自动 | Zìdòng | Automatic |
| 续延 | Xùyán | Renew; extend |
| 依 | Yī | According to; rely on |
| 此 | Cǐ | Literary Chinese for 这个 |
| 类推 | Lèituī | Reason by analogy; analogy |
| 纪律 | Jìlǜ | Discipline |
| 自觉 | Zìjué | Consciously |

| 遵守 | Zūnshǒu | Adhere to; abide by |
| 社会 | Shèhuì | Social; society |
| 公德 | Gōngdé | Social ethics; morality |
| 职业 | Zhíyè | Occupation; profession |
| 道德 | Daòdé | Ethics |
| 维护 | Wéihù | Protect |
| 声誉 | Shēngyù | Reputation; fame; prestige |
| 利益 | Lìyì | Interest; benefit |
| 严格 | Yángé | Strict; rigorous |
| 修改 | Xiūgǎi | Revise; modify; amend |
| 规章制度 | Guīzhāng zhìdù | Rule system[25] |
| 程序 | Chéngxù | Procedure; process |
| 休息 | Xiūxi | Rest breaks |
| 休假 | Xiūjià | Vacation; holiday |
| 实行 | Shíxíng | Implement; carry out |
| 工时 | Gōngshí | Man-hour |
| 执行 | Zhíxíng | Carry out; implement |
| 行政 | Xíngzhèng | Administrative |
| 管理 | Guǎnlǐ | Manage |
| 部门 | Bùmén | Department; branch; section |

---

25 Law Practice Tip: This system of rules for employees is usually found in the Employee Handbook.

| | | |
|---|---|---|
| 批准 | Pīzhǔn | Approve; approval |
| 不定时工作 | Bìdíngshí gōngzuò | Flexible working hours |
| 综合工时 | Zōnghé gōngshí | Aggregate working hours[26] |
| 的 | De | 的 is often used without the term it modifies. Here it might be translated as "in situations where…or when" |
| 加班 | Jiābān | Work overtime |
| 征得 | Zhēngdé | Obtain |
| 书面 | Shūmiàn | Written |
| 享受 | Xiǎngshòu | Enjoy |
| 权利 | Quánlì | Rights |
| 报酬 | Bàochóu | Compensation; pay |
| 支付 | Zhīfù | Pay (money); payment |
| 方式 | Fāngshì | Way; manner; method |
| 根据 x 而 y | Gēnjù x ér y | Based on x, y happens |
| 变更 | Biàngēng | Change; amend |
| 相应 | Xiāngyìng | Correspondingly |
| 提高 | Tígāo | Raise; increase; improve |
| 降低 | Jiàngdī | Reduce; lower |

26 Background Tip: The former is similar to "flex time" in the U.S. The latter is a system which calculates a worker's hours on an annual basis, allowing for more hours during busy periods and less hours during slow periods.

| 待遇 | Dàiyù | Treatment; pay; wages; salary |
|---|---|---|
| 当 | Dāng | While |
| 工资 | Gōngzī | Wages |
| 标准 | Biāozhǔn | Standard |
| 调整 | Tiáozhěng | Adjust; regulate; revise |
| 直至 | Zhízhì | Until; up to |
| 解除 | Jiěchú | Terminate (before the end of a contract term) |
| 保护 | Bǎohù | Protect |
| 条件 | Tiáojiàn | Requirements; conditions |
| 危害 | Wēihài | Harm |
| 防护 | Fánghù | Protect; shelter |
| 享有 | Xiǎngyǒu | Have; enjoy (rights; benefits; prestige; etc.) |
| 提供 | Tígōng | Provide; offer |
| 保险 | Bǎoxiǎn | Insurance[27] |
| 其他 | Qítā | Other (matters) |
| 按照 | Ànzhào | In accordance with |
| 小城镇 | Xiǎo chéngzhèn | Small cities and towns |
| 综合 | Zōnghé | Comprehensive |
| 住房 | Zhùfáng | Housing |

---

27 Law Practice Tip: Social Security in China includes: pensions, unemployment, medical, disability, maternity, and childcare.

| | | |
|---|---|---|
| 公积金 | Gōngjījīn | Public reserve fund |
| 负伤 | Fùshāng | Be wounded; injured |
| 医疗 | Yīliáo | Medical treatment |
| 疾病 | Jíbìng | Disease; sickness; illness |
| 符合 | Fúhé | Conform to; comply with |
| 计划生育 | Jìhuà shēngyù | Family planning |
| 职工 | Zhígōng | Staff and workers |
| 产假 | Chǎnjià | Maternity leave |
| 特殊 | Tèshū | Special |
| 保障 | Bǎozhàng | Ensure; guarantee; safeguard[28] |
| 项目 | Xiàngmù | Project |
| 前述 | Qiánshù | Aforementioned |
| 退回 | Tuìhuí | Send back |
| 撤回 | Chèhuí | Recall; withdraw |
| 培训 | Péixùn | Training |
| 定期 | Dìngqī | Regularly |
| 进行 | Jìnxíng | Carry out; conduct |
| 保密 | Bǎomì | Keep something a secret; confidential |
| 以及 | Yǐjí | As well as; and; too (literary Chinese for 跟 and 和) |

---

28 Background Tip: The Social Safeguard Plan includes social security.

| 未 | Wèi | Literary Chinese for 还没 |
| 包括但不限于 | Bāokuò dàn bùxiànyú | Including but not limited to |
| 泄漏 | Xièlòu | Leak (information); divulge |
| 商业秘密 | Shāngyè mìmì | Trade secret |
| 利用 | Lìyòng | Use; utilize |
| 获利 | Huòlì | Profit |
| 利益冲突 | Lìyì chōngtū | Conflict of interest |
| 从事 | Cóngshì | Engage in |
| 投资 | Tóuzī | Invest; investment |
| 创业 | Chuàngyè | To start an undertaking |
| 雇用 | Gùyòng | Hire |
| 保证 | Bǎozhèng | Guarantee; ensure |
| 如实 | Rúshí | Strictly according to the facts |
| 直接 | Zhíjiē | Direct |
| 相关 | Xiāngguān | Related |
| 依法 | Yīfǎ | Legally; in accordance with the law |
| 并且 | Bìngqiě | And; moreover |
| 存在 | Cúnzài | Exist |
| 竞业 | Jìngyè | Competing industry |
| 限制 | Xiànzhì | Restrict; limit |
| 及时 | Jíshí | Timely; promptly |
| 递交 | Dìjiāo | Submit |

| | | |
|---|---|---|
| 有效 | Yǒuxiào | Valid; effective |
| 凭证 | Píngzhèng | Proof; prove |
| 因 x 而 y | Yīn x ér y | To y because of x |
| 迟延 | Chíyán | Delay |
| 造成 | Zàochéng | Cause; bring about |
| 后果 | Hòuguǒ | Consequence; aftermath |
| 承担 | Chéngdān | Assume; bear |
| 责任 | Zérèn | Responsibility; liability |
| 信息 | Xìnxí | Information |
| 资料 | Zīliào | Data; materials |
| 证明 | Zhèngmíng | Proof |
| 属 | Shǔ | Belong to |
| 诚信 | Chéngxìn | Good faith |
| 行为 | Xíngwéi | Act; conduct; behavior |
| 需 (需要) | Xū (Xūyào) | Need to |
| 财物 | Cáiwù | Property; belongings |
| 移交 | Yíjiāo | Transfer; handover |
| 退工 | Tuìgōng | Return (a worker); resign |
| 严重 | Yánzhòng | Serious; material |
| 违反 | Wéifǎn | Violate (a law) |
| 其中 | Qízhōng | Among |
| 违纪 | Wéijì | Prohibit |

| 卖淫嫖娼 | Màiyín piáochāng | Prostitution and whoring |
|---|---|---|
| 收容 | Shōuróng | Detained for rehabilitation |
| 公安 | Gōng'ān | Public security |
| 治安拘留 | Zhì'ān jūliú | Administrative detention (lit. detention to maintain order) |
| 处罚 | Chǔfá | Penalize; punish |
| 劳动教养 | Laódòng jiàoyǎng | Education through forced labor |
| 查实 | Cháshí | Check and verify (lit. check the truthfulness of accuracy of) |
| 应聘 | Yìngpìn | Accept an offer of employment |
| 虚假 | Xūjiǎ | False; untrue |
| 情节 | Qíngjié | Circumstances; situation |
| 轻重 | Qīngzhòng | Weight; degree of seriousness; relative importance (lit. heavy or light) |
| 视 | Shì | Look at; regard; inspect |
| 立即 | Lìjí | Immediately |
| 失职 | Shīzhí | Neglect one's duty; dereliction of duty |
| 营私 | Yíngsī | Seek private gain |
| 舞弊 | Wǔbì | Fraud |
| 营私舞弊 | Yíngsī wǔbì | Embezzle; be guilty of graft and corruption; engage in fraudulent practices |
| 损害 | Sǔnhài | Harm; damage |

| 任务 | Rènwù | Duty |
|---|---|---|
| 拒 | Jù | Refuse; resist |
| 改正 | Gǎizhèng | Correct; amend |
| 追究 (追究责任) | Zhuījiū (Zhuījiū zérèn) | Investigate and affix responsibility or liability |
| 刑事 | Xíngshì | Criminal |
| 患病 | Huànbìng | Become sick; fall ill |
| 另行 | Lìngxíng | Separate; other; alternatively |
| 胜任 | Shèngrèn | Be competent; succeed |
| 仍 | Réng | Still |
| 之间 | Zhījiān | Between; among |
| 拖欠 | Tuōqiàn | Be in arrears |
| 费 | Fèi | Expenses; fees |
| 提前 | Tíqián | In advance |
| 形式 | Xíngshì | Form |
| 即使 | Jíshǐ | Even if |
| 仅 | Jǐn | Only |
| 亦 | Yì | Also; too |
| 辞职 | Cízhí | Resign |
| 违约 | Wéiyuē | Breach; violate (a contract) |
| 赔偿 | Péicháng | Compensate |
| 损失 | Sǔnshī | Loss (financial; economic; etc.) |

| 释义 | Shìyì | Explain the meaning (of a word, etc.) |
|---|---|---|
| 所称 x 系指 y | Suǒchēng x xìzhǐ y | The term x refers to y |
| 若 | Ruò | Literary Chinese for 如果 |
| 除 x 之外 | Chú x zhīwài | Except for x |
| 附件 | Fùjiàn | Appendix; annex |
| 必要 | Bìyào | Necessary; essential; indispensible |
| 补充 | Bǔchōng | Supplementary |
| 事宜 | Shìyí | Relevant matters |
| 公证 | Gōngzhèng | Notarization |
| 费用 | Fèiyòng | Expenses |
| 自理 | Zìlǐ | Take care of things by oneself |
| 申办 | Shēnbàn | Apply for and handle; process |
| 边防 | Biānfáng | Border |
| 通行证 | Tōngxíngzhèng | Pass |
| 便利 | Biànlì | Facilitate |
| 资格 | Zīgé | Qualifications |
| 申报 | Shēnbào | Report or declare (to an authority) |
| 评定 | Píngdìng | Evaluate |
| 专业 | Zhuānyè | Specialized |
| 技术 | Jìshù | Technology; skill |
| 职称 | Zhíchēng | Professional title |
| 从 | Cōng | Follow; obey; 服从 |

| 遵循 | Zūnxún | Follow; abide by; adhere to |
| 作为 | Zuòwéi | Use as; regard as |
| 以 x 为准 | Yǐ x wéizhǔn | X prevails |
| 连带责任 | Liándài zérèn | Joint liability |
| 争议 | Zhēngyì | Dispute |
| 提交 | Tíjiāo | Submit; refer |
| 调解 | Tiáojiě | Mediation; mediate |
| 委员会 | Wěiyuánhuì | Committee |
| 向 x 申请 | Xiàng x shēnqǐng | Apply to x for |
| 黄埔 | Huángpǔ | Huangpu[29] |
| 区 | Qū | District (local administrative district)[30] |
| 仲裁 | Zhòngcái | Arbitration |
| 对 x 不服 | Duì x bùfú | Do not obey; submit to x |
| 向 x 起诉 | Xiàng x qǐsù | Sue; start a lawsuit at |
| 法院 | Fǎyuàn | Court |
| 判决 | Pànjué | Judgment |
| 向 x 上诉 | Xiàng x shàngsù | Appeal to x |
| 第二中级 | Dì'èr Zhōngjí | The Second Intermediate Court[31] |

---

29 Background Tip: Huangpu is a district in Shanghai.

30 Background Tip: 区 is a term used for administrative areas. For example, large municipalities are divided into multiple 区, usually translated as "districts." Likewise, the term is used for larger administrative regions or areas such as 自治区 or "autonomous regions/areas."

31 Law Practice Tip: In China, there are two levels of trial court.

| 终审 | Zhōngshěn | Final (lit. the end of a law case) |
|---|---|---|
| 知悉 | Zhīxī | Know; learn of |
| 送达 | Sòngdá | Serve on; deliver to |
| 认可 | Rènkě | Approve; recognize |
| 否则 | Fǒuzé | If not; otherwise; or else |
| 就 | Jiù | With regards to; as for |
| 规范 | Guīfàn | Standard; norm |
| 性 | Xìng | Suffix for -ness, -ity, -ive; -ize |
| 实施 | Shíshī | Put into effect; implement; carry out |
| 盖章 | Gàizhāng | Chop; affix seal; stamp (v.)[32] |
| 生效 | Shēngxiào | Go into effect; become effective |
| 文本 | Wénběn | Text |
| 持 | Chí | Hold |
| 效力 | Xiàolì | Effectiveness; validity |
| 经办人 | Jīngbànrén | Person handling this |

---

32 Law Practice Tip: In China, companies have a single official chop (stamp) which is used to "sign" documents and authorize bank transactions. They use a red ink pad. A common tactic in a partnership dispute is to abscond with the company chop. This chop has the same effect as a corporate seal in the U.S., but is used to "sign" all manner of official documents. The English word "chop" is used in China as both a noun and a verb, e.g. "take the chop and chop the invoice."

# Chapter 5
# Property Law

# 物 权 法
Wù　Quán　Fǎ

# A. Introduction to China's Property Law System

By *Wang Kai*, Esq.

By all accounts, China nowadays hosts some of the world's hottest commercial real estate markets. That certainly is a far cry from the early 1950s, when the newly founded People's Republic launched a sweeping land reform to establish the so-called Socialist Public Land Ownership System. The principal aim at that time was to nationalize the urban real property ownership and simultaneously collectivize rural land ownership.

The year 1978 witnessed the implementation of a set of new reform policies, most notably the Household Responsibility System (HRS). The introduction of the HRS signaled, for years to come, the inevitable fragmentation of China's collective land ownership if rural and urban productivity were to be incentivized at all.

In 2007, having had a spectacular economic performance over the past three decades, China passed its much-awaited Property Rights Law.

The 247-article Law codifies and updates the pre-existing legal system of property rights, consisting of relevant provisions of the General Principles of Civil Law, the Land Administration Law, the Urban Real Estate Administration Law, the Law on Rural Land Contracting, and the Security Law. The Law covers three categories of property rights, namely Ownership (所有权) (Part Two), Usufructuary (用益物权) (Part Three) and Security (担保物权) (Part Four).

The Law defines ownership as "the right to possess, use, seek profits from and dispose the property." For the first time in PRC's history, the principle of equal protection is extended to private property, in addition to property owned by the state and collectives. The Law also recognizes additional types of real property ownership rights, such as the partitioned ownership of building areas and common ownership. Further refining a civil law concept, the

Law codifies the second category of property rights — usufructuary rights. A usufructuary right is defined as "the right to possess, use and seek proceeds from the real property owned by someone else in accordance with law." It allows individuals and other legal persons to use the land and other natural resources owned by the state and the collectives. Usufructuary rights include right to the contracted management of land (土地承包经营权), construction land use right (建设用地使用权), right to use house sites (宅基地使用权) and easement (地役权). It provides that the term of a contract for cultivated land shall be 30 years and that the holder of such right may renew the term of the contract upon the expiration of the original term. More important, it allows the holder of such right to assign, exchange or transfer the right provided such transaction is not for non-agricultural use. As to the right to use construction land, the law differentiates the right separately established on the surface of or above or under the land, regulates the creation, transfer, use and mortgage of the right, and allows renewal of the right upon the expiration of its initial term, which is currently up to 70 years. The third category under the Law is property rights for security. The law amends, supplements and updates the Security Law with respect to provisions on security interests, and includes the general principles and provisions on mortgage (抵押权), pledge (质权) and lien (留置权). It further improves the system of property rights for security, extends the scope of collaterals, and revises the rules for the realization of security rights.

The property law system before was fragmented, ambiguous, inconsistent and lacking uniformity, especially in the areas of ownership rights, land use rights, mortgage regulations, and the title registration process. Although still far from perfect, the Law aims to correct those shortcomings by offering stronger protection of ownership rights, allowing renewal of land use rights, broadening the parameters of mortgage regulations, and adopting a uniformed registration process.

# B. Text of Property Rights Law (2007)[1]

## 中华人民共和国主席 令

### 第六十二号

《中华人民共和国物 权法》已 由中华人民共和国第十届 全国人民代表大会第五次会议 于 2007年3月16日通过, 现 予 公布, *自*2007年10月1日*起*施行。

中华人民共和国主席 **胡锦涛**

2007年3月16日

---

1 Source: Zhonghua Renmin Gongheguo wu quan fa [Property Rights Law (P.R.C.)] (promulgated by the Nat'l People's Cong., Mar. 16, 2007, effective Oct. 1, 2007) *available at* http://www.gov.cn/flfg/2007-03/19/content_554452.htm (last visited Jun. 3, 2011).

# 中华人民共和国物权法

## (2007年3月16日第十届全国人民代表大会第五次会议通过）

第一编 总 则

第一章 基本原则

第一条 为了 维护国家基本经济 制度,维护社会主义 市场经济秩序,明确物的归属,发挥物的效用,保护权利人的物权,根据 宪法,制定本法。

第二条 因物的归属和利用 而 产生的民事关系,适用本法。

本法所称物,包括 不动产和动产。法律规定权利作为物权客体 的,依照 其规定。

本法所称物权,是指权利人依法对特定的物享有 直接 支配和排他的权利,包括所有权、用益物权和担保物权。

第三条 国家在社会主义初级 阶段,坚持公有制 为 主体、多种所有制 经济共同发展的基本经济制度。

国家巩固 和发展公有制经济,鼓励、支持和引导 非公有制经济的发展。

国家实行社会主义市场经济,保障 一切市场主体的平等法律地位和发展权利。

第四条 国家、集体、私人的物权和其他权利人的物权受法律保护,任何 单位和个人不得侵犯。

第五条 物权的种类和内容,由法律规定。

第六条 不动产物权的设立、变更、转让和消灭,应当依照法律规定登记。动产物权的设立和转让,应当依照法律规定交付。

第七条 物权的取得和行使,应当遵守法律,尊重社会公德,不得损害公共利益和他人合法 权益。

第八条 其他相关法律对物权另有特别规定的,依照其规定。

第二章 物权的设立、变更、转让和消灭

第一节 不动产登记

第九条 不动产物权的设立、变更、转让和消灭,经依法登记,发生 效力;未经登记,不发生效力,但法律另有规定的除外。

依法属于国家所有的自然 资源,所有权可以不登记。

第十条 不动产登记,由不动产所在地的登记机构 办理。

国家对不动产实行统一登记制度。统一登记的范围、登记机构和登记办法,由法律、行政法规规定。

第十一条 当事人 申请登记，应当根据不同登记事项 提供 权属 证明和不动产界址、面积等必要 材料。

第十二条 登记机构应当履行 下列 职责：

（一）查验申请人提供的权属证明和其他必要材料；

（二）就 有关登记事项询问申请人；

（三）如实、及时登记有关事项；

（四）法律、行政法规规定的其他职责。

申请登记的不动产的有关情况需要进一步证明的，登记机构可以要求申请人补充材料，必要时可以实地 查看。

第十三条 登记机构不得有下列行为：

（一）要求对不动产进行 评估；

（二）以年检等名义进行重复登记；

（三）超出登记职责范围的其他行为。

第十四条 不动产物权的设立、变更、转让和消灭，依照法律规定应当登记的，自 记载于不动产登记簿 时发生效力。

第十五条 当事人之间 订立有关设立、变更、转让和消灭不动产物权的合同，除法律另有规定或者合同另有约定 外，自合同成立时生效；未办理物权登记的，不影响合同效力。

第十六条 不动产登记簿是物权归属和内容的根据。不动产登记簿由登记机构管理。

第十七条 不动产权属证书是权利人享有该不动产物权的证明。不动产权属证书记载的事项，应当与不动产登记簿一致；记载不一致的，除有证据证明不动产登记簿确有错误外，以不动产登记簿为准。

第十八条 权利人、利害关系人可以申请查询、复制登记资料，登记机构应当提供。

第十九条 权利人、利害关系人认为不动产登记簿记载的事项错误的，可以申请更正登记。不动产登记簿记载的权利人书面同意更正或者有证据证明登记确有错误的，登记机构应当予以更正。

不动产登记簿记载的权利人不同意更正的，利害关系人可以申请异议登记。登记机构予以异议登记的，申请人在异议登记之日起十五日内不起诉，异议登记失效。异议登记不当，造成权利人损害的，权利人可以向申请人请求损害赔偿。

第二十条 当事人签订买卖房屋或者其他不动产物权的协议，为保障将来 实现物权，按照约定可以向登记机构申请预告登记。预告登记后，未经预告登记的权利人同意，处分该不动产的，不发生物权效力。

预告登记后，债权消灭或者自能够进行不动产登记之日起三个月内未申请登记的，预告登记失效。

第二十一条 当事人提供虚假材料申请登记，给他人造成损害的，应当承担赔偿责任。

因登记错误，给他人造成损害的，登记机构应当承担赔偿责任。登记机构赔偿后，可以向造成登记错误的人追偿。

第二十二条 不动产登记费 按件 收取，不得按照不动产的面积、体积或者价款的比例收取。具体 收费 标准由国务院有关部门会同价格 主管部门规定。

第二节 动产交付

第二十三条 动产物权的设立和转让，自交付时发生效力，但法律另有规定的除外。

第二十四条 船舶、航空器和机动车等物权的设立、变更、转让和消灭，未经登记，不得对抗 善意 第三人。

第二十五条 动产物权设立和转让前，权利人已经依法占有该动产的，物权自法律行为生效时发生效力。

第二十六条 动产物权设立和转让前，第三人依法占有该动产的，负有交付义务的人可以通过转让请求第三人返还 原物的权利代替交付。

第二十七条 动产物权转让时，双方又约定由出让人 继续占有该动产的，物权自该约定生效时发生效力。

第三节 其他规定

第二十八条 因人民法院、仲裁 委员会的法律文书或者人民政府的征收决定等，导致物权设立、变更、转让或者消灭的，自法律文书或者人民政府的征收决定等生效时发生效力。

第二十九条 因继承或者受遗赠取得物权的，自继承或者受遗赠开始时发生效力。

第三十条 因合法建造、拆除房屋等事实行为设立或者消灭物权的，自事实行为成就时发生效力。

第三十一条 依照本法第二十八条至第三十条规定享有不动产物权的，处分该物权时，依照法律规定需要办理登记的，未经登记，不发生物权效力。

第三章 物权的保护

第三十二条 物权受到侵害的，权利人可以通过和解、调解、仲裁、诉讼等途径 解决。

第三十三条 因物权的归属、内容发生争议的，利害关系人可以请求确认权利。

第三十四条 无权占有不动产或者动产的，权利人可以请求返还 原物。

第三十五条 妨害物权或者可能妨害物权的，权利人可以请求排除妨害或者消除 危险。

第三十六条 造成不动产或者动产毁损的，权利人可以请求修理、重作、更换或者恢复 原状。

第三十七条 侵害物权，造成权利人损害的，权利人可以请求损害赔偿，也可以请求承担其他民事责任。

第三十八条 本章规定的物权保护方式，可以单独适用，也可以根据权利被侵害的情形合并适用。

侵害物权，除承担民事责任外，违反行政

管理规定的, 依法承担行政责任; **构成 犯罪**的, **依法 _追究_ 刑事 _责任_**。

第二编 所有权

第四章 一般规定

第三十九条 所有权人对自己的不动产或者动产, 依法享有占有、使用、**收益**和处分的权利。

第四十条 所有权人有权在自己的不动产或者动产上设立用益物权和担保物权。用益物权人、担保物权人行使权利, 不得损害所有权人的权益。

第四十一条 法律规定专属于国家所有的不动产和动产, 任何单位和个人不能取得所有权。

第四十二条 为了公共利益的需要, 依照法律规定的**权限**和**程序**可以征收集体所有的土地和单位、个人的房屋及其他不动产。

征收集体所有的土地, 应当依法**足额** 支付土地**补偿费**、**安置** 补助费、地上**附着物**和**青苗的补偿费**等**费用**, 安排**被征收地农民**的社会**保障**费用, 保障被征地农民的生活, 维护被征地农民的合法权益。

征收单位、个人的房屋及其他不动产, 应当**依法给予 拆 迁**补偿, 维护被征收人的合法权益; 征收个人**住宅**的, 还应当保障被征收人的**居住 条件**。

任何单位和个人不得**贪污**、**挪用**、**私分**、**截留**、**拖欠**征收补偿费等费用。

第四十三条 国家对**耕地**实行**特殊**保护, **严格 限制**农用地转为建设用地, **控制建设用地总量**。不得违反法律规定的权限和程序征收集体所有的土地。

第六章 业主的建筑物区分所有权

第七十条 业主对**建筑物**内的住宅、经营性**用房**等**专有 部分**享有所有权, 对专有部分以外的共有部分享有共有和**共同**管理的权利。

第七十三条 **建筑区划**内的**道路**, 属于业主共有, 但属于**城镇**公共道路的除外。建筑区划内的绿地, 属于业主共有, 但属于城镇公共绿地或者**明示**属于个人的除外。建筑区划内的其他公共**场所**、公用**设施**和**物业 服务**用房, 属于业主共有。

第八十一条 业主可以**自行**管理建筑物及其**附属**设施, 也可以**委托**物业服务**企业**或者其他管理人管理。

对建设单位**聘请**的物业服务企业或者其他管理人, 业主有权依法更换。

第八十二条 物业服务企业或者其他管理人根据业主的委托管理建筑区划内的建筑物及其附属设施, 并接受业主的**监督**。

第八十三条 业主应当遵守法律、法规**以及**管理规约。

业主大会和业主委员会, 对**任意 弃置 垃圾**、**排放 污染物**或者噪声、违反规定**饲养**动物、**违章 搭建**、**侵占 通道**、**拒付**物业费等损害他人合法权益的行为, 有权依照 法律、法规以及管理规约, 要求行为人停止侵害、消除危险、排除妨害、赔偿**损失**。业主对侵害自己合法权益的行为, 可以依法向人民法院提起诉讼。

### 第七章 相邻关系

第八十六条 不动产权利人应当为相邻权利人用水、**排水**提供必要的**便利**。

对自然**流水**的利用, 应当在不动产的相邻权利人之间**合理 分配**。对自然流水的排放, 应当尊重自然**流向**。

第八十七条 不动产权利人对相邻权利人因**通行**等**必须**利用其土地的, 应当提供必要的便利。

第八十八条 不动产权利人因建造、**修缮**建筑物以及**铺设 电线**、**电缆**、**水管**、**暖气**和**燃气 管线**等必须利用相邻土地、建筑物的, 该土地、建筑物的权利人应当提供必要的便利。

第八十九条 建造建筑物, 不得违反国家有关**工程**建设标准, **妨碍**相邻建筑物的**通风**、**采光**和**日照**。

第九十条 不动产权利人不得违反国家规定弃置**固体 废物**, 排放**大气**污染物、水污染物、噪声、**光**、**电磁波辐射**等**有害 物质**。

第九十一条 不动产权利人**挖掘**土地、建造建筑物、铺设管线以及**安装 设备**等, 不得**危及**相邻不动产的**安全**。

### 第三编 用益物权

### 第十四章 地役权

第一百五十六条 地役权人有权按照合同约定, 利用他人的不动产, **以**提高自己的不动产的**效益**。

**前款**所称他人的不动产为**供役地**, 自己的不动产为**需役地**。

第一百五十七条 设立地役权, 当事人应当**采取**书面**形式**订立地役权合同。

地役权合同一般包括下列条款:

(一) 当事人的**姓名**或者**名称和住所**;

(二) 供役地和需役地的**位置**;

(三) 利用**目的和方法**;

(四) 利用**期限**;

(五) 费用及其支付方式;

(六) 解决争议的方法。

第一百五十八条 地役权自地役权合同**生效**时设立。当事人要求登记的, 可以向登记机构申请地役权登记; 未经登记, 不得对抗善意第三人。

第一百六十一条 地役权的期限由当事人约定, 但不得**超过**土地承包经营权、建设用地使用权等用益物权的**剩余**期限。

第一百六十二条 土地所有权人享有地役权或者**负担**地役权的, 设立土地承包经营权、宅基地使用权时, 该土地承包经营权人、宅基地使用权人继续享有或者负担已设立的地役权。

第四编 担保物权

第十五章 一般规定

第一百七十八条 担保法与本法的规定不一致的,适用本法。

第十六章 抵押权

第一节 一般抵押权

第一百八十条 **债务人**或者第三人有权处分的下列**财产**可以抵押:

(一)建筑物和其他土地附着物;

(二)建设用地使用权;

(三)以**招标**、**拍卖**、**公开 协商**等方式取得的**荒地**等土地承包经营权;

(四)**生产设备**、**原材料**、**半成品**、**产品**;

(五)正在建造的建筑物、船舶、航空器;

(六)**交通运输 工具**;

(七)法律、行政法规未**禁止**抵押的其他财产。

抵押人可以将前款**所列**财产一并抵押。

第一百八十一条 经当事人书面协议,企业、**个体 工商 户**、**农业**生产经营者可以**将**现有的以及将有的生产设备、原材料、半成品、产品抵押,债务人不履行**到期**债务或者发生当事人约定的实现抵押权的情形,债权人有权就实现抵押权时的动产**优先受偿**。

第一百八十七条 以本法第一百八十条第一款第一**项**至第三项规定的财产或者第五项规定的正在建造的建筑物抵押的,应当办理抵押登记。抵押权自登记时设立。

第一百八十八条 以本法第一百八十条第一款第四项、第六项规定的财产或者第五项规定的正在建造的船舶、航空器抵押的,抵押权自抵押合同生效时设立;未经登记,不得对抗善意第三人。

第一百八十九条 企业、个体工商户、农业生产经营者以本法第一百八十一条规定的动产抵押的,应当向抵押人**住所地**的工商行政管理部门办理登记。抵押权自抵押合同生效时设立;未经登记,不得对抗善意第三人。

依照本法第一百八十一条规定抵押的,不得对抗**正常**经营活动中已支付合理价款并取得抵押财产的**买受人**。

第十七章 质权

第一节 动产质权

第二百一十二条 质权自**出质人**交付质押财产时设立。

第二节 权利质权

第二百二十三条 债务人或者第三人有权处分的下列权利可以出质:

(一)**汇票**、**支票**、**本票**;

(二)**债券**、**存款单**;

（三）仓单、提单；

（四）可以转让的**基金 份额**、**股权**；

（五）可以转让的**注册 商标 专用权**、**专利权**、**著作权**等**知识产权**中的财产权；

（六）**应收账款**；

（七）法律、行政法规规定可以出质的其他财产权利。

第二百二十四条 以汇票、支票、本票、债券、存款单、仓单、提单出质的，当事人应当订立书面合同。质权自权利**凭证交**付质权人时设立；没有权利凭证的，质权自有关部门办理出质登记时设立。

# C. Vocabulary of Property Rights Law (2007)

| Chinese | Pinyin | English |
|---|---|---|
| 主席 | Zhǔxí | Chairman |
| 令 | Lìng | Decree |
| 物 | Wù | Property |
| 权 | Quán | Authority; power; right |
| 已 | Yǐ | 已经 |
| 由 x | Yóu x | By x |
| 届 | Jiè | Session |
| 全国人民代表大会 | Quánguó Rénmín Dàibiǎo Dàhuì | National People's Congress (NPC) |
| 会议 | Huìyì | Meeting |
| 于 | Yú | In; on |
| 通过 | Tōngguò | Pass; enact |
| 现 | Xiàn | 现在 |
| 予 | Yǔ | Give (literary Chinese) |
| 公布 | Gōngbù | Promulgate |

| 自 x 起 | Zì x qǐ | Beginning from x |
|---|---|---|
| 施行 | Shīxíng | Come into force |
| 胡锦涛 | Hú Jǐntāo | Hu Jintao[2] |
| 目录 | Mùlù | Table of contents |
| 编 | Biān | Part[3] |
| 总则 | Zǒngzé | General principles |
| 章 | Zhāng | Chapter[4] |
| 基本 | Jīběn | Basic |
| 原则 | Yuánzé | Principle |
| 设立 | Shèlì | Establish; set up |
| 变更 | Biàngēng | Change; amend |
| 转让 | Zhuǎnràng | Transfer possession |
| 消灭 | Xiāomiè | Eliminate; expire; abolish; extinguish |
| 节 | Jié | Section[5] |
| 不动产 | Bùdòngchǎn | Real property (lit. immovable property) |
| 登记 | Dēngjì | Registration |
| 动产 | Dòngchǎn | Movable property |

---

2 Law Practice Tip: After a statute is passed by the NPC or NPCSC, it must be signed by the President before it can take effect.

3 Law Practice Tip: Chinese laws and regulations typically consist of: parts (编), chapters (章), sections (节), and articles (条).

4 Law Practice Tip: There is no standard English translation for this term and related terms such as 条 tiáo (Article). In part, this is because their usage in Chinese is not standardized.

5 Law Practice Tip: There is no standard English translation for this term and related terms such as 条 tiáo (Article). In part, this is because their usage in Chinese is not standardized.

| 交付 | Jiāofù | Handover; deliver |
| 规定 | Guīdìng | Stipulation; provision |
| 保护 | Bǎohù | Protect |
| 所有权 | Suǒyǒuquán | Ownership; title (lit. right of ownership) |
| 一般 | Yībān | General |
| 集体 | Jítǐ | Collective |
| 私人 | Sīrén | Private |
| 业主 | Yèzhǔ | Owner; proprietor |
| 建筑物 | Jiànzhùwù | Building |
| 区分 | Qūfēn | Separate; delineate[6] |
| 相邻 | Xiānglín | Neighbor; neighboring |
| 关系 | Guānxì | Relations; relationship |
| 共有 | Gòngyǒu | Publicly owned; public |
| 取得 | Qǔdé | Obtain; acquire |
| 用益物权 | Yòngyìwùquán | Usufructuary rights |
| 土地 | Tǔdì | Land |
| 承包经营 | Chéngbāo jīngyíng | Contracted management rights |
| 建设用地 | Jiànshè yòngdì | Land used for construction |
| 使用权 | Shǐyòngquán | Right of use; right to use |

---

6 Law Practice Tip: In the West, the term condominium is used to refer to a building with multiple owners. Most often these are residential condominiums. In China, the term can also be used to refer to offices and retail shops individually owned in a common building.

| 宅基地 | Zháijīdì | Curtilage (house site) |
| 地役权 | Dìyìquán | Easement (lit. land service right) |
| 担保物权 | Dānbǎo wùquán | Security interest in property |
| 抵押 | Dǐyá | Mortgage |
| 额 | É | Amount |
| 质权 | Zhìquán | Pledge right (e.g. right to use as collateral) |
| 权利 | Quánlì | Right |
| 留置权 | Liúzhìquán | Lien right |
| 占有 | Zhànyǒu | Possession |
| 附则 | Fùzé | Supplementary provisions |
| 为了 | Wèile | In order to; for the sake of |
| 维护 | Wéihù | Protect |
| 经济 | Jīngjì | Economy; economic |
| 制度 | Zhìdù | System (political or administrative) |
| 社会主义 | Shèhuìzhǔyì | Socialism; socialist |
| 市场 | Shìchǎng | Market |
| 秩序 | Zhìxù | Order |
| 明确 | Míngquè | Make clear and definite; clarify |
| 归属 | Guīshǔ | Ownership |
| 发挥 | Fāhuī | Give free reign to; bring into play |
| 效用 | Xiàoyòng | Usefulness; effectiveness |
| 权利人 | Quánlìrén | Right owner |

| 根据 | Gēnjù | Based on; according to |
|---|---|---|
| 宪法 | Xiànfǎ | Constitution |
| 制定 | Zhìdìng | Formulate; enact |
| 因 x 而 y | Yīn x ér y | To y because of x |
| 利用 | Lìyòng | Use; utilize |
| 产生 | Chǎnshēng | Cause; bring about |
| 民事 | Mínshì | Civil |
| 适用 | Shìyòng | Apply |
| 所称 y 包括 z | Suǒchēng y bāokuò z | The term y as it is used in x includes z |
| 法律 | Fǎlǜ | Law |
| 作为 | Zuòwéi | Use as; regard as |
| 客体 | Kètǐ | Object |
| 的 | De | 的 is often used without the term it modifies. Here the missing term could be 时候 (time, i.e. "when") or 情况 (circumstances) |
| 依照 | Yīzhào | In accordance with |
| 其 | Qí | Literary Chinese for 他的 |
| 所称 x 是指 y | Suǒchēng x shìzhǐ y | The term x refers to y |
| 依法 | Yīfǎ | Legally; in accordance with the law |
| 特定 | Tèdìng | Specific; specified; specifically designated |
| 享有 | Xiǎngyǒu | Have or enjoy (rights, benefits, prestige, etc.) |

| | | |
|---|---|---|
| 直接 | Zhíjiē | Direct |
| 支配 | Zhīpèi | Control |
| 排他的 | Páitādē | Exclusive |
| 初级 | Chūjí | Initial |
| 阶段 | Jiēduàn | Stage |
| 坚持 | Jiānchí | Unremitting; persist |
| 公有制 | Gōngyǒuzhì | Public ownership |
| 为 | Wéi | Take; treat as |
| 主体 | Zhǔtǐ | Principal part; main part |
| 多种 | Duōzhǒng | Diverse; multiple |
| 制 (制度) | Zhì (Zhìdù) | System (political or administrative) |
| 发展 | Fāzhǎn | Development |
| 巩固 | Gǒnggù | Consolidate; strengthen |
| 鼓励 | Gǔlì | Encourage |
| 支持 | Zhīchí | Support |
| 引导 | Yǐndǎo | Guide; lead |
| 非 | Fēi | Non-; un- |
| 实行 | Shíxíng | Implement; carry out |
| 保障 | Bǎozhàng | Ensure; guarantee; safeguard |
| 一切 | Yīqiè | All; every |
| 地位 | Dìwèi | Status; position |
| 任何 | Rènhé | Any |

| 单位 | Dānwèi | Entity[7] |
|---|---|---|
| 不得 | Bùdé | Must not; may not |
| 侵犯 | Qīnfàn | Violate; infringe upon (a right) |
| 种类 | Zhǒnglèi | Kind; type; variety |
| 内容 | Nèiróng | Content |
| 行使 | Xíngshǐ | Exercise (a right) |
| 遵守 | Zūnshǒu | Adhere to; abide by |
| 尊重 | Zūnzhòng | Respect; esteem |
| 公德 | Gōngdé | Social ethics; morality |
| 损害 | Sǔnhài | Harm; damage |
| 利益 | Lìyì | Interest; benefit |
| 合法 | Héfǎ | Legal |
| 权益 | Quányì | Rights and interests |
| 相关 | Xiāngguān | Related |
| 另有 | Lìngyǒu | Other; additional; otherwise |
| 经 (经过 ) | Jīng (Jīngguò) | Go through; be x'd |
| 发生 | Fāshēng | Occur; happen |
| 效力 | Xiàolì | Effectiveness; validity |
| 未 | Wèi | Literary Chinese for 还没 |

---

7 Law Practice Tip: Dānwèi is used to describe the organization to which you belong, e.g. your employer. In the past, when there was no private economy, the Dānwèi played a much more significant role in the lives of its workers. It provided housing, schools, hospitals, cafeterias, etc.

| | | |
|---|---|---|
| 但法律另有规定的除外 | Dàn fǎlù lìngyǒu guīdìngde chúwài | Except as otherwise provided by law |
| 属于 | Shǔyú | Belong to; fall within |
| 自然 | Zìrán | Nature; natural |
| 资源 | Zīyuán | Natural resources |
| 所在地 | Suǒzàidì | Local (lit. the place where it is located) |
| 机构 | Jīgòu | Organization; structure |
| 办理 | Bànlǐ | Handle; take care of |
| 统一 | Tǒngyī | Unified |
| 范围 | Fànwéi | Scope |
| 办法 | Bànfǎ | Method |
| 行政 | Xíngzhèng | Administrative |
| 法规 | Fǎguī | Administrative laws and regulations[8] |
| 当事人 | Dāngshìrén | Parties; party |
| 申请 | Shēnqǐng | Apply for |
| 事项 | Shìxiàng | Item; matter |
| 提供 | Tígōng | Provide; offer |
| 权属 | Quánshǔ | Ownership (lit. to whom the right belongs) |
| 证明 | Zhèngmíng | Proof |

---

8 Law Practice Tip: "行政法规" are legislations adopted by the State Council. They are the third level of legislation in China, only lower than the Constitution and Laws passed by National People's Congress or its Standing Committee.

| 界址 | Jièzhǐ | Boundaries |
|---|---|---|
| 面积 | Miànji | Area |
| 必要 | Bìyào | Necessary; essential; indispensible |
| 材料 | Cáiliào | Materials |
| 履行 | Lǚxíng | Perform; fulfill; carry out |
| 下列 | Xiàliè | The following; set forth below |
| 职责 | Zhízé | Duty; responsibility; obligation |
| 查验 | Cháyàn | Inspect |
| 就 | Jiù | With regards to; as for |
| 有关 | Yǒuguān | Relevant |
| 询问 | Xúnwèn | Inquire about |
| 如实 | Rúshí | Strictly according to the facts |
| 及时 | Jíshí | Timely; promptly |
| 进一步 | Jìnyībù | Further |
| 补充 | Bǔchōng | Supplement |
| 实地 | Shídì | Site |
| 查看 | Chákàn | Inspect; examine |
| 行为 | Xíngwéi | Act; conduct; behavior |
| 进行 | Jìnxíng | Carry out; conduct |
| 评估 | Pínggū | Evaluation; appraisal |
| 年检 | Niánjiǎn | Annual inspection |
| 名义 | Míngyì | Titular; in the name of; as a pretext |

| | | |
|---|---|---|
| 重复 | Chóngfù | Repeat; duplicate |
| 超出 | Chāochū | Exceed; overstep |
| 自 x 时 | Zì x shí | Beginning from x |
| 记载 | Jìzǎi | Record; put down in writing |
| 登记簿 | Dēngjìbù | Registration book; registry |
| 之间 | Zhījiān | Between; among |
| 订立 | Dìnglì | Enter into (a contract) |
| 合同 | Hétóng | Contract |
| 除 x 另有 y 外 | Chú x lìngyǒu y wài | Unless x has y; except for situations when x has y |
| 约定 | Yuēdìng | Agreed on |
| 成立 | Chénglì | Form; establish |
| 影响 | Yǐngxiǎng | Affect; influence |
| 权属证书 | Quánshǔ zhèngshū | Certificate of ownership |
| 该 | Gāi | That[9] |
| 与 | Yǔ | And; together with |
| 一致 | Yīzhì | Identical (views or opinions) |
| 确 | Què | Really; indeed |
| 错误 | Cuòwù | Mistake |
| 以 x 为 y | Yǐ x wéi y | Take x as y |

---

9 Law Practice Tip: In modern legal English, the term "that" is used. In older legal English, the term "said" is used.

| | | |
|---|---|---|
| 准 | Zhǔn | Controlling |
| 利害关系人 | Lìhài guānxì rén | Interested person |
| 查询 | Cháxún | Search; look for |
| 复制 | Fùzhì | Duplicate; copy |
| 资料 | Zīliào | Data; materials |
| 更正 | Gēngzhèng | Correct; correction |
| 书面 | Shūmiàn | Written |
| 证据 | Zhèngjù | Evidence; proof |
| 予以 | Yǔyǐ | 予以 and 加以 both mean "to do x." In English, we would not translate either |
| 异议 | Yìyì | Objection; opposition |
| 起诉 | Qǐsù | Sue; start a lawsuit |
| 失效 | Shīxiào | Become invalid |
| 不当 | Bùdàng | Inappropriate |
| 造成 | Zàochéng | Cause; bring about |
| 向 x 请求 y | Xiàng x qǐngqiú y | Ask y from x |
| 赔偿 | Péicháng | Compensation |
| 签订 | Qiāndìng | Sign (a contract, agreement) |
| 房屋 | Fángwū | Housing |
| 协议 | Xiéyì | Agreement |
| 将来 | Jiānglái | Future |
| 实现 | Shíxiàn | Realize; achieve; bring about |

| 按照 | Ànzhào | In accordance with |
|------|--------|--------------------|
| 预告 | Yùgào | Advance notice |
| 处分 | Chǔfèn | Handle; dispose of |
| 债权 | Zhàiquán | Creditor's claim |
| 虚假 | Xūjiǎ | False; untrue |
| 承担 | Chéngdān | Assume; bear |
| 责任 | Zérèn | Responsibility; liability |
| 追偿 | Zhuīcháng | Recovery; recourse |
| 费 | Fèi | Expenses; fees |
| 按件 (按照文件) | Ànjiàn (Ànzhàowénjiàn) | Based on each document |
| 收取 | Shōuqǔ | Collect; receive |
| 体积 | Tǐjī | Volume; bulk |
| 价款 | Jiàkuǎn | Price |
| 比例 | Bǐlì | Proportion |
| 具体 | Jùtǐ | Concrete; specific |
| 收费 | Shōufèi | Fees; charges |
| 标准 | Biāozhǔn | (an official) Standard |
| 国务院 | Guówùyuàn | State Council |
| 部门 | Bùmén | Department; branch; section |
| 价格 | Jiàgé | Price |
| 主管 | Zhǔguǎn | Responsible for; in charge of |
| 船舶 | Chuánbó | Boats and ships |

| 航空器 | Hángkōngqì | Aircraft |
|---|---|---|
| 机动车 | Jīdòngchē | Motor vehicle |
| 对抗 | Duìkàng | Resist; oppose |
| 善意 | Shànyì | Good faith |
| 第三人 | Dìsānrén | Third party |
| 负有 | Fùyǒu | Bear; carry |
| 义务 | Yìwù | Duties; obligations |
| 请求 | Qǐngqiú | Request; ask |
| 返还原物 | Fǎnhuányuánwù | Return original items |
| 代替 | Dàitì | Replace; substitute |
| 出让人 | Chūràngrén | Transferor; seller |
| 继续 | Jìxù | Continue to; continuously |
| 人民法院 | Rénmín Fǎyuàn | People's Court |
| 仲裁 | Zhòngcái | Arbitration |
| 委员会 | Wěiyuánhuì | Committee |
| 法律文书 | Fǎlǜ wénshū | Legal document |
| 政府 | Zhèngfǔ | Government |
| 征收 | Zhēngshōu | Expropriate; taking; eminent domain |
| 导致 | Dǎozhì | Lead to; result in |
| 继承 | Jìchéng | Inherit |
| 遗赠 | Yízèng | Bequest |
| 建造 | Jiànzào | Build; construct |

| | | |
|---|---|---|
| 拆除 | Chāichú | Demolish |
| 事实 | Shìshí | Fact (ual) |
| 侵害 | Qīnhài | Infringe on |
| 和解 | Héjiě | Settlement; conciliation |
| 调解 | Tiáojiě | Mediation |
| 诉讼 | Sùsòng | Litigation |
| 途径 | Tújìng | Means; ways |
| 解决 | Jiějué | Resolve |
| 争议 | Zhēngyì | Dispute |
| 确认 | Quèrèn | Affirm; confirm |
| 返还 | Fǎnhuán | Return |
| 原物 | Yuánwù | Original property |
| 妨害 | Fánghài | Impair; jeopardize |
| 排除 | Páichú | Remove; eliminate |
| 消除 | Xiāochú | Eliminate |
| 危险 | Wēixiǎn | Danger; hazard |
| 毁损 | Huǐsǔn | Damage; impair |
| 修理 | Xiūlǐ | Repair |
| 重作 | Chóngzuò | Remake |
| 更换 | Gēnghuàn | Replace |
| 恢复 | Huīfù | Restore |
| 原状 | Yuánzhuàng | Original condition |

| | | |
|---|---|---|
| 方式 | Fāngshì | Way; manner; method |
| 单独 | Dāndú | Alone; on its own |
| 合并 | Hébìng | Merge; combine; jointly |
| 违反 | Wéifǎn | Violate (a law) |
| 构成 | Gòuchéng | Form; constitute |
| 犯罪 | Fànzuì | Commit a crime |
| 追究……责任 | Zhuījiū……zérèn | Investigate and affix responsibility or liability |
| 刑事 | Xíngshì | Criminal |
| 收益 | Shōuyì | Income; profit; earnings |
| 专 | Zhuān | Exclusive |
| 权限 | Quánxiàn | Authority; power |
| 程序 | Chéngxù | Procedure; process |
| 足额 | Zú'é | Fully; full amount |
| 支付 | Zhīfù | Pay (money) |
| 补偿 | Bǔcháng | Compensate |
| 安置 | Ānzhì | Find a place for; help resettle |
| 补助 | Bǔzhù | Subsidy |
| 附着物 | Fùzhuówù | Fixtures |
| 青苗的补偿费 | Qīngmiáo de bǔchángfèi | Green sprout compensation |

10 Law Practice Tip: Compensation for crops that have started to grow but have not yet been harvested and sold. It is required under the Land Management Law as well.

| 费用 | Fèiyòng | Expenses |
| 被 | Bèi | Passive marker for the following verb |
| 农民 | Nóngmín | Farmers |
| 社会保障 | Shèhuì bǎozhàng | Social security[11] |
| 给予 | Jǐyǔ | Give |
| 拆 | Chāi | Demolish; demolition |
| 迁 | Qiān | Relocation |
| 住宅 | Zhùzhái | Residence |
| 居住 | Jūzhù | Live; reside |
| 条件 | Tiáojiàn | Requirements; conditions |
| 贪污 | Tānwū | Corruption; graft |
| 挪用 | Nuóyòng | Divert; embezzle |
| 私分 | Sīfēn | Divide privately or secretly |
| 截留 | Jiéliú | Withhold; keep sth. intended for others |
| 拖欠 | Tuōqiàn | Be in arrears |
| 耕地 | Gēngdì | Arable land |
| 特殊 | Tèshū | Special |
| 严格 | Yángé | Strict; rigorous |
| 限制 | Xiànzhì | Restrict; limit |
| 控制 | Kòngzhì | Control; restrict |

11 Law Practice Tip: Social Security in China includes: pensions, unemployment, medical, disability, maternity, and childcare.

| 总量 | Zǒngliàng | Total quantity |
| 建筑物 | Jiànzhùwù | Buildings |
| 用房 | Yòngfáng | Building; room used for x |
| 专有 | Zhuānyǒu | Exclusive |
| 部分 | Bùfèn | Parts; sections |
| 共同 | Gòngtóng | Together; jointly |
| 建筑区划 | Jiànzhùqūhuà | Construction zoning plan |
| 道路 | Dàolù | Roads |
| 城镇 | Chéngzhèn | Cities and towns |
| 明示 | Míngshì | Express; expressly |
| 场所 | Chǎngsuǒ | Location; place |
| 设施 | Shèshī | Facilities |
| 物业 | Wùyè | Realty; property |
| 服务 | Fúwù | Service |
| 自行 | Zìxíng | By oneself |
| 附属 | Fùshǔ | Affiliated; attached |
| 委托 | Wěituō | Entrust; delegate; consign |
| 企业 | Qǐyè | Enterprise |
| 聘请 | Pìnqǐng | Hire |
| 并 | Bìng | And; moreover |
| 监督 | Jiāndū | Control; supervise |
| 以及 | Yǐjí | As well as; and; too (literary Chinese |

| | | meaning the same as 跟 and 和) |
|---|---|---|
| 规约 | Guīyuē | Stipulation (in an agreement) |
| 大会 | Dàhuì | Assembly; association |
| 任意 | Rènyì | Willful; arbitrary |
| 弃置 | Qìzhì | Discard |
| 垃圾 | Lājī | Trash; garbage |
| 排放 | Páifàng | Discharge (of gas or pollutants) |
| 污染物 | Wūrǎnwù | Pollutants |
| 噪声 | Zàoshēng | Noise |
| 饲养 | Sìyǎng | Raise |
| 违章 | Wéizhāng | Break the rules; illegal |
| 搭建 | Dājiàn | Build; construction |
| 侵占 | Qīnzhàn | Occupy; seize |
| 通道 | Tōngdào | Passage way |
| 拒付 | Jùfù | Refuse to pay |
| 损失 | Sǔnshī | Loss (financial, economic, etc.) |
| 排水 | Páishuǐ | Drain off water |
| 便利 | Biànlì | Facilitate |
| 流水 | Liúshuǐ | Running water |
| 合理 | Hélǐ | Reasonable |
| 分配 | Fēnpèi | Distribute; assign |
| 流向 | Liúxiàng | Direction of the flow |

| | | |
|---|---|---|
| 通行 | Tōngxíng | Access |
| 必须 | Bìxū | Shall; must |
| 修缮 | Xiūshàn | Repair |
| 铺设 | Pūshè | Build |
| 电线 | Diànxiàn | Electric wires |
| 电缆 | Diànlǎn | Electric cables |
| 水管 | Shuǐguǎn | Water pipe |
| 暖气 | Nuǎnqì | Steam heating |
| 燃气 | Ránqì | Gas |
| 管线 | Guǎnxiàn | Pipeline |
| 工程 | Gōngchéng | Engineering |
| 妨碍 | Fáng'ài | Hinder; obstruct |
| 通风 | Tōngfēng | Ventilation |
| 采光 | Cǎiguāng | Lighting |
| 日照 | Rìzhào | Sunshine |
| 固体 | Gùtǐ | Solid |
| 废物 | Fèiwù | Waste; trash |
| 大气 | Dàqì | Atmosphere; air |
| 光 | Guāng | Light |
| 电磁波辐射 | Diàncíbō fúshè | Electromagnetic wave radiation |
| 有害 | Yǒuhài | Destructive; harmful |
| 物质 | Wùzhì | Material; matter |

| 挖掘 | Wājué | Excavate |
|---|---|---|
| 安装 | Ānzhuāng | Install |
| 设备 | Shèbèi | Equipment |
| 危及 | Wēijí | Endanger; imperil |
| 安全 | Ānquán | Safety; security |
| 以 | Yǐ | In order to |
| 效益 | Xiàoyì | Beneficial results; productivity |
| 前款 | Qiánkuǎn | Preceding clause; above provision |
| 供役地 | Gōngyìdì | Servient tenement |
| 需役地 | Xūyìdì | Dominant tenement |
| 采取 | Cǎiqǔ | Adopt; take |
| 形式 | Xíngshì | Form |
| 条款 | Tiáokuǎn | Provision; clause |
| 姓名 | Xìngmíng | Name and surname (full name) |
| 名称 | Míngchēng | Name (of an entity) |
| 住所 | Zhùsuǒ | Residence; domicile |
| 位置 | Wèizhì | Place; location |
| 目的 | Mùdì | Purpose |
| 方法 | Fāngfǎ | Method; way |
| 期限 | Qīxiàn | Time limit; term |
| 生效 | Shēngxiào | Go into effect; become effective |
| 超过 | Chāoguò | Exceed |

| 剩余 | Shèngyú | Remaining |
| 负担 | Fùdān | Bear (a burden) |
| 债务人 | Zhàiwùrén | Debtor |
| 财产 | Cáichǎn | Property |
| 招标 | Zhāobiāo | Invite bids; public tender |
| 拍卖 | Pāimài | Auction |
| 公开 | Gōngkāi | Open; public |
| 协商 | Xíeshāng | Consult; discuss |
| 荒地 | Huāngdì | Wasteland; undeveloped land |
| 生产 | Shēngchǎn | Production; manufacture |
| 原材料 | Yuáncáiliào | Raw materials |
| 半成品 | Bànchéngpǐn | Semi-finished products |
| 产品 | Chǎnpǐn | Products |
| 交通运输 | Jiāotōng yùnshū | Transportation |
| 工具 | Gōngjù | Means; tools; instruments |
| 禁止 | Jìnzhǐ | Prohibited |
| 所列 | Suǒliè | Listed (lit. which are listed or set forth in x) |
| 一并 | Yībìng | Altogether |
| 个体工商户 | Gètǐ gōngshāng hù | Individual businessman |
| 农业 | Nóngyè | Agriculture |

| | | |
|---|---|---|
| 经营者 | Jīngyíngzhě | Business operator[12] |
| 将 | Jiāng | Literary Chinese for 把 |
| 到期 | Dàoqī | Come to term; mature |
| 优先 | Yōuxiān | Priority |
| 偿 | Cháng | Compensation |
| 项 | Xiàng | Clause |
| 住所地 | Zhùsuǒdì | Place of residence; domicile |
| 正常 | Zhèngcháng | Regular; normal |
| 买受人 | Mǎishòurén | Buyer |
| 出质人 | Chūzhìrén | Pledgor; mortgagor |
| 汇票 | Huìpiào | Draft; money order |
| 支票 | Zhīpiào | Check (from a bank) |
| 本票 | Běnpiào | Cashier's check |
| 债券 | Zhàiquàn | Bond |
| 存款单 | Cúnkuǎndān | Deposit certificate |
| 仓单 | Cāngdān | Warehouse receipt |
| 提单 | Tídān | Bill of lading |
| 基金 | Jījīn | Fund |
| 份额 | Fèn'é | Share; portion |

---

12 Law Practice Tip: Europe uses the term "undertakings" and the U.S. uses the term "business operators." Here 者 (same as 的人) refers to both individuals and entities engaged in business. See Article 12 in the text for the statutory definition of this term.

| 股权 | Gǔquán | Stock rights |
| --- | --- | --- |
| 注册 | Zhùcè | Register |
| 商标 | Shāngbiāo | Trademark |
| 专用权 | Zhuānyòngquán | Exclusive right to use |
| 专利权 | Zhuānlìquán | Patent (right) |
| 著作权 | Zhùzuòquán | Copyright (lit. right to a work) |
| 知识产权 | Zhīshí chǎnquán | Intellectual property rights |
| 财产权 | Cáichǎnquán | Property right |
| 应收账款 | Yīngshōu zhàngkuǎn | Accounts receivable |
| 凭证 | Píngzhèng | Proof; prove |

# D. Text of Property Law Circular 171 (2006)[13]

## 关于规范 房地产 市场 外资 准入和管理的意见

各省、自治区、直辖市人民政府，国务院各部委、各直属机构：

今年以来，我国房地产领域 外商 投资 增长较快，境外机构和个人在境内购买房地产也比较活跃。为 促进房地产市场健康 发展，*经*国务院同意，现*就*规范房地产市场外资准入和管理提出以下意见：

一、规范外商投资房地产市场准入

（一）境外机构和个人在**境内**投资购买非自用房地产，应当**遵循 商业 存在**的原则，按照外商投资房地产的**有关 规定**，**申请 设立**外商投资企业；经有关**部门 批准**并**办理**有关登记后，

方可按照 核准的经营 范围 从事 相关 业务。

（二）外商投资设立房地产企业，投资总额 超过1000万美元（含1000万美元）*的*，注册资本金 不得 低于投资总额的50%。投资总额低于1000万美元的，注册资本金**仍 按 现行**规定**执行**。

（三）设立外商投资房地产企业，*由* 商务主管部门和**工商 行政** 管理 机关 依法批准设立和办理注册登记手续，颁发 一年期《外商投资企业批准证书》和《营业 执照》。企业付清土地使用权 出让金后，凭 上述证照到土地管理部门申办《国有土地使用证》，根据《国有土地

---

13 Source: Guan yu gui fan fang di chan shi chang wai zi zhun ru he guan li de yi jian [Opinions on Normalizing the Supervision of and Permitting the Entry of Foreign Capital in the Housing Market (P.R.C.)] (promulgated by the Ministry of Housing and Urban-Rural Development of the People's Republic of China, Jul. 26, 2006, effective Jul. 26, 2006) *available at* http://www.mohurd.gov.cn/zcfg/jswj/fdcy/200611/t20061101_157771.htm (last visited Sep. 21, 2011).

使用证》到商务主管部门**换发** 正式的《外商投资企业批准证书》，再到工商行政管理机关换发与《外商投资企业批准证书》经营**期限** 一致的《营业执照》，到**税务**机关办 理税务登记。

（四）外商投资房地产企业的**股权**和**项目**转让，**以及境外投资者** 并购境内房地产企业，由商务主管等部门**严格** 按照有关**法律 法规**和**政策** 规定 **进行** 审批。投资者应**提交 履行**《国有土地使用权出让合同》、《**建设 用地 规划 许可证**》、《建设工程规划许可证》等的**保证 函**，《国有土地使用证》，建设（房地产）主管部门的**变更 备案 证明**，以及税务机关**出具**的相关**纳税证明材料**。

（五）境外投资者**通过**股权转让及其他**方**式并购境内房地产企业，或收购**合资企业 中方**股权的，**须 妥善 安置 职工、处理 银行 债务、并以自有**资金**一次性** 支付全部转让金。对有不**良 记录**的境外投资者，**不允许**其在境内进行上述活动。

二、加强外商投资企业房地产开发经营管理

（六）对投资房地产未取得《外商投资企业批准证书》和《营业执照》的境外投资者，不得进行房地产开发和经营活动。

（七）外商投资房地产企业注册资本金未全部**缴付**的，未取得《国有土地使用证》的，或开发项目资本金未达到项目投资总额**35%**的，不得办理境内、境外**贷款**，**外汇**管理部门不予批准

该企业的外汇**借款 结汇**。

（八）外商投资房地产企业的中外投资各方，不得以任何形式在合同、**章程**、股权转让协议以及其他文件中，**订立**保证任何一方**固定 回报**或**变相**固定回报的**条款**。

（九）外商投资房地产企业应当**遵守**房地产有关法律法规和政策规定，严格执行土地出让合同约定及规划许可 批准的期限和条件。有关部门要加强对外商投资房地产企业开发、**销售**等经营活动的**监管**，发现**囤积**土地和**房源**、**哄抬 房价**等**违法违规**行为的，要根据国**办发**［2006］37号文件及其他有关规定**严肃 查处**。

三、严格境外机构和个人购房管理

（十）境外机构在境内设立的**分支、代表**机构（经批准从事经营房地产业的企业**除外**）和在境内工作、学习时间超过一年的境外个人可以购买**符合**实际需要的自用、**自住 商品房**，不得购买非自用、非自住商品房。在境内没有设立分支、代表机构的境外机构和在境内工作、学习时间一年以下的境外个人，不得购买商品房。**港澳台 地区 居民**和**华侨 因**生活需要，可在境内**限购**一定面积的自住商品房。

（十一）符合规定的境外机构和个人购买自用、自住商品房必须采取**实名制**，并**持 有效**证明（境外机构应持我政府有关部门批准设立**驻**境内机构的证明，境外个人应持其来境内工作、学习，经我方批准的证明，**下同**）到土地和

房地产主管部门办理相应的土地使用权及房屋产权登记手续。房地产产权登记部门必须严格按照自用、自住原则办理境外机构和个人的产权登记,对不符合条件的不予登记。

(十二)外汇管理部门要严格按照有关规定和本意见的要求审核外商投资企业、境外机构和个人购房的资金汇入和结汇,符合条件的允许汇入并结汇;相关房产转让所得人民币资金经 合规性审核并确认按规定办理纳税等手续后,方允许购汇 汇出。

四、进一步强化和落实监管责任

(十三)各地区、特别是城市人民政府要切实 负起 责任,高度 重视当前外资进入房地产市场可能引发的问题, 进一步加强领导,落实监管责任。各地不得擅自 出台对外商投资房地产企业的优惠政策,已经出台的要清理 整顿并予以 纠正。建设部、商务部、发展改革委、国土资源部、人民银行、税务总局、工商总局、银

监会、外汇局等有关部门要及时制定有关操作细则,加强对各地落实规范房地产市场外资准入和管理政策的指导和监督 检查,对擅自降低企业注册资本金和项目资本金比例,以及管理不到位出现其他违法违规行为的,要依法查处。同时,要进一步加大对房地产违规跨境 交易和汇兑违法 违规行为的查处力度。

(十四)完善市场监测 分析工作机制。建设部、商务部、统计局、国土资源部、人民银行、税务总局、工商总局、外汇局等有关部门要建立健全外资进入房地产市场信息 监测 系统,完善外资房地产信息网络。有关部门要加强协调配合,强化对跨境资本流动的监测,尽快实现外资房地产统计数据的信息共享。

建设部　商务部　发展改革委

人民银行　工商总局　外汇局

二〇〇六年七月十一日

# E. Vocabulary of Property Law Circular 171 (2006)

| Chinese | Pinyin | English |
| --- | --- | --- |
| 规范 | Guīfàn | Standardize; normalize |
| 房地产 | Fángdìchǎn | Real estate |
| 市场 | Shìchǎng | Market |
| 外资 | Wàizī | Foreign investment |
| 准入 | Zhǔnrù | Permit to enter |
| 管理 | Guǎnlǐ | Management |
| 意见 | Yìjiàn | Opinion |
| 各 | Gè | Each; every |
| 省 | Shěng | Province |
| 自治 | Zìzhì | Autonomous |
| 区 | Qū | Region[14] |
| 直辖 | Zhíxiá | Directly under jurisdiction (of the Central Government) |

14 Background Tip: 区 is a term used for administrative areas. For example, large municipalities are divided into multiple 区, usually translated as "districts." Likewise, the term is used for larger administrative regions or areas such as 自治区 or "autonomous regions/areas."

| 市 | Shì | City; municipality |
| 人民 | Rénmín | People; People's |
| 政府 | Zhèngfǔ | Government |
| 国务院 | Guówùyuàn | State Council |
| 部委 | Bùwěi | Ministries and commissions |
| 直属 | Zhíshǔ | Directly under[15] |
| 机构 | Jīgòu | Organization; structure |
| 领域 | Lǐngyù | Area |
| 外商 | Wàishāng | Foreign (commercial) |
| 投资 | Tóuzī | Investment |
| 增长 | Zēngzhǎng | Grow; increase |
| 境外 | Jìngwài | Foreign (lit. outside the border) |
| 购买 | Gòumǎi | Purchase |
| 活跃 | Huóyuè | Brisk; active; dynamic |
| 为 | Wèi | For the sake of; in order to |
| 促进 | Cùjìn | Promote; advance |
| 健康 | Jiànkāng | Healthy |
| 发展 | Fāzhǎn | Development |
| 经 | Jīng | Be x'd |
| 就 | Jiù | With regard to; as for |

15 Background Tip: Zhíshǔ refers to agencies that are directly under the State Council but are not a member of the cabinet.

| 境内 | Jìngnèi | Domestic (lit. within the borders) |
|------|---------|-----------------------------------|
| 非 | Fēi | Non-; un- |
| 自用 | Zìyòng | Self (personal) use |
| 遵循 | Zūnxún | Follow; abide by; adhere to |
| 商业 | Shāngyè | Commercial |
| 存在 | Cúnzài | Existence; presence |
| 原则 | Yuánzé | Principle |
| 按照 | Ànzhào | Based on; in accordance with |
| 有关 | Yǒuguān | Relevant |
| 规定 | Guīdìng | Stipulation; provision |
| 申请 | Shēnqǐng | Apply for |
| 设立 | Shèlì | Establish; set up |
| 企业 | Qǐyè | Enterprise |
| 部门 | Bùmén | Department; branch; section |
| 批准 | Pīzhǔn | Approve; approval |
| 办理 | Bànlǐ | Handle; take care of |
| 登记 | Dēngjì | Registration |
| 方 | Fāng | Same as 才 |
| 核准 | Hézhǔn | Authorized |
| 经营 | Jīngyíng | Engage in or run a business |

| 范围 | Fànwéi | Scope[16] |
|---|---|---|
| 从事 | Cóngshì | Engage in |
| 相关 | Xiāngguān | Related |
| 业务 | Yèwù | Business |
| 总额 | Zǒng'é | Total amount |
| 超过 | Chāoguò | Exceed |
| 含 | Hán | Including |
| 的 | De | 的 is often used without the term it modifies. Here the missing term could be 时候 (time, i.e. "when") or 情况 (circumstance) |
| 注册 | Zhùcè | Registered |
| 资本金 | Zīběnjīn | Capital[17] |
| 不得 | Bùdé | Must not; may not |
| 低于 | Dīyú | Less than |
| 仍 | Réng | Still |
| 按 (按照) | Àn (Ànzhào) | Based on; in accordance with |
| 现行 | Xiànxíng | Current |
| 执行 | Zhíxíng | Carry out; implement |

---

16 Law Practice Tip: In the U.S., scope of business is not a critical issue. In China, the government strictly enforces a company's declared scope of business. This is in part because many types of business activities require government approval.

17 Law Practice Tip: In China, registered capital refers to the amount of capital the investors have pledged to pay. This is to be distinguished from paid in capital which is the amount actually paid. Paid in capital typically must be verified by an accounting firm. Various rules and regulations set minimum thresholds for registered capital required for entities depending upon the kind of activity the entity will engage in.

| 由 x | Yóu x | By x |
|---|---|---|
| 商务 | Shāngwù | Commercial |
| 主管 | Zhǔguǎn | Responsible for; in charge of |
| 工商 | Gōngshāng | Industrial and commercial |
| 行政 | Xíngzhèng | Administrative |
| 机关 | Jīguān | Organ (administrative or government) |
| 依法 | Yīfǎ | Legally; in accordance with the law |
| 手续 | Shǒuxù | Process; procedure |
| 颁发 | Bānfā | Issue; promulgate |
| 一年期 | Yīniánqī | One year (term) |
| 证书 | Zhèngshū | Certificate |
| 营业 | Yíngyè | Business |
| 执照 | Zhízhào | License |
| 付清 | Fùqīng | Pay in full; pay off |
| 使用权 | Shǐyòngquán | Right of use; right to use |
| 出让金 | Chūràngjīn | Transfer fee |
| 凭 | Píng | Rely on; based on |
| 上述 | Shàngshù | Above mentioned |
| 申办 | Shēnbàn | Apply for and handle; process |
| 国有 | Guóyǒu | State owned |
| 证 | Zhèng | Permit |
| 根据 | Gēnjù | Based on; according to |

| 换发 | Huànfā | Reissue |
|------|--------|---------|
| 正式 | Zhèngshì | Formal |
| 与 | Yǔ | And; together with |
| 期限 | Qīxiàn | Time limit; term |
| 一致 | Yīzhì | Identical |
| 税务 | Shuìwù | Taxation (bureau) |
| 股权 | Gǔquán | Stock rights |
| 项目 | Xiàngmù | Project |
| 以及 | Yǐjí | As well as; and; too (literary Chinese meaning the same as 跟 and 和) |
| 者 | Zhě | 者 is literary Chinese and is used after an adjective or verb as a substitute for a person, entity, or thing[18] |
| 并购 | Bìnggòu | Merge (lit. combine by purchase) |
| 严格 | Yángé | Strict; rigorous |
| 法律 | Fǎlù | Law |
| 法规 | Fǎguī | Administrative laws and regulations[19] |
| 政策 | Zhèngcè | Government policy |
| 进行 | Jìnxíng | Carry out; conduct |

18 Law Practice Tip: In modern legal Chinese, it is often used to indicate both natural and legal persons, as it is here.

19 Law Practice Tip: "行政法规" are legislations adopted by the State Council. They are the third level of legislation in China, only lower than the Constitution and Laws passed by National People's Congress or its Standing Committee.

| 审批 (审查批准) | Shěnpī (Shěnchá pīzhǔn) | Examination and approval |
|---|---|---|
| 提交 | Tíjiāo | Submit; refer |
| 履行 | Lǚxíng | Perform; fulfill; carry out |
| 合同 | Hétóng | Contract |
| 建设 | Jiànshè | Construction |
| 用地 | Yòngdì | Land use |
| 规划 | Guīhuà | Plan |
| 许可证 | Xǔkězhèng | Permit; license (literally certificate of approval) |
| 工程 | Gōngchéng | Construction engineering |
| 等 | Děng | Etc. |
| 保证 | Bǎozhèng | Guarantee; ensure |
| 函 | Hán | Letter; document |
| 变更 | Biàngēng | Change; amend |
| 备案 | Bèi'àn | Put on record; filed |
| 证明 | Zhèngmíng | Proof |
| 出具 | Chūjù | Provide |
| 纳税 | Nàshuì | Pay taxes |
| 材料 | Cáiliào | Materials |
| 通过 | Tōngguò | Go through |
| 方式 | Fāngshì | Way; manner; method |
| 合资企业 | Hézīqǐyè | Joint venture |

| 中方 | Zhōngfāng | Chinese side or party |
| 须 | Xū | Shall |
| 妥善 | Tuǒshàn | Appropriately; properly |
| 安置 | Ānzhì | Find a place for; arrange for |
| 职工 | Zhígōng | Staff and workers |
| 处理 | Chǔlǐ | Handle; deal with |
| 银行 | Yínháng | Bank |
| 债务 | Zhàiwù | Debt; liability |
| 并 | Bìng | And; moreover |
| 自有 | Zìyǒu | Private; privately owned |
| 一次性 | Yīcìxìng | Once; one time |
| 支付 | Zhīfù | Pay (money) |
| 不良 | Bùliáng | Bad (lit. not good) |
| 记录 | Jìlù | Record |
| 允许 | Yǔnxǔ | Allow; permit |
| 未 | Wèi | Literary Chinese for 还没 |
| 缴付 | Jiǎofù | Paid in[20] |
| 贷款 | Dàikuǎn | Loan |
| 外汇 | Wàihuì | Foreign currency or exchange |
| 予 | Yǔ | Give (literary Chinese) |

20 Law Practice Tip: Companies must hire an accounting firm to verify that its registered capital has been paid in.

| 该 | Gāi | That[21] |
|---|---|---|
| 借款 | Jièkuǎn | Loan |
| 结汇 | Jiéhuì | Convert foreign exchange |
| 章程 | Zhāngchéng | Articles of Association[22] |
| 订立 | Dìnglì | Enter into (a contract) |
| 固定 | Gùdìng | Fixed; set |
| 回报 | Huíbào | Return |
| 变相 | Biànxiàng | Covert; disguised |
| 条款 | Tiáokuǎn | Provision; clause |
| 遵守 | Zūnshǒu | Adhere to; abide by |
| 销售 | Xiāoshòu | Sell |
| 监管 (监督管理) | Jiānguǎn (Jiāndū guǎnlǐ) | Supervision and management |
| 囤积 | Túnjī | Hoard |
| 房源 | Fángyuán | Housing resources |
| 哄抬 | Hōngtái | Drive up |
| 房价 | Fángjià | Home prices |
| 违法违规 | Wéifǎ wéiguī | Illegal (lit. violate laws and regulations) |
| 办发 | Bànfā | Issue |
| 严肃 | Yánsù | Strict |

---

21 Law Practice Tip: In modern legal English, the term "that" is used. In older legal English, the term "said" is used.

22 Law Practice Tip: In the U.S., the term would be Articles of Incorporation. The practice in China is to say Articles of Association. The latter term is often used in the U.S. for unincorporated entities.

| | | |
|---|---|---|
| 查处 | Cháchǔ | Investigate and handle |
| 分支 | Fēnzhī | Branch |
| 代表 | Dàibiǎo | Representative |
| 除外 | Chúwài | With the exception of x |
| 符合 | Fúhé | Conform to; comply with |
| 自住 | Zìzhù | Personal residence |
| 商品房 | Shāngpǐnfáng | Commodity housing |
| 港澳台 (香港 澳门台湾) | GǎngÀoTái (Xiānggǎng Àomén Táiwān) | Hong Kong, Macao, and Taiwan |
| 地区 | Dìqū | Region |
| 居民 | Jūmín | Resident |
| 华侨 | Huáqiáo | Overseas Chinese |
| 因 | Yīn | 因为 |
| 限购 | Xiàn'gòu | Limit purchase |
| 实名制 | Shímíngzhì | System of actual names |
| 持 | Chí | Hold; have |
| 有效 | Yǒuxiào | Valid; effective |
| 驻 | Zhù | Based; stationed |
| 下同 | Xiàtóng | The same applies below |
| 本 | Běn | Literary Chinese for 这个 |
| 审核 | Shěnhé | Examine and verify |
| 汇入 | Huìrù | Inbound remittance |

| 经 (过) x 后 | Jīng (guò) x hòu | After going through x |
|---|---|---|
| 合规性 | Héguīxìng | Lawful |
| 确认 | Quèrèn | Affirm; confirm |
| 购汇 | Gòuhuì | Purchase foreign currency |
| 汇出 | Huìchū | Outbound remittance |
| 落实 | Luòshí | Implement |
| 切实 | Qièshí | Realistically; feasibly; conscientiously |
| 负起 | Fùqǐ | Bear; take |
| 责任 | Zérèn | Responsibility; liability |
| 高度 | Gāodù | High degree |
| 重视 | Zhòngshì | Treat as important |
| 引发 | Yǐnfā | Trigger |
| 领导 | Lǐngdǎo | Leadership |
| 擅自 | Shànzì | Unauthorized |
| 出台 | Chūtái | Unveil |
| 优惠 | Yōuhuì | Preferential |
| 清理 | Qīnglǐ | Sort out |
| 整顿 | Zhěngdùn | Rectify |
| 予以 | Yǔyǐ | 予以 and 加以 both mean "to do x." <br><br> In English, we would not translate either |
| 纠正 | Jiūzhèng | Correct |
| 建设部 | Jiànshè Bù | Ministry of Construction |

| 商务部 | Shāngwù Bù | Ministry of Commerce |
|---|---|---|
| 发展改革委 (员会) | Fāzhǎn Gǎigé Wěi (yuánhuì) | National Development and Reform Commission |
| 国土资源部 | Guótǔ Zīyuán Bù | Ministry of Land and Resources |
| 税务总局 | Shuìwù Zǒng Jú | State Administration of Taxation |
| 工商总局 | Gōngshāng Zǒng Jú | State Administration of Industry and Commerce |
| 银监会 (银行监督会) | Yín Jiān Huì (Yínháng Jiāndū Huì) | China Banking Regulatory Commission |
| 外汇局 | Wàihuì Jú | State Administration of Foreign Exchange |
| 操作 | Cāozuò | Operational |
| 细则 | Xìzé | Detailed provisions |
| 检查 | Jiǎnchá | Examination; inspection |
| 降低 | Jiàngdī | Reduce; lower |
| 比例 | Bǐlì | Proportion |
| 到位 | Dàowèi | Reach goal; meet standard |
| 跨境 | Kuàjìng | Cross-border |
| 交易 | Jiāoyì | Business transaction or deal |
| 汇兑 | Huìduì | Currency exchange |
| 力度 | Lìdù | Strength |
| 监测 | Jiāncè | Monitor |

| 分析 | Fēnxī | Analyze |
| 统计局 | Tǒngjì Jú | Bureau of Statistics |
| 建立 | Jiànlì | Establish |
| 健全 | Jiànquán | Strengthen; perfect |
| 信息 | Xìnxí | Information |
| 系统 | Xìtǒng | System |
| 完善 | Wánshàn | Improve; perfect |
| 网络 | Wǎngluò | Network |
| 协调 | Xiétiáo | Coordinate |
| 配合 | Pèihé | Cooperation |
| 尽快 | Jìnkuài | As quickly as possible |
| 数据 | Shùjù | Data |
| 共享 | Gòngxiǎng | Share |

# Chapter 6
# Intellectual Property / Criminal Law

# 知识产权法/刑法

Zhī　Shí　Chǎn　Quán　Fǎ　Xíng　Fǎ

# A. Introduction to China's Intellectual Property Law System

By *Luckie Hong*, Registered Foreign Lawyer, Jones Day Law Firm

One of the most common business mistakes made by international investors is to fail to adequately protect their intellectual property rights before they come to China. It is noteworthy that, as of 2008, there is relatively little copyright litigation in China and that the largest volume of IPR litigation involves only domestic parties.

China's intellectual property laws are comparatively new. After the Cultural Revolution (1966-1976), a modern IP system emerged in China with the implementation of Reform and Opening-up. China promulgated the Trademark Law, the Patent Law, the Copyright Law, and the Unfair Competition Law over the past 20 years, and also enacted narrower laws to protect geographical indications, trade secrets, new plant varieties, and layout designs of integrated circuits. Below is a brief summary of the four basic elements of China's IP law system: patent, trademark, copyright, and unfair competition.

Patent: China's first patent law was enacted in 1984 and has been amended twice (1992 and 2000). To comply with the Trade-Related Aspects of Intellectual Property Rights Agreement (TRIPs), the 2000 amendment extended the duration of patent protection to 20 years from the date of filing a patent application. Chemical and pharmaceutical products, as well as food, beverages, and flavorings are all now patentable. As a signatory to the 1994 Patent Cooperation Treaty, China will perform international patent searches and preliminary examinations of patent applications. Under China's patent law, a foreign patent application filed by a person or firm without a business office in China must apply through an authorized patent agent, while initial preparation may be done by anyone. Patents are filed with China's State Intellectual Property Office (SIPO) in Beijing, while SIPO offices at the provincial and municipal level are responsible for administrative enforcement.

Trademark: China's trademark law was first adopted in 1982 and revised in 1993 and 2001. The 2001 trademark law extended registration to collective marks, certification marks and three-dimensional symbols, as required by TRIPs. China joined the Madrid Protocol in 1989, which requires reciprocal trademark registration for member countries. China has a 'first-to register' system that requires no evidence of prior use or ownership, thus foreign companies seeking to distribute their products in China are advised to register their marks and/or logos with the Trademark Office. As with patent registration, foreign parties must use the services of approved Chinese agents when submitting a trademark application, however foreign attorneys or the Chinese agents also may prepare the application.

Copyright: China's copyright law was established in 1990 and amended in October 2001. The latest implementing rules came into force on September 15, 2002. Unlike patent and trademark protection, copyrighted works do not require registration for protection. Protection is granted to individuals from countries belonging to international copyright conventions or bilateral agreements of which China is a member. However, copyright owners may wish to voluntarily register with China's National Copyright Administration (NCA) to establish evidence of ownership, should enforcement actions become necessary.

Unfair Competition: China's Unfair Competition Law provides some protection for unregistered trademarks, packaging, trade dress and trade secrets. The Fair Trade Bureau, under the State Administration for Industry and Commerce (SAIC) is responsible for the interpretation and implementation of the Unfair Competition Law. According to TRIPs, China is required to protect undisclosed information submitted to Chinese agencies in obtaining regulatory approval for pharmaceutical and chemical entities from disclosure or unfair commercial use. China's State Drug Administration and Ministry of Agriculture oversee the marketing approval of pharmaceuticals and agricultural chemicals, respectively. It is anticipated that China's Anti-Monopoly Law (effective August 1, 2008) will also have an impact in this area.

# B. Text of Intellectual Property/ Criminal Law

## 中华人民共和国刑法

1979年7月1日第五届 全国人民代表大会第二次会议 通过 1997年3月14日第八届全国人民代表大会第五次会议修订第七节 侵犯 知识 产权 罪

第二百一十七条 *以* 营利 *为* 目的, *有下* 列 侵犯 著作权 情形 *之一*, 违法 所得 数额较大 **或者** 有其他 **严重 情节** 的, 处三年以下 **有期徒刑** 或者 拘役, 并处 或者 单处 **罚金**; 违法所得数额巨大或者有其他特别严重情节的, 处三年以上七年以下有期徒刑, 并处罚金:

(一) 未 经著作权人许可, 复制 发行 其 文字 作品、音乐、电影、电视、录像作品、计算机 软件 及其他作品的;

(二) 出版他人享有 专有出版权的图书的;

(三) 未经录音 录像 制作 者许可, 复制 发行其制作的录音录像的;

(四) 制作、**出售** 假冒他人署名的美术作品的。

第十四条 **明知** 自己的 行为会发生 危害社会的结果, 并且希望或者 **放任** 这种结果发生, **因而 构成 犯罪** 的, 是 **故意犯罪**。

故意犯罪, 应当负 刑事 责任。

《最高人民法院 关于 审理 非法出版物刑事案件 具体 应用 法律 若干问题的解释》
已 于1998年12月11日由最高人民法院审判 委员会第1032次会议通过, 现 予 公布,
自1998年12月23日起 施行。
1998年12月17日

第二条 以营利为目的, 实施刑法 第二百一十七条所 列侵犯著作权行为 之一, 个人违法所得数额在五万元以上, 单位违法所得数额在二十万元以上的, 属于 "违法所得数额较大"; 具有下列情形之一的, 属于 "有其他严重情节":

(一)因侵犯著作权曾经两次以上被追究行政责任或者民事责任, 两年内又实施刑法第二百一十七条所列侵犯著作权行为之一的;

(二)个人非法经营数额在二十万元以上, 单位非法经营数额在一百万元以上的;

(三)造成其他严重后果的。

第三条 刑法第二百一十七条第(一)项中规定的 "复制发行", 是指 行为人以营利为目的, 未经著作权人许可而实施的复制、发行或者既复制又发行其文字作品、音乐、电影、电视、录像作品、计算机软件及其他作品的行为。

第十七条 本解释所称 "经营数额", 是指 以非法出版物的定价数额乘以行为人经营的非法出版物数量所得的数额。

本解释所称 "违法所得数额", 是指获利数额。

非法出版物没有定价或者以境外 货币定价的, 其单价数额应当按照行为人实际出售的价格 认定。

《最高人民法院、最高人民检察院关于办理侵犯知识产权刑事案件
具体应用法律若干问题的解释》
2004年11月2日最高人民法院审判委员会第1331次会议、2004年11月11日最高人民检察院第十届检察委员会第28次会议通过)(法释〔2004〕19号)

第五条 以营利为目的, 实施刑法第 二百一十七条所列侵犯著作权行为之一, 违法

所得数额在三万元以上的，属于"违法所得数额较大"；具有下列情形之一的，属于"有其他严重情节"，应当以侵犯著作权罪判处三年以下有期徒刑或者拘役，并处或者单处罚金：

（一）非法经营数额在五万元以上的；

（二）未经著作权人许可，复制发行其文字作品、音乐、电影、电视、录像作品、计算机软件及其他作品，复制品数量合计在一千张（份）以上的；

（三）其他严重情节的情形。

《最高人民法院 最高人民检察院关于办理侵犯知识产权刑事案件
具体应用法律若干问题的解释（二）》

（2007年4月4日最高人民法院审判委员会第1422次会议、最高人民检察院第十届检察委员会第75次会议
通过）法释〔2007〕6号

发布时间：2007-04-07

为维护社会主义市场 经济 秩序，依法惩治侵犯知识产权犯罪活动，根据刑法、刑事诉讼法有关规定，现就办理侵犯知识产权刑事案件具体应用法律的若干问题解释如下：

第一条 以营利为目的，未经著作权人许可，复制发行其文字作品、音乐、电影、电视、录像作品、计算机软件及其他作品，复制品数量合计在五百张（份）以上的，属于刑法第二百一十七条规定的"有其他严重情节"；复制品数量在二千五百张（份）以上的，属于刑法第二百一十七条规定的"有其他 特别严重情节"。

第二条 刑法第二百一十七条侵犯著作权罪中的"复制发行"，包括复制、发行或者既复制又发行的行为。

侵权产品的持有人 通过 广告、征订等方式 推销侵权产品的，属于刑法第二百一十七条规定的"发行"。

非法出版、复制、发行他人作品，侵犯著作权构成犯罪的，按照侵犯著作权罪定罪处罚。

第七条 以前发布的司法解释与本解释不一致的，以本解释为准。

# C. Vocabulary of Intellectual Property/Criminal Law

| Chinese | Pinyin | English |
|---------|--------|---------|
| 刑法 | Xíngfǎ | Criminal Law |
| 届 | Jiè | Session |
| 全国人民代表大会 | Quánguó Rénmín Dàibiǎo Dàhuì | National People's Congress (NPC) |
| 会议 | Huìyì | Meeting |
| 通过 | Tōngguò | Enact; pass |
| 修订 | Xiūdìng | Revised; amended |
| 节 | Jié | Section[1] |
| 侵犯 | Qīnfàn | Violate; infringe upon (a right) |
| 知识 | Zhīshi | Intellectual |
| 产权 | Chǎnquán | Property |
| 罪 | Zuì | Crime |

---

1 Law Practice Tip: Chinese laws and regulations typically consist of: parts (编), chapters (章), sections (节), and articles (条). There is no definitive English translation for these terms.

| | | |
|---|---|---|
| 条 | Tiáo | Article[2] |
| 以 x 为 y | Yǐ x wéi y | Take x as y |
| 营利 | Yínglì | Seek a profit |
| 目的 | Mùdì | Purpose |
| 有……之一 | Yǒu……zhīyī | Have one of… |
| 下列 | Xiàliè | The following; set forth below |
| 著作权 | Zhùzuòquán | Copyright (lit. right to a work) |
| 情形 | Qíngxíng | Circumstance; situation |
| 违法 | Wéifǎ | Illegal |
| 所得 | Suǒdé | What you have obtained |
| 数额 | Shù'é | Amount |
| 或者 | Huòzhě | Or |
| 严重 | Yánzhòng | Serious; material |
| 情节 | Qíngjié | Circumstance; situation |
| 的 | De | 的 is often used without the term it Here the missing term could be 时候 (time, i.e. "when") or 情况 (circumstance) |
| 处 | Chǔ | Sentence to |

---

2 Law Practice Tip: Chinese laws and regulations typically consist of: parts (编), chapters (章), sections (节), and articles (条). There is no definitive English translation for these terms.

| 有期 | Yǒuqī | Fixed term |
|---|---|---|
| 徒刑 | Túxíng | Sentence; imprisonment |
| 拘役 | Jūyì | Detention |
| 并 | Bìng | And; moreover |
| 单 | Dān | Only; solely |
| 罚金 | Fájīn | Fine |
| 巨大 | Jùdà | Huge; enormous |
| 以上 | Yǐshàng | More than |
| 未 | Wèi | Literary Chinese for 还没 |
| 经 (经过) | Jīng (Jīngguò) | Go through; be x'd |
| 许可 | Xǔkě | Approval; permission |
| 复制 | Fùzhì | Duplicate; copy |
| 发行 | Fāxíng | Distribute |
| 其 | Qí | Literary Chinese for 他的 |
| 文字 | Wénzì | Written |
| 作品 | Zuòpǐn | Works |
| 录像 | Lùxiàng | Video recording |
| 计算机 | Jìsuànjī | Computer |
| 软件 | Ruǎnjiàn | Software |
| 及 | Jí | And; as well as (literary Chinese meaning the same as 跟 and 和) |
| 出版 | Chūbǎn | Publish |

| 享有 | Xiǎngyǒu | Have; enjoy (rights; benefits; prestige; etc.) |
| 专有 | Zhuānyǒu | Exclusive |
| 录音 | Lùyīn | Sound recording |
| 制作 | Zhìzuò | Make; produce |
| 者 | Zhě | 者 is literary Chinese and is used after an adjective or verb as a substitute for a person, entity, or thing[3] |
| 出售 | Chūshòu | Sell |
| 假冒 | Jiǎmào | Fake; imitation |
| 署名 | Shǔmíng | Sign one's name; signed |
| 美术 | Měishù | Art |
| 明知 | Míngzhī | Clearly know; knowingly |
| 行为 | Xíngwéi | Act; conduct; behavior |
| 发生 | Fāshēng | Occur; happen |
| 危害 | Wēihài | Harm |
| 社会 | Shèhuì | Social; society |
| 结果 | Jiéguǒ | Result |
| 并且 | Bìngqiě | And; moreover |
| 放任 | Fàngrèn | Indifferent |

---

3 Law Practice Tip: In modern legal Chinese, it is often used to indicate both natural and legal persons as it is here.

| 因而 | Yīn'ér | Thus |
|---|---|---|
| 构成 | Gòuchéng | Form; constitute |
| 犯罪 | Fànzuì | Crime |
| 故意 | Gùyì | Intentional |
| 负 | Fù | Bear (e.g. responsibility) |
| 刑事 | Xíngshì | Criminal |
| 责任 | Zérèn | Responsibility; liability |
| 法院 | Fǎyuàn | Court |
| 关于 | Guānyú | Relating to |
| 审理 | Shěnlǐ | Try; hear a case |
| 非法 | Fēifǎ | Illegal |
| 物 | Wù | Things |
| 案件 | Ànjiàn | Case |
| 具体 | Jùtǐ | Concrete; specific |
| 应用 | Yīngyòng | Apply; use |
| 法律 | Fǎlù | Law |
| 若干 | Ruògān | Several |
| 解释 | Jiěshì | Interpret; interpretation |
| 已 | Yǐ | 已经 |
| 于 | Yú | In; on |
| 由 x | Yóu x | By x |

| 审判委员会 | Shěnpàn Wěiyuánhuì | Judicial Adjudication Committee[4] |
|---|---|---|
| 现 | Xiàn | 现在 |
| 予 | Yǔ | Give (literary Chinese) |
| 公布 | Gōngbù | Promulgate |
| 自 x 起 | Zì x qǐ | Beginning from x |
| 施行 | Shīxíng | Come into force |
| 实施 | Shíshī | Put into effect; implement; carry out |
| 所 | Suǒ | Which |
| 列 | Liè | Set forth; list |
| 之一 | Zhīyī | 的一个 |
| 个人 | Gèrén | Individual |
| 单位 | Dānwèi | Entity[5] |
| 属于 | Shǔyú | Belong to; fall within |
| 具有 | Jùyǒu | Fully possess; have |
| 曾 | Céng | Previously; 已经 |
| 追究责任 | Zhuījiū zérèn | Investigate and affix responsibility or liability |
| 行政 | Xíngzhèng | Administrative |

4 Law Practice Tip: In China, every court has a judicial adjudication committee that consists of high ranking leaders of the court. Even though they don't review cases as a judge, they play a dominant role in framing important judicial policies, as well as handling complicated cases. It has been hotly debated whether an internal organ like this harms the independence of the judges.

5 Law Practice Tip: Dānwèi is used to describe the organization to which you belong, e.g. your employer. In the past, when there was no private economy, the Dānwèi played a much more significant role in the lives of its workers. It provided housing, schools, hospitals, cafeterias, etc. In modern Chinese is it often best translated as "entity."

| | | |
|---|---|---|
| 经营 | Jīngyíng | Engage in or run a business |
| 后果 | Hòuguǒ | Consequence; aftermath |
| 项 | Xiàng | Clause |
| 民事 | Mínshì | Civil[6] |
| 规定 | Guīdìng | Stipulate; provide |
| 是指 | Shìzhǐ | This refers to; means |
| 行为人 | Xíngwéirén | Actor |
| 既 x 又 y | Jì x yòu y | Not only x but also y |
| 本 | Běn | Literary Chinese for 这个 |
| 所称 y 是指 z | Suǒchēng y shìzhǐ z | The term y means z |
| 以 x 乘以 y | Yǐ x chéngyǐ y | Take x and multiply it times y |
| 定价 | Dìngjià | Set price |
| 数量 | Shùliàng | Quantity; amount |
| 获利 | Huòlì | Profit |
| 境外 | Jìngwài | Foreign (lit. outside the border) |
| 货币 | Huòbì | Currency |
| 单价 | Dānjià | Unit price |
| 按照 | Ànzhào | In accordance with |
| 实际 | Shíjì | Actual; realistic; in practice |

---

6 Law Practice Tip: In China, there are three ways to enforce IPR. The first two, criminal prosecution and administrative action, are initiated by the government (although typically at the request of the holder of the IPR). The third, a civil claim, is enforced privately through a civil lawsuit.

| 价格 | Jiàgé | Price |
|---|---|---|
| 认定 | Rèndìng | Determine; establish |
| 检察院 | Jiǎncháyuàn | Procuratorate (prosecutor) |
| 办理 | Bànlǐ | Handle; take care of |
| 法释 | Fǎshì | Legal interpretation |
| 判处 | Pànchǔ | Sentence |
| 合计 | Héjì | Total |
| 发布 | Fābù | Issue |
| 维护 | Wéihù | Protect |
| 市场 | Shìchǎng | Market |
| 经济 | Jīngjì | Economy |
| 秩序 | Zhìxù | Order |
| 惩治 | Chéngzhì | Punish |
| 活动 | Huódòng | Activity; act |
| 诉讼 | Sùsòng | Procedure (in litigation)[7] |
| 有关 | Yǒuguān | Relevant |
| 就 | Jiù | With regards to; as for |
| 如下 | Rúxià | As set forth below |
| 侵权 (侵犯知识产权) | Qīnquán (Qīnfàn zhīshi chǎnquán) | Violate intellectual property rights |

---

7 Law Practice Tip:诉讼 when used together with 民事 or 刑事 means "procedure" i.e. "criminal procedure" or "civil procedure."

| 持有人 | Chíyǒurén | Holder; bearer |
| 通过 | Tōngguò | Go through |
| 广告 | Guǎnggào | Advertisement |
| 征订 | Zhēngdìng | Solicit orders |
| 方式 | Fāngshì | Way; manner; method |
| 推销 | Tuīxiāo | Market; promote sales |
| 司法 | Sīfǎ | Judicial |
| 与 | Yǔ | And; together with |
| 一致 | Yīzhì | Identical (views or opinions) |
| 准 | Zhǔn | Controlling |

# Chapter 7
# Anti-Trust Law

# 反垄断法

Fǎn    Lǒng    Duàn    Fǎ

# A. Introduction to China's Anti-Monopoly Law System

By *Xue Yi* , Partner of Zhong Lun Law Firm, Beijing

China's emerging anti-monopoly law system plays an increasingly important role in today's Chinese economy. Although multiple state administrations had previously issued a number of rules regulating certain kinds of monopolistic conduct, China has not had any comprehensive anti-monopoly legislation until the Anti-Monopoly Law of the People's Republic of China (AML) was issued in 2007 and took effect in 2008. The AML is often considered as a crucial step in China's transition to a market economy. Dubbed China's "economic constitution," the AML is China's first comprehensive competition law.

For foreign investors and undertakings, the AML covers the following three areas of private party conduct: concentration of undertakings (mergers), monopoly agreements, and abuse of dominant market position. Several regulatory authorities with different powers and functions are in charge of anti-monopoly issues. The Ministry of Commerce (MOFCOM) is responsible for concentration of undertakings. The National Development and Reform Commission (NDRC) is responsible for price-related monopoly agreements and abuse of market dominant position. The State Administration for Industry and Commerce (SAIC) is responsible for non-price-related monopoly agreements and abuse of market dominant position. The State Council's Anti-monopoly Commission (SCAC) serves as the lead government supervisory authority on anti-monopoly matters.

Due to the broad, general nature of the AML, SCAC, MOFCOM, SAIC, and NDRC have issued or proposed a number of implementing rules; a testament to the growing complexity of the PRC anti-trust regulatory regime and the determination of the regulators to swiftly build up a functioning enforcement mechanism.

A.  Monopoly Agreements

In accordance with the AML and the implementing rules issued by SAIC and NDRC, undertakings are prohibited from concluding the following horizontal monopoly agreements: (1) price fixing, (2) volume restriction, (3) market division, (4) technology restriction, (5) boycotting a transaction, and (6) bid-rigging; as well as concluding any of the following vertical monopoly agreements with its trading counterparty: (1) resale price fixing, (2) resale price floor, (3) geographical market restriction, (4) exclusive dealing, and (5) vertical tender or auction collusion.

B.  Abuse of Market Dominant Position

Neither the AML nor the draft implementing rules from SAIC and NDRC provide a specific definition of "abuse of dominance." Instead, the AML enumerates a set of instances of abuse of dominant market position that are generally in line with international competition practice. Conduct amounting to abuse of dominance includes both exclusionary (e.g. refusal to deal and exclusive dealing) and exploitative conduct (e.g. monopolistic pricing, predatory pricing, tying, and customer discrimination). The draft implementing rules from SAIC and NDRC add no new types of abusive conduct, but provide more detailed guidelines to use in determining specific instances of abuse of dominant market position.

C.  Concentration of Undertakings

"Concentration of undertakings" refers to the merger of undertakings or an undertaking that obtains controlling power over another business operator through acquisition of equity or assets, or through conclusion of contracts and other means. Where the turnover realized by the participating undertakings reaches the threshold as provided in the Provisions of the State Council on the Thresholds for Declaring Concentration of Undertakings (《国务院关于经营者集中申报标准的规定》), the undertakings must file an application with MOFCOM.

# B. Text of Anti-Monopoly Law[1]

# 中华人民共和国主席 令

## 第 六十八 号

　　《中华人民共和国反 垄断法》已 由中华人民共和国第十届 全国人民代表大会 常务委员会第二十九次会议于2007年8月30日通过, 现 予 公布, *自*2008年8月1日*起* 施行。

中华人民共和国主席 **胡锦涛**

2007年8月30日

---

1 Source: Zhonghua Renmin Gongheguo fan long duan fa [Anti-monopoly Law (P.R.C.)] (promulgated by the Nat'l People's Cong., Aug. 30, 2007, effective Aug. 1, 2008) *available at* http://www.gov.cn/flfg/2007-08/30/content_732591.htm (last visited May 30, 2011).

# 中华人民共和国反垄断法
## （2007年8月30日第十届全国人民代表大会常务委员会第二十九次会议通过）

第一章 总则

第一条 为了 预防和制止垄断行为，保护市场公平竞争，提高 经济 运行 效率，维护 消费者 利益和社会 公共利益，促进社会主义市场经济健康 发展，制定本法。

第二条 中华人民共和国境内经济活动中的垄断行为，适用本法；中华人民共和国境外的垄断行为，对境内市场竞争产生排除、限制影响的，适用本法。

第三条 本法规定的垄断行为包括：

（一）经营者达成垄断协议；

（二）经营者滥用市场支配地位；

（三）具有或者可能具有排除、限制竞争效果的经营者集中。

第七条 国有经济占 控制地位的关系 国

民经济命脉和国家安全的**行业 以及 依法 实行** 专营专卖的行业，国家对其经营者的合法经营活动**予以**保护，并对经营者的经营行为及其**商品**和服务的**价格**依法实施 **监管**和**调控**，维护消费者利益，促进**技术 进步**。

前款规定行业的经营者应当依法经营，**诚实 守信**，严格 **自律**，接受社会公众的监督，**不得 利用**其控制地位或者专营专卖地位损害消费者利益。

**第八条** 行政机关和**法律、法规 授权**的具有**管理公共事务 职能**的**组织**不得滥用行政权力，排除、限制竞争。

**第九条 国务院 设立**反垄断委员会，**负责组织、协调、指导**反垄断工作，**履行 下列 职责：**

（一）**研究 拟订 有关**竞争**政策；**

（二）组织调查、**评估**市场总体竞争状况，**发布评估报告；**

（三）制定、发布反垄断**指南；**

（四）协调反垄断行政**执法**工作；

（五）国务院规定的**其他**职责。

国务院反垄断委员会的**组成**和工作**规则**由国务院规定。

**第十条** 国务院规定的**承担反垄断执法职责的机构**（以下统称国务院反垄断执法机构）**依照**本法规定，负责反垄断执法工作。

国务院反垄断执法机构**根据**工作**需要**，可以授权省、自治区、**直辖市 人民政府 相应**的机构，依照本法规定负责有关反垄断执法工作。

**第十二条 本法所称**经营者，**是指 从事**商品**生产**、经营或者**提供**服务的**自然人、法人**和其他组织。

本法所称**相关市场**，是指经营者在一定**时期内就 特定**商品或者服务（以下统称商品）**进行竞争**的商品**范围**和**地域**范围。

第二章 垄断协议

**第十三条 禁止**具有竞争关系的经营者达成下列垄断协议：

（一）**固定**或者**变更**商品价格；

（二）限制商品的生产**数量**或者**销售数量；**

（三）**分割**销售市场或者**原材料 采购**市场；

（四）限制购买新技术、新**设备**或者限制**开发新技术、新产品；**

（五）**联合 抵制 交易；**

（六）国务院反垄断执法机构**认定**的其他垄断协议。

本法所称垄断协议，是指排除、限制竞争的协议、决定或者其他**协同**行为。

**第十四条 禁止**经营者与交易**相对人**达成下列垄断协议：

（一）固定向第三人**转售**商品的价格；

（二）**限定**向第三人转售商品的最低价格；

（三）国务院反垄断执法机构认定的其他垄断协议。

第十五条 经营者**能够 证明**所达成的协议**属于**下列**情形** 之一的, 不适用本法第十三条、第十四条的规定:

(一) 为**改进技术**、研究开发新产品的;

(二) 为提高产品**质量**、**降低** 成本、**增进效率**, 统一产品**规格**、**标准**或者实行专业化 分工的;

(三) 为提高中小经营者经营效率, 增强中小经营者竞争力的;

(四) 为**实现** 节约 能源、保护**环境**、救灾**救助**等社会公共利益的;

(五) 因经济**不景气**, 为**缓解**销售量严重**下降**或者生产**明显** 过剩的;

(六) 为**保障** 对外 贸易和对外经济合作中的正当利益的;

(七) 法律和国务院规定的其他情形。

属于前款第一**项** 至第五项情形, 不适用本法第十三条、第十四条规定的, 经营者还应当证明所达成的协议不会严重限制相关市场的竞争, **并且**能够**使**消费者分享 由此产生的利益。

第三章 滥用市场支配地位

第十七条 禁止具有市场支配地位的经营者从事下列滥用市场支配地位的行为:

(一) **以不公平**的高价销售商品或者以不公平的低价购买商品;

(二) 没有正**当理由**, 以**低于**成本的价格销售商品;

(三) 没有正当理由, **拒绝**与交易相对人进行交易;

(四) 没有正当理由, 限定交易相对人只能与其进行交易或者只能与其**指定**的经营者进行交易;

(五) 没有正当理由**搭售**商品, 或者在交易时**附加**其他不合理的交易**条件**;

(六) 没有正当理由, 对条件**相同**的交易相对人在交易价格等交易条件上实行**差别 待遇**;

(七) 国务院反垄断执法机构认定的其他滥用市场支配地位的行为。

本法所称市场支配地位, 是指经营者在相关市场内具有能够控制商品价格、数量或者其他交易条件, 或者能够**阻碍**、影响其他经营者**进入**相关市场**能力**的市场地位。

第十八条 认定经营者具有市场支配地位, 应当**依据下列因素**:

(一) **该经营者**在相关市场的市场**份额**, 以及相关市场的竞争状况;

(二) 该经营者控制销售市场或者原材料采购市场的能力;

(三) 该经营者的**财力**和技术条件;

(四) 其他经营者对该经营者在交易上的**依赖 程度**;

(五) 其他经营者进入相关市场的**难易**

程度；

（六）与认定该经营者市场支配地位有关的其他因素。

第十九条 有下列情形之一的，可以**推定**经营者具有市场支配地位：

（一）一个经营者在相关市场的市场份额**达到二分之一的**；

（二）两个经营者在相关市场的市场份额合计达到三分之二的；

（三）三个经营者在相关市场的市场份额合计达到四分之三的。

有前款第二项、第三项规定的情形，**其中**有的经营者市场份额**不足十分之一的**，不应当推定该经营者具有市场支配地位。

**被推定**具有市场支配地位的经营者，有**证据**证明不具有市场支配地位的，不应当认定其具有市场支配地位。

第四章 经营者集中

第二十条 经营者集中是指下列情形：

（一）经营者合并；

（二）经营者**通过 取得 股权**或者资产的**方式**取得对其他经营者的控制权；

（三）经营者通过**合同**等方式取得对其他经营者的控制权或者能够对其他经营**者施加决定 性**影响。

第二十一条 经营者集中达到国务院规定的**申报**标准的，经营者应当**事先** *向*国务院反垄断执法机构*申报*，未申报的不得实施集中。

第五章 滥用行政权力排除、限制竞争

第三十三条 行政机关和法律、法规授权的具有管理公共事务职能的组织不得滥用行政权力，实施下列行为，**妨碍**商品在**地区**之间的**自由 流通**：

（一）对**外地**商品**设定 歧视性收费 项目**、实行歧视性收费标准，或者规定歧视性价格；

（二）对外地商品规定与**本地 同类**商品不同的技术**要求、检验**标准，或者对外地商品**采取 重复**检验、重复**认证**等歧视性技术**措施**，限制外地商品进入本地市场；

（三）采取**专门 针**对外地商品的行政许**可**，限制外地商品进入本地市场；

（四）**设置** 关卡或者采取其他**手段**，阻碍外地商品进入或者本地商品**运出**；

（五）妨碍商品在地区之间自由流通的其他行为。

第六章 对涉嫌垄断行为的调查

第三十九条 反垄断执法机构调查涉嫌垄断行为，可以采取下列措施：

（一）进入被调查的经营者的**营业 场所**

或者其他有关场所进行**检查**；

（二）**询问**被调查的经营者、**利害关系人**或者其他有关**单位**或者**个人**，要求其**说明**有关情况；

（三）**查阅**、**复制**被调查的经营者、利害关系人或者其他有关单位或者个人的有关**单证**、协议、**会计 账簿**、**业务 函电**、**电子 数据**等**文件**、**资料**；

（四）**查封**、**扣押** 相关证据；

（五）**查询**经营者的银行**账户**。

采取前款规定的措施，应当向反垄断执法机构**主要**负责人**书面**报告，并**经 批准**。

第八章 附则

第五十五条 经营者依照有关**知识产权**的法律、行政法规规定**行使**知识产权的行为，不适用本法；但是，经营者滥用知识产权，排除、限制竞争的行为，适用本法。

# C. Vocabulary of Anti-Monopoly Law

| Chinese | Pinyin | English |
|---|---|---|
| 主席 | Zhǔxí | President (lit.Chairman)[2] |
| 令 | Lìng | Decree |
| 反 | Fǎn | Anti- |
| 垄断 | Lǒngduàn | Monopoly |
| 已 | Yǐ | 已经 |
| 由 x | Yóu x | By x |
| 届 | Jiè | Session |
| 全国人民代表大会 | Quánguó Rénmín Dàibiǎo Dàhuì | National People's Congress (NPC) |
| 常务委员会 | Chángwù Wěiyuánhuì | Standing Committee (of the NPC) |
| 会议 | Huìyì | Meeting |
| 通过 | Tōngguò | Enact; pass |

2 Background Tip: When Mao Zedong led China, this Chinese term was translatd in to English as "Chairman." After Mao, the translation was changod to "President."

| | | |
|---|---|---|
| 现 | Xiàn | 现在 |
| 予 | Yǔ | Give (literary Chinese) |
| 公布 | Gōngbù | Promulgate |
| 自 x 起 | Zì x qǐ | Beginning from x |
| 施行 | Shīxíng | Come into force |
| 胡锦涛 | Hú Jǐntāo | Hu Jintao (PRC President)[3] |
| 目录 | Mùlù | Table of contents |
| 章 | Zhāng | Chapter[4] |
| 总则 | Zǒngzé | General principles |
| 协议 | Xiéyì | Agreement |
| 滥用 | Lànyòng | Abuse |
| 市场 | Shìchǎng | Market |
| 支配 | Zhīpèi | Controlling; dominant |
| 地位 | Dìwèi | Status; position |
| 经营者 | Jīngyíngzhě | Business operator[5] |
| 者 | Zhe | 者 is literary Chinese and is used after an adjective or verb as a substitute for a person, entity, or thing[6] |

3 Law Practice Tip: After a statute is passed by the NPC or NPCSC, it must be signed by the President before it can take effect.

4 Law Practice Tip: There is no standard English translation for this term and related terms such as 条 tiáo (Article). In part, this is because their usage in Chinese is not standardized.

5 Law Practice Tip: Europe uses the term "undertakings" and the U.S. uses the term "business operators." Here 者 (same as 的人) refers to both individuals and entities engaged in business. See Article 12 in the text for the statutory definition of this term.

6 Law Practice Tip: In modern legal Chinese, 者 is often used, as it is here, to indicate both natural and legal persons.

| 集中 | Jízhōng | Concentrations |
| 行政 | Xíngzhèng | Administrative |
| 权力 | Quánlì | Power |
| 排除 | Páichú | Remove; eliminate |
| 限制 | Xiànzhì | Restrict; limit |
| 竞争 | Jìngzhēng | Competition |
| 涉嫌 | Shèxián | Suspected of a crime |
| 行为 | Xíngwéi | Act; conduct; behavior |
| 调查 | Diàochá | Investigate |
| 责任 | Zérèn | Bear responsibility for |
| 附则 | Fùzé | Supplementary provisions |
| 条 | Tiáo | Article[7] |
| 为了 | Wèile | In order to; for the sake of |
| 预防 | Yùfáng | Prevent |
| 制止 | Zhìzhǐ | Limit; restrict |
| 保护 | Bǎohù | Protect |
| 公平 | Gōngpíng | Fair |
| 提高 | Tígāo | Raise; increase; improve |
| 经济 | Jīngjì | Economy |

---

7 Law Practice Tip: Chinese laws and regulations typically consist of: parts (编), chapters (章), sections (节), and articles (条). There is no definitive English translation for these terms.

| 运行 | Yùnxíng | Operation; function |
|---|---|---|
| 效率 | Xiàolǜ | Efficiency |
| 维护 | Wéihù | Protect |
| 消费者 | Xiāofèizhě | Consumer |
| 利益 | Lìyì | Interests; benefits |
| 社会 | Shèhuì | Social; society |
| 公共 | Gōnggòng | Public |
| 促进 | Cùjìn | Promote; advance |
| 主义 | Zhǔyì | -ism |
| 健康 | Jiànkāng | Healthy |
| 发展 | Fāzhǎn | Development |
| 制定 | Zhìdìng | Formulate; enact |
| 境内 | Jìngnèi | Domestic (lit. within the borders) |
| 活动 | Huódòng | Activity |
| 适用 | Shìyòng | Apply |
| 境外 | Jìngwài | Foreign (lit. outside the border) |
| 产生 | Chǎnshēng | Cause; bring about |
| 影响 | Yǐngxiǎng | Affect; influence |
| 的 | De | 的 is often used without the term it modifies. Here the missing term could be 时候 (time, i.e. "when") or 情况 (circumstance) |

| 规定 | Guīdìng | Stipulate; provide |
|------|---------|--------------------|
| 包括 | Bāokuò | Include |
| 达成 | Dáchéng | Reach (e.g. an agreement) |
| 具有 | Jùyǒu | Fully possess; have |
| 效果 | Xiàoguǒ | Result; effect |
| 国有 | Guóyǒu | State-owned |
| 占 | Zhàn | Hold; occupy |
| 控制 | Kòngzhì | Controlling |
| 关系 (到) | Guānxì (dào) | Affect |
| 国民 | Guómín | National |
| 命脉 | Mìngmài | Lifeblood |
| 行业 | Hángyè | Trade; profession; industry |
| 以及 | Yǐjí | As well as; and; too (literary Chinese meaning the same as 跟 and 和) |
| 依法 | Yīfǎ | Legally; in accordance with the law |
| 实行 | Shíxíng | Implement; carry out |
| 专营专卖 | Zhuānyíng zhuānmài | Monopoly |
| 其 | Qí | Literary Chinese for 他 |
| 合法 | Héfǎ | Legal |
| 予以 | Yǔyǐ | 予以 and 加以 both mean "to do x." In English, we would not translate either |
| 并 | Bìng | And; moreover |

| | | |
|---|---|---|
| 及 | Jí | And; as well as (literary Chinese meaning the same as 跟 and 和) |
| 商品 | Shāngpǐn | Goods; merchandise |
| 服务 | Fúwù | Service |
| 价格 | Jiàgé | Price |
| 实施 | Shíshī | Put into effect; implement; carry out |
| 监管 | Jiānguǎn | Oversee; supervise |
| 调控 | Tiáokòng | Regulate and control |
| 技术 | Jìshù | Technology |
| 进步 | Jìnbù | Progress; advances |
| 前款 | Qiánkuǎn | Preceding clause; above provisions |
| 应当 | Yīngdāng | Shall; must[8] |
| 诚实 | Chéngshí | Honest |
| 守信 | Shǒuxìn | Trustworthy |
| 严格 | Yán'gé | Strict; rigorous |
| 自律 | Zìlǜ | Self-regulate |
| 接受 | Jiēshòu | Receive; accept |
| 公众 | Gōngzhòng | Public |
| 监督 | Jiāndū | Control; supervision |

---

8 Law Practice Tip: In legal English, there is a difference between "must" and "shall." "Shall" has several meanings including "must" and "will." In modern legal English the trend is to avoid using "shall." When "shall" is used in the mandatory sense, then the word "must" is used.

| 不得 | Bùdé | Must not; may not |
| 利用 | Lìyòng | Use; utilize |
| 损害 | Sǔnhài | Harm; damage |
| 机关 | Jīguān | Organ (administrative, government) |
| 法律 | Fǎlù | Law |
| 法规 | Fǎguī | Administrative laws and regulations[9] |
| 授权 | Shòuquán | Authorize |
| 管理 | Guǎnlǐ | Manage |
| 事务 | Shìwù | Affairs; matters (political or economic) |
| 职能 | Zhínéng | Function; role |
| 组织 | Zǔzhī | Organization |
| 国务院 | Guówùyuàn | State Council |
| 设立 | Shèlì | Establish; set up |
| 负责 | Fùzé | In charge of; responsible for |
| 协调 | Xiétiáo | Coordinate |
| 指导 | Zhǐdǎo | Guide; direct |
| 履行 | Lǚxíng | Perform; fulfill; carry out |
| 下列 | Xiàliè | The following; set forth below |
| 职责 | Zhízé | Duty; responsibility; obligation |

9 Law Practice Tip: "行政法规"are legislations adopted by the State Council. They are the third level of legislation in China, only lower than the Constitution and Laws passed by National People's Congress or its Standing Committee.

| 研究 | Yánjiū | Look into; research the possibility of |
|------|--------|----------------------------------------|
| 拟订 | Nǐdìng | Formulate; draw up; draft |
| 有关 | Yǒuguān | Relevant |
| 政策 | Zhèngcè | Government policy |
| 评估 | Pínggū | Evaluate; evaluation |
| 总体 | Zǒngtǐ | Aggregate; as a whole; overall |
| 状况 | Zhuàngkuàng | Condition; state; situation |
| 发布 | Fābù | Issue |
| 报告 | Bàogào | Report |
| 指南 | Zhǐnán | Guide; guidelines |
| 执法 | Zhífǎ | Enforcement of the law |
| 其他 | Qítā | Other |
| 组成 | Zǔchéng | Composition; formation |
| 规则 | Guīzé | Rule; regulation |
| 承担 | Chéngdān | Assume; bear |
| 机构 | Jīgòu | Organization; organ |
| 统称 | Tǒngchēng | Collectively referred to as |
| 依照 | Yīzhào | In accordance with |
| 根据 | Gēnjù | Based on; according to |
| 需要 | Xūyào | Need; demand; require |
| 省 | Shěng | Provinces |
| 自治区 | Zìzhìqū | Autonomous regions |

| | | |
|---|---|---|
| 直辖市 | Zhíxiáshì | Municipalities directly under control of Central Government |
| 人民政府 | Rénmín zhèngfǔ | People's government |
| 相应 | Xiāngyìng | Corresponding |
| 所称 y 是指 z | Suǒchēng y shìzhǐ z | The term y means z |
| 从事 | Cóngshì | Engage in |
| 生产 | Shēngchǎn | Produce; manufacture |
| 提供 | Tígōng | Provide; offer |
| 自然人 | Zìrán rén | Natural person[10] |
| 法人 | Fǎrén | Legal person (i.e. legally established entity) |
| 相关市场 | Xiāngguān shìchǎng | Related market[11] |
| 时期 | Shíqī | Time period |
| 就 | Jiù | With regards to; as for |
| 特定 | Tèdìng | Specific; specified; specifically designated |
| 进行 | Jìnxíng | Carry out; conduct |
| 范围 | Fànwéi | Scope |
| 地域 | Dìyù | Region |
| 禁止 | Jìnzhǐ | Prohibited |
| 固定 | Gùdìng | Fixed; set |

---

10 Law Practice Tip: This is a legal term of art. Natural persons are individuals. Legal persons are entities created by law (e.g. a corporation).

11 Law Practice Tip: In January 2009, China's Ministry of Commerce further defined the term "related market" in the Guidance on Definition of Related Market.

| | | |
|---|---|---|
| 变更 | Biàngēng | Change; amend |
| 数量 | Shùliàng | Quantity; amount |
| 销售 | Xiāoshòu | Sales |
| 分割 | Fēn'gē | Divide |
| 原材料 | Yuáncáiliào | Raw materials |
| 采购 | Cǎigòu | Purchase |
| 购买 | Gòumǎi | Purchase |
| 设备 | Shèbèi | Equipment |
| 开发 | Kāifā | Develop |
| 产品 | Chǎnpǐn | Product |
| 联合 | Liánhé | Jointly |
| 抵制 | Dǐzhì | Refuse to cooperate; boycott |
| 交易 | Jiāoyì | Business transaction or deal |
| 认定 | Rèndìng | Determine; establish |
| 协同 | Xiétóng | Concerted |
| 与 | Yǔ | And; together with |
| 相对人 | Xiāngduìrén | Opposite party |
| 转售 | Zhuǎnshòu | Resale |
| 限定 | Xiàndìng | Restrict; limit |
| 能够 | Nénggòu | Capable of |
| 证明 | Zhèngmíng | Prove |
| 属于 | Shǔyú | Belong to; fall within |

| 情形 | Qíngxíng | Circumstances; situations |
|---|---|---|
| 之一 | Zhīyī | 的一个 |
| 改进 | Gǎijìn | Improve; upgrade |
| 质量 | Zhìliàng | Quality |
| 降低 | Jiàngdī | Reduce; lower |
| 成本 | Chéngběn | (manufacturing or production) Costs |
| 增进 | Zēngjìn | Enhance; promote |
| 统一 | Tǒngyī | Unify |
| 规格 | Guīgé | Norms; standards |
| 标准 | Biāozhǔn | Standards |
| 专业 | Zhuānyè | Specialization |
| 化 | Huà | -ize (lit. change to x) |
| 分工 | Fēngōng | Division of labor |
| 增强 | Zēngqiáng | Strengthen; increase |
| 实现 | Shíxiàn | Realize; achieve; bring about |
| 节约 | Jiéyuē | Save; conserve |
| 能源 | Néngyuán | Energy |
| 环境 | Huánjìng | Environment |
| 救灾 | Jiùzāi | Help people in a disaster |
| 救助 | Jiùzhù | Render aid |
| 不景气 | Bùjǐngqì | Depression |
| 缓解 | Huǎnjiě | Ease; relieve |

| 严重 | Yánzhòng | Seriously; materially |
| 下降 | Xiàjiàng | Decline; decrease |
| 明显 | Míngxiǎn | Obviously; clearly |
| 过剩 | Guòshèng | Excess; surplus |
| 保障 | Bǎozhàng | Ensure; guarantee; safeguard |
| 对外 | Duìwài | Foreign |
| 贸易 | Màoyì | Trade |
| 合作 | Hézuò | Cooperation |
| 正当 | Zhèngdàng | Proper; legitimate |
| 项 | Xiàng | Clause |
| 至 | Zhì | 到 |
| 并且 | Bìngqiě | And; moreover |
| 使 | Shǐ | Cause; to allow |
| 分享 | Fēnxiǎng | Share in... |
| 由此 | Yóucǐ | From this |
| 以 | Yǐ | Same meaning as 把 and 用 |
| 理由 | Lǐyóu | Reason |
| 低于 | Dīyú | Lower than |
| 拒绝 | Jùjué | Refuse |
| 指定 | Zhǐdìng | Appointed; designated |
| 搭售 | Dāshòu | Tie or pair up (of unsalable goods with salable goods) |

| | | |
|---|---|---|
| 附加 | Fùjiā | Add on |
| 合理 | Hélǐ | Reasonable |
| 条件 | Tiáojiàn | Requirements; conditions |
| 相同 | Xiāngtóng | Identical |
| 差别 | Chābié | Differentiate |
| 待遇 | Dàiyù | Treatment |
| 阻碍 | Zǔ'ài | Obstruct; hinder |
| 进入 | Jìnrù | Enter |
| 能力 | Nénglì | Ability; capability; capacity |
| 依据 | Yījù | Follow; act in accordance with |
| 因素 | Yīnsù | Factors; elements |
| 该 | Gāi | That[12] |
| 份额 | Fèn'é | Share; portion |
| 财力 | Cáilì | Financial resources |
| 依赖 | Yīlài | Dependence |
| 程度 | Chéngdù | Degree (level or extent) |
| 难易 | Nányì | Difficulty (lit. difficulty/ease) |
| 推定 | Tuīdìng | Infer; deduce; presume |
| 达到 | Dádào | Reach |
| x分之y | x Fēnzhī y | Indicates a fraction |

---

12 Law Practice Tip: In modern legal English the term "that" is used. In older legal English the term "said" is used.

| | | |
|---|---|---|
| 合计 | Héjì | Total |
| 其中 | Qízhōng | Among |
| 不足 | Bùzú | Less than |
| 被 | Bèi | Passive marker for the following verb |
| 证据 | Zhèngjù | Evidence; proof |
| 合并 | Hébìng | Merge |
| 通过 | Tōngguò | Go through |
| 取得 | Qǔdé | Obtain; acquire |
| 股权 | Gǔquán | Stock rights |
| 资产 | Zīchǎn | Property; assets |
| 方式 | Fāngshì | Way; manner; method |
| 权 | Quán | Authority; power; right |
| 合同 | Hétóng | Contract |
| 施加 | Shījiā | Exert (effort or pressure) |
| 决定 (性) | Juédìng (xìng) | Decisive; conclusive |
| 性 | Xìng | Suffix for -ness, -ity, -ive, -ize |
| 申报 | Shēnbào | Report or declare (to an authority) |
| 事先 | Shìxiān | In advance |
| 向 x 申报 | Xiàng x shēnbào | Report or declare to x |
| 未 | Wèi | Literary Chinese for 还没 |
| 妨碍 | Fáng'ài | Hinder; obstruct |
| 地区 | Dìqū | Area; region |

| 自由 | Zìyóu | Free; freely |
| 流通 | Liútōng | Circulate |
| 外地 | Wàidì | Refers to places outside the locality one is in (e.g. 外地人 is used to describe outsiders or people not from here) |
| 设定 | Shèdìng | Set up; establish |
| 歧视 | Qíshì | Discriminate; discriminatory |
| 收费 | Shōufèi | Fee; charge |
| 项目 | Xiàngmù | Project |
| 本地 | Běndì | Local |
| 同类 | Tónglèi | Same kind |
| 要求 | Yāoqiú | Demands; requirements |
| 检验 | Jiǎnyàn | Inspect |
| 采取 | Cǎiqǔ | Take; adopt |
| 重复 | Chóngfù | Repeat; duplicate |
| 认证 | Rènzhèng | Authenticate; approve |
| 措施 | Cuòshī | Measures |
| 专门 | Zhuānmén | Specialized |
| 针对 | Zhēnduì | Aimed or directed at |
| 许可 | Xǔkě | Approval; permission |
| 设置 | Shèzhì | Set up; install |

| 关卡 | Guānqiǎ | Checkpoint |
|---|---|---|
| 手段 | Shǒuduàn | Method |
| 运出 | Yùnchū | Ship out |
| 营业 | Yíngyè | Business |
| 场所 | Chǎngsuǒ | Location; place |
| 检查 | Jiǎnchá | Examine; inspect |
| 询问 | Xúnwèn | Inquire about |
| 利害关系人 | Lìhài guānxì rén | Interested person |
| 单位 | Dānwèi | Entity[13] |
| 个人 | Gèrén | Individual |
| 说明 | Shuōmíng | Explain |
| 查阅 | Cháyuè | Refer to; review |
| 复制 | Fùzhì | Duplicate; copy |
| 单证 | Dānzhèng | Documents; invoices |
| 会计 | Kuàijì | Accounting |
| 账簿 | Zhàngbù | Account book |
| 业务 | Yèwù | Business |
| 函电 | Hándiàn | Correspondence |
| 电子 | Diànzǐ | Electronic |

13 Law Practice Tip: Dānwèi is used to describe the organization to which you belong, e.g. your employer. In the past, when there was no private economy, the Dānwèi played a much more significant role in the lives of its workers. It provided housing, schools, hospitals, cafeterias, etc. In modern Chinese is it often best translated as "entity."

| 数据 | Shùjù | Data |
|------|-------|------|
| 文件 | Wénjiàn | Document; file |
| 资料 | Zīliào | Data; materials |
| 查封 | Cháfēng | Seize |
| 扣押 | Kòuyā | Detain |
| 相关 | Xiāngguān | Related |
| 查询 | Cháxún | Search; look for |
| 账户 | Zhànghù | Bank account |
| 主要 | Zhǔyào | Principal |
| 书面 | Shūmiàn | Written |
| 经 (经过) | Jīng (Jīngguò) | Go through; to be x'd |
| 批准 | Pīzhǔn | Approve; approval |
| 知识产权 | Zhīshí chǎnquán | Intellectual property rights |
| 行使 | Xíngshǐ | Exercise (a right) |

# D. Text of Anti-Monopoly Bureau Decision[14]

# 中华人民共和国商务部 公告[2008]第95号

2008−11−18 15:02 文章 来源：商务部反垄断 局

中华人民共和商务部**收到** 英博 集团 公司（INBEV N.V./S.A.）**收购**AB公司（ANHEUSER−BUSCH COMPANIES INC.）的反垄断**申报** 材料，经 审查，决定 如下：

一、审查程序。2008年9月10日，英博公司向商务部**递交**了申报材料。10月17日和10月23日，英博公司**对**申报材料进行了补充。10月27日，商务部对**此** 项申报进行立案审查，并 发出了立案通知。

二、审查决定。立案后，商务部对申报材料进行了审查，并征求了**政府** 有关部门的意见，听取了相关啤酒行业 协会、国内主要啤酒生产企业、啤酒原料生产企业以及啤酒产品 销售商的意见，根据反垄断法第28条的**规定**，决定对此项并购 不予 禁止。

三、附加的限制性 条件。鉴于此项并购规模 巨大，合并后新企业**市场** 份额较大，竞争 实力 明显 增强，为了 减少可能对中国啤酒未来

---

14 Source: Zhonghua Renmin Gongheguo shang wu bu gong gao (Ministry of Commerce (P.R.C.) Public Announcement, Nov. 18, 2008) *available at* http://file.mofcom.gov.cn/moffile/search/pages/detail.jsp?seqno=12696 (last visited May 30, 2011).

市场竞争产生的不利影响，商务部对审查决定附加限制性条件，要求英博公司履行如下义务：

1、不得增加AB公司在青岛啤酒股份有限公司现有27%的持股比例；

2、如果英博公司的控股股东或控股股东的股东发生变化，必须及时通报商务部；

3、不得增加英博公司在珠江啤酒股份有限公司现有28.56%的持股比例；

4、不得寻求持有华润雪花啤酒（中国）有限公司和北京燕京啤酒有限公司的股份；

如果违反上述任何一项承诺，英博公司必须事先向商务部及时进行申报，商务部批准前，不得实施。

本决定自公告之日起生效。

中华人民共和国商务部

二〇〇八年十一月十八日

# E. Vocabulary of Anti-Monopoly Bureau Decision

| Chinese | Pinyin | English |
| --- | --- | --- |
| 商务部 | Shāngwù Bù | Ministry of Commerce |
| 公告 | Gōnggào | Public announcement |
| 文章 | Wénzhāng | Document |
| 来源 | Láiyuán | Source |
| 反垄断 | Fǎnlǒngduàn | Anti-monopoly |
| 局 | Jú | Bureau |
| 收到 | Shōudào | Receive |
| 英博 | Yīngbó | InBev |
| 集团 | Jítuán | Group |
| 公司 | Gōngsī | Company |
| 收购 | Shōugòu | Purchase; buy |
| 申报 | Shēnbào | Report or declare (to an authority) |
| 材料 | Cáiliào | Materials |
| 经 (经过) | Jīng (Jīngguò) | Go through; be x'd |
| 审查 | Shěnchá | Investigation; review |

| | | |
|---|---|---|
| 决定 | Juédìng | Decide |
| 如下 | Rúxià | As set forth below |
| 程序 | Chéngxù | Procedure; process |
| 向 | Xiàng | 向 and 对 combine with a number of different verbs to generally mean "to" or "for" |
| 递交 | Dìjiāo | Submit |
| 对 (对于) | Duì (Duìyú) | As for; towards |
| 进行 | Jìnxíng | Carry out; conduct |
| 补充 | Bǔchōng | Supplement |
| 此 | Cǐ | Literary Chinese for 这个 |
| 项 | Xiàng | Counter for a wide variety of items including 申报 |
| 立案 | Lì'àn | Place a case on file; lit. set up a case file[15] |
| 并 | Bìng | And; moreover |
| 发出 | Fāchū | Issue |
| 通知 | Tōngzhī | Notice |
| 征求 | Zhēngqiú | Solicit; seek |

---

15 Law Practice Tip: In the filing of law suits and some kinds of applications, the first step taken by the receiving court/agency is to have the court/agency decide if it will accept the filing. This acceptance is called 立案.

| 政府 | Zhèngfǔ | Government |
|---|---|---|
| 有关 | Yǒuguān | Relevant |
| 部门 | Bùmén | Department; branch; section |
| 意见 | Yìjiàn | Opinion |
| 听取 | Tīngqǔ | Listen to (lit. hear and take in) |
| 相关 | Xiāngguān | Related |
| 行业 | Hángyè | Trade; profession; industry |
| 协会 | Xiéhuì | Associations |
| 国内 | Guónèi | Domestic |
| 生产 | Shēngchǎn | Produce; manufacture |
| 企业 | Qǐyè | Enterprise |
| 原料 | Yuánliào | Raw materials |
| 以及 | Yǐjí | As well as; and; too (literary Chinese meaning the same as 跟 and 和) |
| 产品 | Chǎnpǐn | Product |
| 销售商 | Xiāoshòushāng | Sellers |
| 根据 | Gēnjù | Based on; according to |
| 条 | Tiáo | Article[16] |
| 规定 | Guīdìng | Stipulation; provision |

---

16 Law Practice Tip: Chinese laws and regulations typically consist of: parts (编), chapters (章), sections (节), and articles (条). There is no definitive English translation for these terms.

| 并购 | Bìnggòu | Merge (lit. combine by purchase) |
| 不予 | Bùyú | Not grant or give; decline (literary Chinese) |
| 禁止 | Jìnzhǐ | Prohibit |
| 附加 | Fùjiā | Add on |
| 限制 (性) | Xiànzhì (xìng) | Restrict (ive) |
| 条件 | Tiáojiàn | Requirements; conditions |
| 鉴于 | Jiànyú | In light of; whereas |
| 规模 | Guīmó | Scale; scope |
| 巨大 | Jùdà | Huge; enormous |
| 合并 | Hébìng | Merge |
| 市场 | Shìchǎng | Market |
| 份额 | Fèn'é | Share; portion |
| 较大 | Jiàodà | Comparatively large[17] |
| 竞争 | Jìngzhēng | Competition |
| 实力 | Shílì | Strength |
| 明显 | Míngxiǎn | Obviously; clearly |
| 增强 | Zēngqiáng | Strengthen; increase |
| 为了 | Wèile | In order to; for the sake of |
| 减少 | Jiǎnshǎo | Reduce |

---

17 Law Practice Tip: The term "relatively large" is often used in Chinese law. In the Law on Legislation, the term is defined later in the text of the law. In the Criminal Law, the term is typically defined by later interpretations by the Supreme People's Court.

| | | |
|---|---|---|
| 未来 | Wèilái | Future |
| 产生 | Chǎnshēng | Cause; bring about |
| 不利 | Bùlì | Detrimental; harmful; negative |
| 影响 | Yǐngxiǎng | Affect; influence |
| 履行 | Lǚxíng | Perform; fulfill; carry out |
| 义务 | Yìwù | Duty; obligation |
| 增加 | Zēngjiā | Increase |
| 青岛啤酒 | Qīngdǎo Píjiǔ | Qingdao (Tsingtao) Beer |
| 股份有限 | Gǔfèn yǒuxiàn | Limited or Ltd.[18] |
| 现 | Xiàn | 现在 |
| 持股 | Chígǔ | Shareholding (lit. hold shares) |
| 比例 | Bǐlì | Proportion |
| 控股 | Kònggǔ | Controlling |
| 股东 | Gǔdōng | Shareholder |
| 发生 | Fāshēng | Occur; happen |
| 变化 | Biànhuà | Change |
| 及时 | Jíshí | Timely; promptly |
| 通报 | Tōngbào | Notify (an agency) (lit. notify and report) |

---

18 Law Practice Tip: Literally, a Company Limited by Shares. The PRC Company Law allows for two kinds of limited liability corporations: the limited liability company (有限公司) and a company limited by shares (股份有限公司). See Article 3 of the Company Law for a definition of these two kinds of limited liability companies. In English, normally the word Limited or Ltd. would be used for both. In China, if we need to be technically correct, in English we would probably say Company Limited by Shares, e.g. if we were doing a Due Diligence Report on the company. The lay person English reader would not understand this term which is why usually it is simply translated as Limited or Ltd.

| | | |
|---|---|---|
| 珠江啤酒 | Zhūjiāng Píjiǔ | Pearl River Beer |
| 寻求 | Xúnqiú | Seek; look for |
| 持有 | Chíyǒu | Hold; own |
| 华润雪花啤酒 | Huárùn Xuěhuā Píjiǔ | Huarun Xuehua Beer |
| 北京燕京啤酒 | Běijīng Yànjīng Píjiǔ | Beijing Yanjing Beer |
| 股份 | Gǔfèn | Shares; stock |
| 违反 | Wéifǎn | Violate (a law) |
| 上述 | Shàngshù | Above mentioned |
| 承诺 | Chéngnuò | Promise to do something; acceptance |
| 事先 | Shìxiān | In advance |
| 批准 | Pīzhǔn | Approve; approval |
| 实施 | Shíshī | Put into effect; implement; carry out |
| 自 x 起 | Zì x qǐ | Beginning from x |
| 之 | Zhī | Literary Chinese. The modern character would be 的 |
| 生效 | Shēngxiào | Go into effect; become effective |

# Chapter 8
# Environmental Law

# 环境法

Huán    Jìng    Fǎ

# A. Introduction to China's Environmental Laws

By *Tiffany Yajima*, Esq.

As by-products of China's rapid economic growth, pollution and ecological deterioration present China with a growing number of significant environmental challenges. A toxic spill in a major river in Harbin Province in 2005 was only the first in a number of cases that highlight China's environmental problems. That same year, a water supply company in Inner Mongolia was awarded RMB2.88 million as compensation for operating losses after paper companies in the area were found to have polluted the company's main water supply. In 2009, a manganese processing plant in Hunan Province was closed after thousands of children were diagnosed with lead poisoning. To address the country's growing environmental pollution problems, China's environmental protection bureau (EPB) has begun imposing stringent environmental requirements on polluters.

China's first Environmental Protection Law (EPL) was introduced in 1989. It provides the general principles of protection for China's environment and is the foundation for all other environmental laws and regulations in China. Other major environmental laws implement the EPL's enforcement provisions. For example, the Shanghai City Environmental Protection Regulations, included in this chapter, provide stringent city-wide limits on pollutant emissions as well as specific penalties for violations.

Other national laws enforce provisions in the EPL. The National People's Congress Standing Committee approved the Torts Law on December 26, 2009, which provides the general environmental liability principle that a polluter will be held liable for any pollution it creates. The Torts Law takes an important step forward in addressing China's environmental problems by increasing the liabilities for environmental pollution, and its enforcement is vital to protecting the environment.

Additional laws, regulations, ministerial rules, local regulations and rules, and national and local standards include:

- *The PRC Constitution* (providing for government protection of the environment and for pollution prevention and control);
- *The Water Pollution Prevention and Treatment Law* (requiring discharge permits, compliance with state and local discharge standards, and reporting to the local EPB);
- *The Air Pollution Prevention and Treatment Law* (requiring companies to report the discharge of air pollutants to the local EPB);
- *Law on the Prevention and Control of Environmental Pollution by Solid Wastes* (providing standards for hazardous waste disposal);
- *Ministerial rules on land contamination – State Environmental Protection Agency notice and a Ministry of Environmental Protection opinion* (providing general principles to prevent against land or soil contamination and treatment measures);
- *The Environmental Impact Assessment Law* (requiring an environmental impact report for new or expansion projects);
- *Torts Law* (addressing civil liabilities for pollution);
- *Various local environmental regulations* (applicable jurisdictionally and setting forth more stringent limits on pollutant emissions).

# B. Text of Environmental Protection Law[1]

## 中华人民共和国环境 保护法

（1989年12月26日第七届 全国人民代表大会 常务 委员会第十一次会议 通过

1989年12月26日中华人民共和国主席 令第二十二号公布 施行）

第一章 总则

第一条 *为*保护和改善生活环境与 生态环境, 防治 污染和其他 公害, 保障 人体 健康, 促进 社会 主义 现代 化 建设的发展, *制定* 本法。

第二条 本法*所称*环境, *是指* 影响 人类 生存和发展的各种 天然的和经过 人工 改造的自然 因素的**总体**, 包括 **大气**、**水**、**海洋**、**土地**、**矿藏**、**森林**、**草原**、**野生生物**、自然遗迹、人文遗迹、自然保护区、风景 名胜区、城市和乡村等。

第四条 国家制定的环境保护规划 必须 纳入 国民 经济和社会发展计划, 国家采取 有利于环境保护的经济、技术 政策和措施, 使环境

1 Source: Zhonghua Renmin Gongheguo huan jing bao hu fa [Environmental Protection Law (P.R.C.)] (promulgated by the Nat'l People's Cong., Dec. 26, 1989, effective Dec. 26, 1989) *available at* http://zfs.mep.gov.cn/fl/198912/t19891226_75912.htm (last visited Feb. 9, 2010).

保护工作**同**经济建设和社会发展**相 协调**。

第六条 **一切 单位**和个人都有保护环境的**义务**，并有**权** *对*污染和**破坏**环境的单位和个人**进行 检举**和**控告**。

第七条 **国务院**环境保护**行政 主管 部门**，对全国环境保护**工作 实施 统一 监督 管理**。

**县 级 以上 地方人民政府**环境保护行政主管部门，对本**辖区**的环境保护工作实施统一监督管理。

国家海洋行政主管部门、**港 务**监督、**渔政渔港**监督、**军队**环境保护部门和各级公安、**交通**、**铁道**、**民航**管理部门，**依照 有关 法律**的**规定**对环境污染防治实施监督管理。

县级以上人民政府的土地、**矿产**、林业、**农业**、水利行政主管部门，依照有关法律的规定对**资源**的保护实施监督管理。

第八条 对保护和改善环境有**显著 成绩**的单位和个人，*由*人民政府给予 **奖励**。

第二章 环境监督管理

第九条 国务院环境保护行政主管部门制定国家环境质量 **标准**。

**省、自治区、直辖市**人民政府对国家环境质量标准**中 未作规定的项目**，可以制定地方环境质量标准，并**报**国务院环境保护行政主管部门备案。

第十条 国务院环境保护行政主管部门**根据**国家环境质量标准和国家经济、技术**条件**，制定国家**污染物 排放**标准。

省、自治区、直辖市人民政府对国家污染物排放标准中未作规定的项目，可以制定地方污染物排放标准；对国家污染物排放标准中已作规定的项目，可以制定**严于**国家污染物排放标准的地方污染物排放标准。地方污染物排放标准须报国务院环境保护行政主管部门备案。

**凡是** *向*已有地方污染物排放标准的**区域**排放污染物*的*，应当 **执行**地方污染物排放标准。

第十一条 国务院环境保护行政主管部门**建立 监测 制度**，制定监测**规范**，会同有关部门**组织**监测网络，**加强**对环境监测的管理。

国务院和省、自治区、直辖市人民政府的环境保护行政主管部门，应当**定期 发布**环境状况**公报**。

第十二条 县级以上人民政府环境保护行政主管部门，应当会同有关部门对管辖范围内的环境状况进行**调查和评价**，拟订环境保护规划，**经**计划部门综合 **平衡**后，报同级人民政府**批准**实施。

第十三条 建设污染环境的项目，必须**遵守**国家有关建设项目环境保护管理的规定。

建设项目的环境影响**报告书**，必须对建设项目**产生**的污染和对环境的影响作出评价，规定防治措施，经项目主管部门**预审**并依照规定的程序报环境保护行政主管部门批准。环境影响报告书经批准后,计划部门方可批准建设项目设计任务书。

第三章 保护和改善环境

第十七条 各级人民政府对**具有 代表 性**的各种**类型**的自然生态**系统 区域**,**珍稀**、**濒危**的野生**动植物**自然分布区域,重要的**水源 涵养**区域,具有**重大 科学**文化价值的**地质 构造**、著名**溶洞**和化石分布区、**冰川**、**火山**、**温泉**等自然遗迹,以及人文遗迹、**古树名木**,应当采取措施**加以保护,严禁破坏**。

第十九条 **开发 利用**自然资源,必须采取措施保护生态环境。

第二十条 各级人民政府应当加强对农业环境的保护,防治**土壤**污染、土地**沙 盐 渍化**、贫瘠化、**沼泽化**、**地面 沉降**和防治植被破坏、水土**流失**、水源**枯竭**、种源 灭绝以及其他生态失调 现象的发生和发展,*推广*植物病虫害的综合防治,**合理 使用 化肥**、**农药**及**植物生长 激素**。

第四章 防治环境污染和其他公害

第二十四条 产生环境污染和其他公害的单位,必须把环境保护工作纳入计划,建立环境保护责任制度;采取**有效**措施,防治在**生产建设**或者其他活动中产生的**废气**、**废水**、**废渣**、**粉尘**、**恶臭 气体**、**放射性 物质** 以及 **噪声**、**振动**、**电磁波 辐射**等对环境的污染和**危害**。

第二十七条 排放污染物的**企业 事业单位**,必须依照国务院环境保护行政主管部门的规定**申报 登记**。

第二十八条 排放污染物**超过**国家或者地方规定的污染物排放标准的企业事业单位,依照国家规定**缴纳 超标准排污费**,并负责 治理。水污染防治法另有规定的,依照水污染防治法的规定执行。

**征收**的超标准排污费必须用于污染的防治,不得**挪**作他用,**具体**使用办法由国务院规定。

第五章 法律责任

第三十五条 **违反**本法规定,有下列 **行为**之一的,环境保护行政主管部门或者其他依照法律规定**行使**环境监督管理权的部门可以根据不同**情节**,给予**警告**或者处以 **罚款**:

(一)**拒绝**环境保护行政主管部门或者其他依照法律规定行使环境监督管理权的部门**现场 检查**或者在被检查时**弄虚作假**的。

(二)**拒报**或者**谎报**国务院环境保护行政主管部门规定的有关污染物排放申报**事项**的。

(三)不按国家规定缴纳超标准**排污费**的。

(四)引进不符合 我国环境保护规定**要求**的技术和**设备**的。

（五）**将**产生**严重**污染的生产设备**转移**给没有污染防治**能力**的单位使用的。

第三十八条 对违反本法规定，**造成**环境污染**事故**的企业事业单位，由环境保护行政主管部门或者其他依照法律规定行使环境监督管理权的部门根据**所**造成的危害**后果**处以罚款；情节较重的，对有关责任人员由**其 所在**单位或者政府主管**机关**给予行政**处分**。

第四十条 **当事人**对行政**处罚 决定 不服**的，可以在**接到**处罚**通知** 之日起十五日内，*向*作出处罚决定的机关的上一级机关*申请* 复议；对复议决定不服的，可以在接到复议决定之日起十五日内，*向* **人民法院** *起诉*。当事人也可以在接到处罚通知之日起十五日内，**直接**向人民法院起诉。当事人**逾期**不申请复议、也不向人民法院起诉、**又不履行**处罚 决定的，由作出处罚决定的机关申请人民法院**强制**执行。

第四十一条 造成环境污染危害的，有责任排除危害，并对直接受到**损害**的单位或者个人赔**偿 损失**。

赔偿责任和赔偿**金额**的**纠纷**，可以根据当事人的**请求**，由环境保护行政主管部门或者其他依照法律规定行使环境监督管理权的部门**处理**；当事人对处理决定不服的，可以向人民法院起诉。当事人也可以直接向人民法院起诉。

**完全 由于**不可**抗拒**的自然灾害，并经**及时**采取合理措施，**仍然**不能**避免**造成环境污染损害的，**免予 承担**责任。

第六章 **附则**

第四十六条 中华人民共和国**缔结**或者**参加**的与环境保护有关的**国际 条约**，同中华人民共和国法律有不同规定的，**适用**国际条约的规定，*但*中华人民共和国**声明** 保留的**条款** *除外*。

第四十七条 本法*自*公布之日*起*施行。《中华人民共和国环境保护法（**试行**）》同时**废止**。

# C. Vocabulary of Environmental Protection Law

| Chinese | Pinyin | English |
| --- | --- | --- |
| 环境 | Huánjìng | Environment |
| 保护 | Bǎohù | Protection |
| 届 | Jiè | Session |
| 全国人民代表大会 | Quánguó Rénmín Dàibiǎo Dàhuì | National People's Congress (NPC) |
| 常务委员会 | Chángwù Wěiyuánhuì | Standing Committee (of the NPC) |
| 会议 | Huìyì | Meeting |
| 通过 | Tōngguò | Pass; enact |
| 主席 | Zhǔxí | President (lit. Chairman)[2] |
| 令 | Lìng | Decree |
| 公布 | Gōngbù | Promulgate |
| 施行 | Shīxíng | Come into force |

---

2 Background Tip: When Mao Zedong led China, this Chinese term was translated into English as "Chairman." After Mao, the translation was changed to "President."

| 章 | Zhāng | Chapter[3] |
|---|---|---|
| 总则 | Zǒngzé | General principles |
| 条 | Tiáo | Article[4] |
| 为 | Wèi | For the sake of; in order to |
| 改善 | Gǎishàn | Improve |
| 与 | Yǔ | And; together with |
| 生态 | Shēngtài | Ecology (生态环境 ecosystem or environment) |
| 防治 | Fángzhì | Prevent and cure |
| 污染 | Wūrǎn | Pollution |
| 其他 | Qítā | Other |
| 公害 | Gōnghài | Public harms |
| 保障 | Bǎozhàng | Ensure; guarantee; safeguard |
| 人体 | Réntǐ | Human (body) |
| 健康 | Jiànkāng | Health |
| 促进 | Cùjìn | Promote; advance |
| 社会 | Shèhuì | Social; society |
| 主义 | Zhǔyì | -ism |

---

3 Law Practice Tip: Chinese laws and regulations typically consist of: parts (编), chapters (章), sections (节), and articles (条). There is no definitive English translation for these terms.

4 Law Practice Tip: Chinese laws and regulations typically consist of: parts (编), chapters (章), sections (节), and articles (条). There is no definitive English translation for these terms.

| | | |
|---|---|---|
| 现代 | Xiàndài | Modern |
| 化 | Huà | -ize (lit. change to x) |
| 建设 | Jiànshè | Construction |
| 发展 | Fāzhǎn | Development |
| 制定 | Zhìdìng | Formulate; enact |
| 本 | Běn | Literary Chinese for 这个 |
| 所称 x 是指 y | Suǒchēng x shìzhǐ y | The term x refers to y |
| 影响 | Yǐngxiǎng | Affect; influence |
| 人类 | Rénlèi | Human; mankind |
| 生存 | Shēngcún | Existence; survival |
| 各种 | Gèzhǒng | All kinds; various |
| 天然 | Tiānrán | Natural |
| 经过 | Jīngguò | Pass; go through |
| 人工 | Réngōng | Artificial; man-made |
| 改造 | Gǎizào | Transform; reform |
| 自然 | Zìrán | Nature; natural |
| 因素 | Yīnsù | Factors; elements |
| 总体 | Zǒngtǐ | Aggregate; as a whole; overall |
| 包括 | Bāokuò | Including |
| 大气 | Dàqì | Atmosphere; air |
| 海洋 | Hǎiyáng | Ocean |
| 矿藏 | Kuàngcáng | Mineral resources |

| | | |
|---|---|---|
| 森林 | Sēnlín | Forest |
| 草原 | Cǎoyuán | Grass land |
| 野生生物 | Yěshēng shēngwù | Wildlife |
| 遗迹 | Yíjì | Historical remains; vestiges; traces |
| 人文 | Rénwén | Human |
| 区 | Qū | Area[5] |
| 风景 | Fēngjǐng | Scenic; scenery |
| 名胜 | Míngshèng | Well-known |
| 乡村 | Xiāngcūn | Country side |
| 国家 | Guójiā | National |
| 规划 | Guīhuà | Plan[6] |
| 必须 | Bìxū | Shall |
| 纳入 | Nàrù | Incorporate sth. into another; bring in-line with |
| 国民 | Guómín | National |
| 经济 | Jīngjì | Economic; economy |
| 计划 | Jìhuà | Plan |
| 采取 | Cǎiqǔ | Take; adopt |
| 有利 | Yǒulì | Advantageous; favorable |

---

5 Background Tip: 区 is a term used for administrative areas. For example, large municipalities are divided into multiple 区, usually translated as "districts." Likewise, the term is used for larger administrative regions or areas such as 自治区 or "autonomous regions/areas."

6 Law Practice Tip: China is currently in its twelfth five-year Environmental Protection Plan (2011-2015).

| | | |
|---|---|---|
| 于 | Yú | In; on; towards |
| 技术 | Jìshù | Technology; skill |
| 政策 | Zhèngcè | Government policy |
| 措施 | Cuòshī | Measures |
| 使 | Shǐ | Cause; make |
| 同 | Tóng | Together with |
| 相 | Xiāng | Mutually |
| 协调 | Xiétiáo | Coordinate |
| 一切 | Yīqiè | All |
| 单位 | Dānwèi | Entity[7] |
| 个人 | Gèrén | Individual |
| 义务 | Yìwù | Duty; obligation |
| 并 | Bìng | And; moreover |
| 权 | Quán | Authority; power; right |
| 对 | Duì | 对 and 向 combine with a number of different verbs to generally mean "to" or "for" |
| 破坏 | Pòhuài | Destroy |
| 进行 | Jìnxíng | Carry out; conduct |

---

7 Law Practice Tip: Dānwèi is used to describe the organization to which you belong, e.g. your employer. In the past, when there was no private economy, the Dānwèi played a much more significant role in the lives of its workers. It provided housing, schools, hospitals, cafeterias, etc.

| | | |
|---|---|---|
| 检举 | Jiǎnjǔ | Report (an offense) |
| 控告 | Kònggào | Accuse; charge |
| 国务院 | Guówùyuàn | State Council |
| 行政 | Xíngzhèng | Administrative |
| 主管 | Zhǔguǎn | Principally responsible for |
| 部门 | Bùmén | Department; branch; section |
| 工作 | Gōngzuò | Work |
| 实施 | Shíshī | Put into effect; implement; carry out |
| 统一 | Tǒngyī | Unified |
| 监督 | Jiāndū | Control; supervision |
| 管理 | Guǎnlǐ | Management |
| 县 | Xiàn | County |
| 级 | Jí | Level |
| 以上 | Yǐshàng | More than |
| 地方 | Dìfāng | Local |
| 政府 | Zhèngfǔ | Government |
| 辖区 | Xiáqū | Area under one's jurisdiction |
| 港 | Gǎng | Harbor; port |
| 务 | Wù | Affairs |
| 渔政 | Yúzhèng | Fisheries |
| 渔港 | Yúgǎng | Fishing harbor |
| 军队 | Jūnduì | Military |

| 公安 | Gōng'ān | Public security |
|---|---|---|
| 交通 | Jiāotōng | Transportation |
| 铁道 | Tiědào | Railroad |
| 民航 | Mínháng | Civil aviation |
| 依照 | Yīzhào | In accordance with |
| 有关 | Yǒuguān | Relevant |
| 法律 | Fǎlǜ | Law |
| 规定 | Guīdìng | Stipulation; provision |
| 矿产 | Kuàngchǎn | Minerals |
| 林业 | Línyè | Forestry |
| 农业 | Nóngyè | Agriculture |
| 水利 | Shuǐlì | Water conservancy |
| 资源 | Zīyuán | Natural resources |
| 显著 | Xiǎnzhù | Notable; striking |
| 成绩 | Chéngjī | Achievement |
| 由 x | Yóu x | By x |
| 给予 | Jǐyǔ | Give |
| 奖励 | Jiǎnglì | Encourage through rewards |
| 质量 | Zhìliàng | Quality |
| 标准 | Biāozhǔn | Standard |
| 省 | Shěng | Province |
| 自治区 | Zìzhìqū | Autonomous region |

| | | |
|---|---|---|
| 直辖市 | Zhíxiáshì | Municipalities directly under control of the Central government |
| 中 | Zhōng | Within |
| 未 | Wèi | Literary Chinese for 还没 |
| 项目 | Xiàngmù | Project |
| 报 | Bào | Report to |
| 备案 | Bèi'àn | Put on record; file |
| 根据 | Gēnjù | Based on; according to |
| 条件 | Tiáojiàn | Requirements; conditions |
| 污染物 | Wūrǎnwù | Pollutants |
| 排放 | Páifàng | Discharge (of gas or pollutants) |
| 已 | Yǐ | 已经 |
| 严于 | Yányú | Stricter than |
| 须 | Xū | Must; shall |
| 凡是 | Fánshì | All; every |
| 向 | Xiàng | 对 and 向 combine with a number of different verbs to generally mean "to" or "for" |
| 区域 | Qūyù | Area; region |
| 的 | De | 的 is often used without the term it modifies. Here the missing term could be 时候 (time, i.e. "when") or 情况 (circumstance) |

| 应当 | Yīngdāng | Shall; must[8] |
|------|----------|----------------|
| 执行 | Zhíxíng | Carry out; implement |
| 建立 | Jiànlì | Establish |
| 监测 | Jiāncè | Monitoring |
| 制度 | Zhìdù | System (political or administrative) |
| 规范 | Guīfàn | Standardize; normalize |
| 会同 | Huìtóng | Handle jointly with |
| 组织 | Zǔzhī | Organize |
| 网络 | Wǎngluò | Network |
| 加强 | Jiāqiáng | Strengthen |
| 定期 | Dìngqī | Regularly |
| 发布 | Fābù | Issue |
| 状况 | Zhuàngkuàng | Condition; state; situation |
| 公报 | Gōngbào | Bulletin; communique |
| 调查 | Diàochá | Investigate |
| 评价 | Píngjià | Evaluate; assess |
| 拟定 | Nǐdìng | Formulate; draw up; draft |
| 经 (经过) | Jīng (Jīngguò) | Go through; be x'd |
| 综合 | Zōnghé | Integrated; unified |

---

8 Law Practice Tip: In legal English, there is a difference between "must" and "shall." "Shall" has several meanings including "must" and "will." In modern legal English the trend is to avoid using "shall." When "shall" is used in the mandatory sense, then the word "must" is used.

| | | |
|---|---|---|
| 平衡 | Pínghéng | Balance |
| 批准 | Pīzhǔn | Approve; approval |
| 遵守 | Zūnshǒu | Adhere to; abide by |
| 报告书 | Bàogàoshū | Report (statement, e.g. EIS) |
| 产生 | Chǎnshēng | Cause; bring about |
| 预审 | Yùshěn | Preliminary review |
| 程序 | Chéngxù | Procedure; process |
| 方 | Fāng | Same as 才 |
| 可 | Kě | 可以 |
| 设计任务书 | Shèjì rènwùshū | Planning document (lit. plan for who is to take on which responsibility) |
| 具有 | Jùyǒu | Fully possess; have |
| 代表 | Dàibiǎo | Represent |
| 性 | Xìng | Suffix for -ness, -ity, -ive, -ize |
| 类型 | Lèixíng | Type |
| 系统 | Xìtǒng | System |
| 珍稀 | Zhēnxī | Precious; treasured |
| 濒危 | Bīnwēi | Endangered |
| 动植物 | Dòngzhíwù | Plants and animals; flora and fauna |
| 分布区域 | Fēnbùqūyù | Distributed range; range |
| 水源 | Shuǐyuán | Water source |
| 涵养 | Hányǎng | Conserve |

| | | |
|---|---|---|
| 重大 | Zhòngdà | Major; material |
| 科学 | Kēxué | Science |
| 价值 | Jiàzhí | Value; worth |
| 地质 | Dìzhì | Geology |
| 构造 | Gòuzào | Structure |
| 著名 | Zhùmíng | Famous; well known |
| 溶洞 | Róngdòng | Karst caves |
| 化石 | Huàshí | Fossil |
| 冰川 | Bīngchuān | Glaciers |
| 火山 | Huǒshān | Volcano |
| 温泉 | Wēnquán | Hot spring |
| 以及 | Yǐjí | As well as; and; too (literary Chinese meaning the same as 跟 and 和) |
| 古树名木 | Gǔshù míngmù | Famous old trees |
| 加以 | Jiāyǐ | 予以 and 加以 both mean "to do x." In English, we would not translate either |
| 严禁 | Yánjìn | Strictly prohibit |
| 开发 | Kāifā | Develop |
| 利用 | Lìyòng | Use; utilize |
| 土壤 | Tǔrǎng | Soil |
| 沙 | Shā | Sand; desert |
| 盐 | Yán | Salt |

| 渍 | Zì | Saturate; soak |
| 贫瘠 | Pínjí | Barren; infertile |
| 沼泽 | Zhǎozé | Marsh; swamp; bog |
| 地面 | Dìmiàn | Earth's surface; ground |
| 沉降 | Chénjiàng | Subside; settle |
| 被 | Bèi | Passive marker for the following verb |
| 流失 | Liúshī | Run off; wash away |
| 枯竭 | Kūjié | Dried up; exhausted |
| 种源 | Zhǒngyuán | Source of species |
| 灭绝 | Mièjué | Become extinct |
| 失调 | Shītiáo | Imbalance; maladjustment |
| 现象 | Xiànxiàng | Phenomenon |
| 推广 | Tuīguǎng | Popularize; spread; extend |
| 病虫害 | Bìngchónghài | Plant diseases and insect pests |
| 合理 | Hélǐ | Reasonably |
| 使用 | Shǐyòng | Use |
| 化肥 | Huàféi | Fertilizer |
| 农药 | Nóngyào | Pesticide |
| 生长 | Shēngzhǎng | Grow; growth |
| 激素 | Jīsù | Hormone |
| 责任 | Zérèn | Responsibility |
| 有效 | Yǒuxiào | Valid; effective |

| | | |
|---|---|---|
| 生产 | Shēngchǎn | Produce; manufacture |
| 废气 | Fèiqì | Emissions (waste gas or steam) |
| 废水 | Fèishuǐ | Effluent (waste water) |
| 废渣 | Fèizhā | Waste |
| 粉尘 | Fěnchén | Dust |
| 恶臭 | Èchòu | Malodorous; stench |
| 气体 | Qìtǐ | Gas |
| 放射性 | Fàngshèxìng | Radio active |
| 物质 | Wùzhì | Material; matter |
| 噪声 | Zàoshēng | Noise |
| 振动 | Zhèndòng | Vibration |
| 电磁波 | Diàncíbō | Electromagnetic wave |
| 辐射 | Fúshè | Radiation |
| 危害 | Wēihài | Harm |
| 企业 | Qǐyè | Enterprise |
| 事业单位 | Shìyè dānwèi | Institution |
| 申报 | Shēnbào | Report or declare (to an authority) |
| 登记 | Dēngjì | Register |
| 超过 | Chāoguò | Exceed |
| 缴纳 | Jiǎonà | Pay (taxes, fees, etc.) |
| 超 | Chāo | Exceed |
| 费 | Fèi | Expense; fee |

| 负责 | Fùzé | Bear responsibility for |
|---|---|---|
| 治理 | Zhìlǐ | Bring under control |
| 征收 | Zhēngshōu | Levy; impose (a fine) |
| 用于 | Yòngyú | Used for or in |
| 挪 | Nuó | Divert; misappropriate (funds) for another use |
| 他 | Tā | 其他 (other) |
| 具体 | Jùtǐ | Concrete; specific |
| 违反 | Wéifǎn | Violate (a law) |
| 下列 | Xiàliè | The following; set forth below |
| 行为 | Xíngwéi | Act; conduct; behavior |
| 之一 | Zhīyī | 的一个 |
| 行使 | Xíngshǐ | Exercise (a right) |
| 情节 | Qíngjié | Circumstance; situation |
| 警告 | Jǐnggào | Warn; admonish |
| 处以 | Chǔyǐ | Impose; give a sentence of (e.g. a penalty or fine) |
| 罚款 | Fákuǎn | Penalty; fine |
| 拒绝 | Jùjué | Refuse |
| 现场 | Xiànchǎng | Site |
| 检查 | Jiǎnchá | Examination; inspection |
| 弄虚作假 | Nòngxū zuòjiǎ | Practice fraud; cheat |

| 拒报 | Jùbào | Refuse (拒绝) to report |
| --- | --- | --- |
| 谎报 | Huǎngbào | File a false report |
| 事项 | Shìxiàng | Item; matter |
| 按 (按照) | Àn (Ànzhào) | Based on; in accordance with |
| 排污 (排放污染物) | Páiwū<br>(Páifàng wūrǎnwù) | Pollution discharge |
| 引进 | Yǐnjìn | Import; introduce |
| 符合 | Fúhé | Conform to; comply with |
| 我国 | Wǒguó | China (lit. "our country") |
| 要求 | Yāoqiú | Demands; requirement |
| 设备 | Shèbèi | Equipment |
| 将 | Jiāng | Literary Chinese for 把 |
| 严重 | Yánzhòng | Serious; material[9] |
| 转移 | Zhuǎnyí | Shift; transfer; divert |
| 能力 | Nénglì | Ability; capability; capacity |
| 造成 | Zàochéng | Cause; bring about |
| 事故 | Shìgù | Accident |
| 所 | Suǒ | Which |
| 后果 | Hòuguǒ | Consequences; aftermath |

---

9 Law Practice Tip: These kinds of vague standards are sometimes defined in follow-up regulations or interpretations. See, for example, the reading on Intellectual Property/Criminal Law.

| 其 | Qí | Literary Chinese for 他 |
| 所在 | Suǒzài | Local (lit. the place where something or someone is) |
| 机关 | Jīguān | Organ (administrative or government) |
| 处分 | Chǔfèn | Sanction; punish |
| 当事人 | Dāngshìrén | Party |
| 处罚 | Chǔfá | Penalty |
| 决定 | Juédìng | Decision |
| 不服 | Bùfú | Refuse to obey; do not accept |
| 接到 | Jiēdào | Receive |
| 通知 | Tōngzhī | Notice |
| 之 | Zhī | Literary Chinese equivalent of 的 |
| 向 x 申请 y | Xiàng x shēnqǐng y | Apply to x for y |
| 上一级 | Shàngyījí | Next highest level |
| 复议 | Fùyì | Reconsider (a decision) |
| 向 x 起诉 | Xiàng x qǐsù | Sue; start a lawsuit at x |
| 人民法院 | Rénmín Fǎyuàn | People's Court |
| 直接 | Zhíjiē | Directly |
| 逾期 | Yúqī | Exceed time limit; overdue |
| 又 | Yòu | Moreover |
| 履行 | Lǚxíng | Perform; fulfill; carry out |
| 强制 | Qiángzhì | Mandatory; compulsory |

| 损害 | Sǔnhài | Harm; damage |
| 赔偿 | Péicháng | Compensate |
| 损失 | Sǔnshī | Loss (financial, economic, etc.) |
| 金额 | Jīn'é | Amount |
| 纠纷 | Jiūfēn | Dispute |
| 请求 | Qǐngqiú | Request; ask |
| 处理 | Chǔlǐ | Handle; deal with |
| 完全 | Wánquán | Completely |
| 由于 | Yóuyú | Due to; as a result of |
| 抗拒 | Kàngjù | Resist; defy |
| 灾害 | Zāihài | Calamity; disaster |
| 及时 | Jíshí | Timely; promptly |
| 仍然 | Réngrán | Still; yet |
| 避免 | Bìmiǎn | Avoid |
| 免予 | Miǎnyǔ | Avoid; avert (being given) |
| 承担 | Chéngdān | Assume; bear |
| 附则 | Fùzé | Supplementary provisions |
| 缔结 | Dìjié | Conclude (an agreement) |
| 参加 | Cānjiā | Join in; participate in |
| 国际 | Guójì | International |
| 条约 | Tiáoyuē | Treaty |
| 适用 | Shìyòng | Apply |

| | | |
|---|---|---|
| 但 x 除外 | Dàn x chúwài | With the exception of x |
| 声明 | Shēngmíng | Stated; declared |
| 保留 | Bǎoliú | Reservation |
| 条款 | Tiáokuǎn | Provision; clause |
| 自 x 起 | Zì x qǐ | Beginning from x |
| 试行 | Shìxíng | Trial[10] |
| 废止 | Fèizhǐ | Abolish; nullify |

---

10 Law Practice Tip: In China, it is common to issue new laws and rules in a "trial," i.e. temporary version. Some trial versions remain on the books for several years before the final version is promulgated.

# D. Text of Shanghai City Environmental Protection Regulations[11]

## 上海市人民代表大会 常务 委员会 公告

### 第54号

《上海市环境 保护 条例》已 *由* 上海市第十二届人民代表大会常务委员会第二十三次会议 于 2005年10月28日通过, 现 予 公布, *自* 2006年5月1日*起* 施行。

上海市人民代表大会常务委员会

2005年10月28日

---

11 Source: Shanghai shi huan jing bao hu tiao li [Shanghai City Environmental Protection Regulations] (promulgated by the Standing Comm. Shanghai City People's Cong., Oct. 28, 2005, effective May 1, 2006) *available at* http://www.shanghai.gov.cn/shanghai/node2314/node3124/node3177/node3185/userobject6ai206.html (last visited Jun. 3, 2011).

# 上海市环境保护条例

（1994 年12月8日上海市第十届人民代表大会常务委员会第十四次会议通过，根据1997年5月27日上海市第十届人民代表大会常务委员会第三十六次会议《关于 修改〈上海市环境保护条例〉的决定》修正，2005年10月28日上海市第十二届人民代表大会常务委员会第二十三次会议修订）

第一章 总则

第一条 为了保护和改善 本市环境，保障市民身体健康，促进 经济和社会的可持续 发展，根据《中华人民共和国环境保护法》和其他 有关 法律、行政 法规，结合本市实际情况，制定本条例。

第二条 本条例适用 于本市行政区域内的环境保护及 其 相关的管理 活动。

第三条 本市坚持环境保护与经济、社会发展并重的方针，实行环境与发展综合 决策，促进循环经济发展，实现经济效益、社会效益和环境效益的统一。

第四条 本市各级 人民政府 应当 对本行政区域的环境质量 负责，实行环境保护行政首长负责制。每届政府应当根据环境保护规划，制定任期内的环境保护目标和年度 实施 计划，并

保证一定的财政 资金 投入环境保护工作。

各级人民政府应当每年向同级人民代表大会或者其常务委员会报告环境保护工作以及任期内的环境保护目标实现情况。

街道办事处根据所在区、县人民政府的要求，开展本辖区内有关的环境保护工作。

第五条 市环境保护局（以下简称市环保局）是本市环境保护行政主管 部门，对全市环境保护工作实施统一监督管理，并负责组织实施本条例。区、县环境保护行政主管部门（以下简称区、县环保部门）对本行政区域内的环境保护工作实施统一监督管理，业务上同时受市环保局的领导。

市环保局和区、县环保部门（以下统称环保部门）所属的环境监察 机构，负责本行政区域内环境保护情况的监督检查，对环境污染 事故

和纠纷 进行 调查、提出 处理意见, 并负责征收 排污 费。环保部门可以*在* *法定* *权限* *范围* *内* *委托*其所属的环境监察机构实施行政处罚和行政**强制** 措施。

环保部门应当**建立** **检举**、**控告** **制度**, 公布**投诉**电话。对属于环保部门**职责**范围的检举和控告, 应当**依法处理**; 对属于其他管理部门职责范围的检举和控告, 应当**按照** **规定** 转送相关管理部门处理, 并**告知** 当事人。

第六条 市环保局应当**加强**对区、县环保部门的监督。对区、县环保部门作出的**违法**的行政**许可**、行政处罚或者其他决定, 市环保局应当**责令其改正**; 对区、县环保部门应当依法处理的**事项**不予处理*的*, 市环保局应当责令其改正。

## 第二章 规划、**区划**和**标准**

第十条 市环保局应当**会同**本市有关部门组织**编制**市环境保护规划和相关环境保护**专项**规划, *报*市人民政府*批准*。

区、县环保部门应当根据市环境保护规划和相关环境保护专项规划, 结合本区、县实际, 会同有关部门编制区、县环境保护规划, 报区、县人民政府批准; 区、县人民政府在批准前应当**征求**市环保局的意见。

环境保护规划应当**纳入**市和区、县国民经济和社会发展计划、城市**总体**规划。

*经*批准后的环境保护规划和相关环境保护专项规划, 由环保部门会同有关部门组织实施。

第十三条 市人民政府可以根据本市实际, 对国家环境质量标准和国家**污染物** 排放标准中**未**作规定的**项目**, 制定**地方标准**; 对国家污染物排放标准中已作规定的项目, 可以制定**严** 于国家污染物排放标准的地方污染物排放标准, *但*法律、行政法规另有规定的*除外*。

## 第三章 环境监督管理

第二十二条 市环保局应当根据国家环境**监测** **技术**要求, 统一组织编制本市环境监测技术**规范**。

环境监测**专业**机构应当根据国家和本市环境监测技术规范开展环境监测, 保证监测**数据**的**准确** **性**, 并对监测数据和监测**结论**负责。

当事人对区、县环保部门**设立**的环境监测机构和其他环境监测专业机构**出具**的与**具体**行政**行为**有关的监测数据有**异议**的, 可以向市环保局设立的环境监测机构**申请** **复核**, 市环保局设立的环境监测机构应当在三十日内出具复核意见; 情况**特殊**的, 可以**延长**三十日出具复核意见。

当事人对市环保局设立的环境监测机构出具的监测数据有异议的, 可以向国家环境保护行政主管部门设立的环境监测机构申请复核。

**复核得出**的监测结论**与** 原监测结论**一致**的, 复核**费用**由申请复核**者** **承担**; 复核得出的监测结论与原监测结论不一致的，复核费用由出具监测数据的**单位**承担。

第四章 环境污染**防治**

第二十八条 排污单位应当按照环境保护**设施**的**设计**要求和排污**许可证**规定的排放要求，制定**操作 规程**，并**保持**环境保护设施**正常运行**。

排污单位的环境保护设施因 **维修**、**故障**等原因无法**达标**排放的，应当**采取 限 产**或者其他措施，**确保**其污染物排放达到规定的标准，并在十二个小时内向区、县环保部门报告；采取措施后**仍**不能达标排放的，应当**立即 停产**，停止排放污染物。

**禁止 擅自 拆除**或者闲置环境保护设施。**直接**向环境排放污染物或者向城市**污水 集中**处理设施排放一类水污染物的排污单位，**确有必要**拆除或者闲置环境保护设施的，应当在拆除或闲置三十日前，向市或者区、县环保部门提出申请。

环保部门**受理**申请后，应当在二十日内作出**审批**决定；不予批准的，应当说明**理由**。

# E. Vocabulary of Shanghai City Environmental Protection Regulations

| Chinese | Pinyin | English |
| --- | --- | --- |
| 人民代表大会 | Rénmín Dàibiǎo Dàhuì | People's Congress[12] |
| 常务委员会 | Chángwù Wěiyuánhuì | Standing Committee (of the NPC) |
| 公告 | Gōnggào | Public announcement |
| 环境 | Huánjìng | Environment |
| 保护 | Bǎohù | Protection |
| 条例 | Tiáolì | Regulation; rule; ordinance[13] |
| 已 | Yǐ | 已经 |
| 由 x | Yóu x | By x |
| 届 | Jiè | Session |
| 会议 | Huìyì | Meeting |
| 于 | Yú | In; on |

12 Background Tip: There are People's Congresses at the national and local levels.

13 Law Practice Tip: There is no standardized Chinese term or English translation for this. Because these are at the city level, in the U.S., they would be called ordinances rather than regulations.

| | | |
|---|---|---|
| 通过 | Tōngguò | Pass; enact |
| 现 | Xiàn | 现在 |
| 予 | Yǔ | Give (literary Chinese) |
| 公布 | Gōngbù | Promulgate |
| 自 x 起 | Zì x qǐ | Beginning from x |
| 施行 | Shīxíng | Come into force |
| 根据 | Gēnjù | Based on; according to |
| 关于 | Guānyú | Relating to |
| 修改 | Xiūgǎi | Revise; modify; amend |
| 决定 | Juédìng | Decision |
| 修正 | Xiūzhèng | Revise; amend; correct |
| 修订 | Xiūdìng | Revise; amend |
| 章 | Zhāng | Chapter[14] |
| 总则 | Zǒngzé | General principles |
| 为了 | Wèile | In order to; for the sake of |
| 改善 | Gǎishàn | Improve |
| 本 | Běn | Literary Chinese for 这个 |
| 保障 | Bǎozhàng | Ensure; guarantee; safeguard |
| 健康 | Jiànkāng | Health |

---

14 Law Practice Tip: There is no standard English translation for this term and related terms such as 条 tiáo (article). In part this is because their usage in Chinese is not standardized.

| 促进 | Cùjìn | Promote; advance |
|------|-------|------------------|
| 经济 | Jīngjì | Economy; economic |
| 社会 | Shèhuì | Social; society |
| 可持续 | Kěchíxù | Sustainable |
| 发展 | Fāzhǎn | Development |
| 其他 | Qítā | Other |
| 有关 | Yǒuguān | Relevant |
| 法律 | Fǎlù | Law |
| 行政 | Xíngzhèng | Administrative |
| 法规 | Fǎguī | Administrative laws and regulations[15] |
| 结合 | Jiéhé | Combine; integrate |
| 实际 | Shíjì | Actual; realistic; in practice |
| 制定 | Zhìdìng | Formulate; enact |
| 适用 | Shìyòng | Apply |
| 于 | Yú | In; on; towards |
| 区域 | Qūyù | Area; region |
| 及 | Jí | And; as well as (literary Chinese meaning the same as 跟 and 和) |
| 其 | Qí | Literary Chinese for 他的 |

---

15 Law Practice Tip: "行政法规" are legislations adopted by the State Council. They are the third level of legislation in China, only lower than the Constitution and Laws passed by National People's Congress or its Standing Committee.

| | | |
|---|---|---|
| 相关 | Xiāngguān | Related |
| 管理 | Guǎnlǐ | Management |
| 活动 | Huódòng | Activity; act |
| 坚持 | Jiānchí | Unremitting; persist |
| 与 | Yǔ | And; together with |
| 并重 | Bìngzhòng | Pay equal attention to |
| 方针 | Fāngzhēn | Policy; guidelines |
| 实行 | Shíxíng | Implement; carry out |
| 综合 | Zōnghé | Integrated; unified |
| 决策 | Juécè | Policy decisions |
| 循环 | Xúnhuán | Cyclical |
| 实现 | Shíxiàn | Realize; achieve; bring about |
| 效益 | Xiàoyì | Beneficial results; productivity |
| 统一 | Tǒngyī | Unify |
| 各级 | Gèjí | All levels |
| 人民政府 | Rénmín zhèngfǔ | People's government |
| 应当 | Yīngdāng | Shall; must[16] |
| 对 | Duì | 对 and 向 combine with a number of different verbs to generally mean "to" or "for" |

---

16 Law Practice Tip: In legal English, there is a difference between "must" and "shall." "Shall" has several meanings including "must" and "will." In modern legal English the trend is to avoid using "shall." When "shall" is used in the mandatory sense, then the word "must" is used.

| 质量 | Zhìliàng | Quality |
|---|---|---|
| 负责 | Fùzé | Bear responsibility for |
| 首长 | Shǒuzhǎng | Department leader |
| 制 (制度) | Zhì (Zhìdù) | System (administrative or political) |
| 规划 | Guīhuà | Planning |
| 任期 | Rènqī | Term of office |
| 目标 | Mùbiāo | Target; goal; objective |
| 年度 | Niándù | Annual |
| 实施 | Shíshī | Put into effect; implement; carry out |
| 计划 | Jìhuà | Plan |
| 并 | Bìng | And; moreover |
| 保证 | Bǎozhèng | Guarantee; ensure |
| 财政 | Cáizhèng | Financial |
| 资金 | Zījīn | Funds; funding |
| 投入 | Tóurù | Invest |
| 向 | Xiàng | 对 and 向 combine with a number of different verbs to generally mean "to" or "for" |
| 报告 | Bàogào | Report |
| 以及 | Yǐjí | As well as; and (literary Chinese meaning the same as 跟 and 和) |
| 情况 | Qíngkuàng | Circumstance; situation |

| 街道办事处 | Jiēdào bànshìchù | Neighborhood office |
|---|---|---|
| 所在 | Suǒzài | Local (lit. the place where something or somebody is) |
| 县 | Xiàn | County |
| 要求 | Yāoqiú | Demands; requirements |
| 开展 | Kāizhǎn | Develop; launch; unfold |
| 辖区 | Xiáqū | Area under one's jurisdiction |
| 局 | Jú | Bureau |
| 以下简称 x | Yǐxià jiǎnchēng x | Abbreviated below as x[17] |
| 主管 | Zhǔguǎn | Responsible for; in charge of |
| 部门 | Bùmén | Department; branch; section |
| 监督 | Jiāndū | Control; supervision |
| 组织 | Zǔzhī | Organize |
| 业务 | Yèwù | Business |
| 受 | Shòu | Receive |
| 领导 | Lǐngdǎo | Leadership |
| 统称 | Tǒngchēng | Collectively referred to as |
| 所属 | Suǒshǔ | Those which fall under x (belong to x) |
| 监察 | Jiānchá | Supervise |
| 机构 | Jīgòu | Organization; structure |

---

17 Law Practice Tip: In modern legal English, the term "below" would be used. In older legal English, the term would be "hereinafter."

| 检查 | Jiǎnchá | Examine; inspect |
|------|---------|------------------|
| 污染 | Wūrǎn | Pollution |
| 事故 | Shìgù | Accident |
| 纠纷 | Jiūfēn | Disputes |
| 进行 | Jìnxíng | Conduct; carry out |
| 调查 | Diàochá | Investigation |
| 提出 | Tíchū | Raise; propose (an idea) |
| 处理 | Chǔlǐ | Handle; deal with |
| 征收 | Zhēngshōu | Levy; impose (a fine) |
| 排污 (排放污染物) | Páiwū (Páifàng wūrǎnwù) | Pollution discharge |
| 费 | Fèi | Fees |
| 在 x 内 | Zài x nèi | Within x |
| 法定 | Fǎdìng | Legally mandated |
| 权限 | Quánxiàn | Authority; power(s) |
| 范围 | Fànwéi | Scope |
| 委托 | Wěituō | Entrust; delegate; consign |
| 处罚 | Chǔfá | Penalize; punish |
| 强制 | Qiángzhì | Mandatory; compulsory |
| 措施 | Cuòshī | Measures; steps |
| 建立 | Jiànlì | Establish |
| 检举 | Jiǎnjǔ | Report (an offense) |
| 控告 | Kònggào | Accuse; charge |

| 投诉 | Tóusù | File or make a complaint |
| 属于 | Shǔyú | Belong to; fall within |
| 职责 | Zhízé | Duty; responsibility; obligation |
| 依法 | Yīfǎ | Legally; In accordance with the law |
| 按照 | Ànzhào | In accordance with |
| 规定 | Guīdìng | Stipulate; provide |
| 转送 | Zhuǎnsòng | Transfer |
| 告知 | Gàozhī | Inform; notify |
| 当事人 | Dāngshìrén | Party |
| 加强 | Jiāqiáng | Strengthen |
| 违法 | Wéifǎ | Illegal |
| 许可 | Xǔkě | Approval; permission |
| 责令 | Zélìng | Order; instruct |
| 改正 | Gǎizhèng | Correct; amend |
| 事项 | Shìxiàng | Items; matters |
| 的 | De | 的 is often used without the term it modifies. Here the missing term could be 时候 (time, i.e. "when") or 情况 (circumstance) |
| 区划 | Qūhuà | Zoning |
| 标准 | Biāozhǔn | Standard |
| 会同 | Huìtóng | Handle jointly with |

| | | |
|---|---|---|
| 编制 | Biānzhì | Draw up; establish |
| 专项 | Zhuānxiàng | Specialized |
| 报 x 批准 | Bào x pīzhǔn | Report to x for approval |
| 征求 | Zhēngqiú | Solicit; seek |
| 纳入 | Nàrù | Incorporate sth. into another; bring in line with |
| 总体 | Zǒngtǐ | Aggregate; as a whole; overall |
| 经 (经过) | Jīng (Jīngguò) | Go through; be x'd |
| 污染物 | Wūrǎnwù | Pollutants |
| 排放 | Páifàng | Discharge (of gas or pollutants) |
| 未 | Wèi | Literary Chinese for 还没 |
| 项目 | Xiàngmù | Project |
| 地方 | Dìfāng | Local |
| 严 | Yán | Strict |
| 于 | Yú | Adjective (-er than x) |
| 但 x 除外 | Dàn x chúwài | With the exception of x |
| 监测 | Jiāncè | Monitor |
| 技术 | Jìshù | Technology |
| 规范 | Guīfàn | Standard; norm |
| 专业 | Zhuānyè | Specialized |
| 数据 | Shùjù | Data |
| 准确 | Zhǔnquè | Accurate; precise |

| 性 | Xìng | Suffix for -ness, -ity, -ive, -ize |
| 结论 | Jiélùn | Conclusion; verdict |
| 设立 | Shèlì | Establish; set up |
| 出具 | Chūjù | Provide |
| 具体 | Jùtǐ | Concrete; specific |
| 行为 | Xíngwéi | Act; conduct; behavior |
| 异议 | Yìyì | Objection |
| 申请 | Shēnqǐng | Apply for |
| 复核 | Fùhé | Review; reexamination |
| 特殊 | Tèshū | Special |
| 延长 | Yáncháng | Prolong; extend |
| 得出 | Déchū | Obtained (here, the x which was obtained from the review) |
| 与 x 一致 | Yǔ x yīzhì | Identical (views or opinions) with x |
| 原 | Yuán | Original |
| 费用 | Fèiyòng | Expenses |
| 者 | Zhě | 者 is literary Chinese and is used after an adjective or verb as a substitute for a person, entity, or thing[18] |
| 承担 | Chéngdān | Assume; bear |

---

18 Law Practice Tip: In modern legal Chinese it is often used, as it is here, to indicate both natural and legal persons.

| | | |
|---|---|---|
| 单位 | Dānwèi | Entity[19] |
| 防治 | Fángzhì | Prevent and cure |
| 设施 | Shèshī | Facilities |
| 设计 | Shèjì | Design; plan |
| 许可证 | Xǔkězhèng | Permit; license (lit. certificate of approval) |
| 操作 | Cāozuò | Operate; operating |
| 规程 | Guīchéng | Rules; regulations |
| 保持 | Bǎochí | Keep; maintain |
| 正常 | Zhèngcháng | Regular; normal |
| 运行 | Yùnxíng | Operate; function |
| 因 | Yīn | 因为 |
| 维修 | Wéixiū | Protect; maintain (maintenance) |
| 故障 | Gùzhàng | Glitch; breakdown; stoppage |
| 达标 (达到目标) | Dábiāo (Dádào mùbiāo) | To reach a set standard |
| 采取 | Cǎiqǔ | Take; adopt |
| 限 | Xiàn | Limit; restrict |
| 产 | Chǎn | Production |
| 确保 | Quèbǎo | Ensure; guarantee |

---

19 Law Practice Tip: Dānwèi is used to describe the organization to which you belong, e.g. your employer. In the past, when there was no private economy, the Dānwèi played a much more significant role in the lives of its workers. It provided housing, schools, hospitals, cafeterias, etc.

| 仍 (仍然) | Réng (Réngrán) | Still; yet |
| 立即 | Lìjí | Immediately |
| 停产 | Tíngchǎn | Cease; stop production |
| 禁止 | Jìnzhǐ | Prohibited |
| 擅自 | Shànzì | Do something without authorization |
| 拆除 | Chāichú | Demolish |
| 闲置 | Xiánzhì | Leave idle or unused |
| 直接 | Zhíjiē | Direct |
| 污水 | Wūshuǐ | Waste water |
| 集中 | Jízhōng | Centralized |
| 确 | Què | Really; indeed |
| 必要 | Bìyào | Necessary; essential; indispensible |
| 受理 | Shòulǐ | Accept (a case) |
| 审批(审查批准) | Shěnpī(Shěnchá pīzhǔn) | Examination and approval |
| 理由 | Lǐyóu | Reason |

# Chapter 9
# **Banking Law**

# 银 行 法

Yín　Háng　Fǎ

# A. Introduction to China's Banking Law System

By *Yang Wantao*, Partner of Zhong Lun Law Firm, Shanghai

Key players in the banking sector of the People's Republic of China (PRC) include the central bank, policy banks, commercial banks, and certain non-banking financial institutions. The People's Bank of China (PBOC) is the central bank. Three policy banks were established in 1994 to primarily handle financing for policy-based projects. Among the commercial banks, the "Big Four" [1] are the most dominant and formidable players. China made concessions in liberalizing its financial services market for foreign investors when accessing to WTO. Now, the China branches of foreign investor invested banks, joint-venture banks, and foreign banks are important players in China's banking market. Non-banking financial institutions in the banking sector in China include urban credit cooperatives, rural credit cooperatives, finance companies, and trust companies.

China's banking law consists of numerous laws, regulations, rules, notices, and policy documents. Major banking laws include the Law of the PRC on the People's Bank of China (PBOC Law), the Law of the PRC on Commercial Banks, and the Law of the PRC on Regulation of and Supervision over the Banking Industry. The history of the enactment and amendment of the PBOC Law reflects the evolution of China's banking regulatory regime.

The PBOC Law was initially enacted in 1995. It authorized the PBOC to take on the role of central bank and regulate the legal tender of the PRC.

---

1 The"Big Four" are the Bank of China, the China Construction Bank, the Agricultural Bank of China and the Industrial and Commercial Bank of China. They used to be wholly state-owned banks and are now publicly listed on stock exchanges.

Under the original 1995 PBOC Law, PBOC used to have a full spectrum of authority in regulating, controlling, and supervising financial institutions and the financial market.

The current PBOC Law took effect on February 1, 2004. The new PBOC Law focuses PBOC's functions and responsibilities relating to formulating and implementing monetary policies. PBOC no longer exercises general authority in direct supervision over financial institutions[2]. Its function is related to preventing systematic financial risks and maintaining financial stability through macro-economic control. The PBOC Law also sets forth PBOC's additional responsibilities and authority, including regulating inter-bank markets and anti-money laundering.

The PBOC Law also grants PBOC certain monetary policy tools, including: setting deposit reserves and basic interest rates; rediscounting; last resort loans to commercial banks; and open market operation in the purchase and sale of government bonds, financial bonds, and foreign exchange. However, PBOC may not directly subscribe to or underwrite government bonds.

---

2 The China Banking Regulatory Commission is responsible for supervision of the business operations and risks of commercial banks and certain non-bank financial institutions.

# B. Law of the People's Republic of China on the People's Bank of China (2003) Text[3]

## 中华人民共和国中国人民银行法

(1995年3月18日第八届 全国人民代表大会第三次会议 通过 根据2003年12月27日第十届全国人民代表大会常务 委员会第六次会议《关于 修改〈中华人民共和国中国人民银行法〉的决定》修正)

第一章 总则

第二条 中国人民银行是中华人民共和国的中央银行。中国人民银行在 国务院 领导 下，制定和执行 货币 政策，防范和化解 金融 风险，维护金融稳定。

第三条 货币政策目标是保持货币币值的稳定，并 以此 促进经济增长。

第四条 中国人民银行履行 下列 职责：

（一）发布 与履行其职责有关的命令和规章；

（二）依法制定和执行货币政策；

（三）发行人民币，管理人民币流通；

（四）监督管理银行间 同业 拆借 市场和

---

3 Source: Zhonghua Renmin Gongheguo Zhongguo ren min yin hang fa [Law on People's Bank of China (P.R.C.)] (promulgated by the Nat'l People's Cong., Mar. 18, 1995, amended Dec. 27, 2003, effective Dec. 27, 2003) *available at* http://www.cbrc.gov.cn/chinese/home/jsp/docView.jsp?docID=2420 (last visited Jun.3, 2009).

银行间**债券**市场;

（五）**实施 外汇**管理，监督管理银行间外汇市场;

（六）监督管理**黄金**市场;

（七）**持有**、管理、经营国家外汇**储备**、黄金储备;

（八）**经理 国库**;

（九）维护**支付**、**清算 系统**的正常 运行;

（十）**指导**、**部署 金融业 反 洗钱**工作，负责反洗钱的**资金 监测**;

（十一）负责金融业的**统计**、**调查**、**分析**和**预测**;

（十二）**作为**国家的中央银行，从事有关的国际金融**活动**;

（十三）国务院**规定**的其他职责。

中国人民银行**为**执行货币政策，可以**依照**本法第四章的有关规定从事金融**业务**活动。

**第五条** 中国人民银行**就** 年度货币供应**量**、**利率**、**汇率**和国务院规定的其他重要**事项**作出的决定，*报*国务院**批准**后执行。

中国人民银行就**前款**规定以外的其他有关货币政策事项作出决定后，**即** 予执行，并报国务院备案。

**第八条** 中国人民银行的全部**资本** *由*国家**出资**，属于 国家所有。

## 第二章 组织 机构

**第十条** 中国人民银行**设 行长**一人，**副行长若干人**。中国人民银行行长的**人选**，根据国务院**总理**的**提名**，由全国人民代表大会决定;全国人民代表大会**闭会 期间**，由全国人民代表大会常务委员会决定，由中华人民共和国**主席 任免**。中国人民银行副行长由国务院总理任免。

**第十二条** 中国人民银行**设立**货币政策委员会。货币政策委员会的职责、**组成和**工作**程序**，由国务院规定，报全国人民代表大会常务委员会备案。中国人民银行货币政策委员会**应当**在国家**宏观 调控**、货币政策制定和**调整**中，**发挥**重要作用。

## 第三章 人民币

**第十六条** 中华人民共和国的**法定**货币是人民币。*以*人民币支付中华人民共和国**境内**的一切公共的和私人的**债务**，任何**单位**和个人**不得 拒收**。

**第十八条** 人民币由中国人民银行**统一 印制**、发行。

中国人民银行发行新**版**人民币，应当**将**发行时间、**面额**、**图案**、**式样**、**规格 予以 公告**。

**第二十条** 任何单位和个人不得印制、**发售代 币 票 券**，**以 代替**人民币在市场上流通。

**第二十二条** 中国人民银行设立人民币发行**库**，在其分支机构设立分支库。分支库**调拨**人民币发行**基金**，应当**按照 上级**库的调拨命令**办理**。任何单位和个人不得**违反**规定，**动用**发行基金。

第四章 业务

第二十三条 中国人民银行为执行货币政策，可以运用下列货币政策工具：

（一）要求 银行业金融机构按照规定的比例 交存 存款 准备金；

（二）确定中央银行基准利率；

（三）为在中国人民银行开立 账户的银行业金融机构办理再贴现；

（四）向 商业银行 提供 贷款；

（五）在公开市场上买卖国债、其他政府债券和金融债券及外汇；

（六）国务院确定的其他货币政策工具。

中国人民银行为执行货币政策，运用前款所列货币政策工具时，可以规定具体的条件和程序。

第二十四条 中国人民银行依照法律、行政法规的规定经理国库。

第二十七条 中国人民银行应当组织或者协助组织银行业金融机构相互 之间的清算系统，协调银行业金融机构相互之间的清算事项，提供清算服务。具体办法由中国人民银行制定。

中国人民银行会同国务院银行业监督管理机构制定支付结算 规则。

第二十八条 中国人民银行根据执行货币政策的需要，可以决定对商业银行贷款的数额、期限、利率和方式，但贷款的期限不得超过一年。

第三十条 中国人民银行不得向地方政府、各级政府部门提供贷款，不得向非银行金融机构以及其他单位和个人提供贷款，但国务院决定中国人民银行可以向特定的非银行金融机构提供贷款的除外。

中国人民银行不得向任何单位和个人提供担保。

第五章 金融监督管理

第三十二条 中国人民银行有权对金融机构以及其他单位和个人的下列行为 进行 检查监督：

（一）执行有关存款准备金管理规定的行为；

（二）与中国人民银行特种贷款有关的行为；

（三）执行有关人民币管理规定的行为；

（四）执行有关银行间同业拆借市场、银行间债券市场管理规定的行为；

（五）执行有关外汇管理规定的行为；

（六）执行有关黄金管理规定的行为；

（七）代理中国人民银行经理国库的行为；

（八）执行有关清算管理规定的行为；

（九）执行有关反洗钱规定的行为。

前款所称中国人民银行特种贷款，是指国务院决定的由中国人民银行向金融机构发放的用于特定目的的贷款。

第三十三条 中国人民银行根据执行货币政策和维护金融稳定的需要，可以建议国务院银行业监督管理机构对银行业金融机构进行检查监督。国务院银行业监督管理机构应当*自* 收到建议之日*起*三十日内予以回复。

第三十五条 中国人民银行根据履行职责的需要，有权要求银行业金融机构**报送 必要的资产负债表**、**利润表**以及其他财务 **会计**、统计**报表和资料**。中国人民银行应当和国务院银行业监督管理机构、国务院其他金融监督管理机构**建立**监督管理**信息 共享 机制**。

### 第六章 财务会计

第三十九条 中国人民银行每一会计年度的**收入 减除 该年度支出**，并按照国务院**财政**部门核定的比例**提取 总准备金后的净利润**，全部**上缴**中央财政。中国人民银行的**亏损**由中央财政**拨款 弥补**。

### 第七章 法律责任

第四十六条 本法第三十二条所列行为违反有关规定，有关法律、行政法规有处**罚规**定*的*，依照其规定**给予处罚**；有关法律、行政法规未作处罚规定的，由中国人民银行**区别**不同**情形**给予**警告，没收 违法 所得**，违法所得五十万元以上的，并*处*违法所得一倍以上五倍以下*罚款*；没有违法所得或者违法所得**不足**五十万元的，处五十万元以上二百万元以下罚款；对**负有 直接**责任的**董事**、高级管理**人**员和其他直接责任人员给予警告，处五万元以上五十万元以下罚款；**构成 犯罪的，依法追究 刑事**责任。

第四十七条 **当事人**对行政处罚**不服**的，可以依照《**中华人民共和国行政诉讼法》**的规定**提起行政诉讼**。

第四十八条 中国人民银行有下列行为之一的，对负有直接责任的**主管人员**和其他直接责任人员，依法给予行政**处分**；构成犯罪的，依法追究刑事责任：

（一）违反本法第三十条第一款的规定提供贷款的；

（二）对单位和个人提供担保的；

（三）**擅自**动用发行基金的。

有前款所列行为之一，**造成 损失的**，负有直接责任的主管人员和其他直接责任人员应当**承担 部分**或者全部赔偿责任。

第四十九条 地方政府、各级政府部门、**社会 团体和个人强令**中国人民银行**及其**工作人员违反本法第三十条的规定提供贷款或者担保的，对负有直接责任的主管人员和其他直接责任人员，依法给予行政处分；构成犯罪的，依法追究刑事责任；造成损失的，应当承担部分或者全部赔偿责任。

第五十条 中国人民银行的工作人员**泄露**国家**秘密**或者所**知悉**的商业秘密，构成犯罪的，依法追究刑事责任；**尚**不构成犯罪的，依法给予行政处分。

# C. Vocabulary of Law of the People's Republic of China on the People's Bank of China (2003)

| Chinese | Pinyin | English |
| --- | --- | --- |
| 届 | Jiè | Session |
| 全国人民代表大会 | Quánguó Rénmín Dàibiǎo Dàhuì | National People's Congress (NPC) |
| 会议 | Huìyì | Meeting |
| 通过 | Tōngguò | Enact; pass |
| 根据 | Gēnjù | Based on; according to |
| 常务委员会 | Chángwù Wěiyuánhuì | Standing Committee (of the NPC) |
| 关于 | Guǎnyú | Related to; regarding |
| 修改 | Xiūgǎi | Revise; modify; amend |
| 决定 | Juédìng | Decision |
| 修正 | Xiūzhèng | Revise; amend; correct |
| 章 | Zhāng | Chapter[4] |

---

4 Law Practice Tip: There is no standard English translation for this term and related terms such as 条 tiáo (Article). In part this is because their usage in Chinese is not standardized.

| 总则 | Zǒngzé | General principles |
| 中央 | Zhōngyāng | Central |
| 在 x 下 | Zài x xià | Under x |
| 国务院 | Guówùyuàn | State Council |
| 领导 | Lǐngdǎo | Leadership |
| 制定 | Zhìdìng | Formulate; enact |
| 执行 | Zhíxíng | Carry out; implement |
| 货币 | Huòbì | Money; monetary |
| 政策 | Zhèngcè | Government policy |
| 防范 | Fángfàn | Look out for; guard against |
| 化解 | Huàjiě | Resolve; dissipate |
| 金融 | Jīnróng | Finance; banking |
| 风险 | Fēngxiǎn | Risk |
| 维护 | Wéihù | Protect |
| 稳定 | Wěndìng | Stability |
| 目标 | Mùbiāo | Target; goal; objective |
| 保持 | Bǎochí | Keep; maintain |
| 币值 | Bìzhí | Value of currency |
| 并 | Bìng | And; moreover |
| 以此 | Yǐcǐ | By this (lit. taking this) |
| 促进 | Cùjìn | Promote; advance |
| 增长 | Zēngzhǎng | Grow; increase |

| | | |
|---|---|---|
| 履行 | Lǚxíng | Perform; fulfill; carry out |
| 下列 | Xiàliè | The following; set forth below |
| 职责 | Zhízé | Duty; obligation; responsibility |
| 发布 | Fābù | Issue |
| 与 | Yǔ | And; together with |
| 其 | Qí | Literary Chinese for 他 or 他的 |
| 有关 | Yǒuguān | Relevant |
| 命令 | Mìnglìng | Order |
| 规章 | Guīzhāng | Rules; regulations |
| 依法 | Yīfǎ | Legally; in accordance with the law |
| 发行 | Fāxíng | Issue (money) |
| 管理 | Guǎnlǐ | Manage |
| 流通 | Liútōng | Circulation |
| 监督 | Jiāndū | Control; supervise |
| 间 | Jiān | Among |
| 同业 | Tóngyè | The same trade or business |
| 拆借 | Chāijiè | Short term loan made at a daily interest rate |
| 银行间同业拆借 | Yínháng jiān tóngyè chāijiè | Inter-bank borrowing and lending |
| 市场 | Shìchǎng | Market |
| 债券 | Zhàiquàn | Bond |

| 实施 | Shíshī | Put into effect; implement; carry out |
|---|---|---|
| 外汇 | Wàihuì | Foreign currency or exchange |
| 黄金 | Huángjīn | Gold |
| 持有 | Chíyǒu | Hold; own |
| 经营 | Jīngyíng | Engage in or run a business |
| 储备 | Chǔbèi | Reserves |
| 经理 (经营管理) | Jīnglǐ (Jīngyíng guǎnlǐ) | Engage in and manage |
| 国库 | Guókù | National Treasury |
| 支付 | Zhīfù | Pay (money); payment |
| 清算 | Qīngsuàn | Clear or settle (an account); settlement; liquidation |
| 系统 | Xìtǒng | System |
| 正常 | Zhèngcháng | Regular; normal |
| 运行 | Yùnxíng | Operations; functions |
| 指导 | Zhǐdǎo | Guide; direct |
| 部署 | Bùshǔ | Delegate; arrange |
| 金融业 | Jīnróngyè | Financial (industry/sector) |
| 反 | Fǎn | Anti- |
| 洗钱 | Xǐqián | Money laundering |
| 资金 | Zījīn | Funds |
| 监测 | Jiāncè | Monitor |
| 统计 | Tǒngjì | Statistics |

| 调查 | Diàochá | Investigation |
|---|---|---|
| 分析 | Fēnxī | Analysis |
| 预测 | Yùcè | Forecast |
| 作为 | Zuòwéi | Use as; be regarded as |
| 从事 | Cóngshì | Engage in |
| 活动 | Huódòng | Activity |
| 规定 | Guīdìng | Stipulate; provide |
| 为 | Wèi | For the sake of; in order to |
| 依照 | Yīzhào | In accordance with |
| 业务 | Yèwù | Business |
| 就 | Jiù | With regards to; concerning |
| 年度 | Niándù | Annual |
| 供应 | Gōngyìng | Supply |
| 量 | Liàng | Quantity |
| 利率 | Lìlù | Interest rate |
| 汇率 | Huìlù | Exchange rate |
| 事项 | Shìxiàng | Items; matters |
| 报 x 批准 | Bào x pīzhǔn | Report to x for approval |
| 批准 | Pīzhǔn | Approve; approval |
| 前款 | Qiánkuǎn | Preceding clause; above provision |
| 即 | Jí | Immediately |
| 予 | Yǔ | Give (literary Chinese) |

| | | |
|---|---|---|
| 备案 | Bèi'àn | Put on record; file |
| 资本 | Zīběn | Capital |
| 由 x | Yóu x | By x |
| 出资 | Chūzī | Capitalize; fund |
| 属于 | Shǔyú | Belong to; fall within |
| 国家所有 | Guójiā suǒyǒu | State owned |
| 组织 | Zǔzhī | Organization |
| 机构 | Jīgòu | Organization; structure |
| 设 | Shè | Establish; arrange |
| 行长 | Hángzhǎng | President of a bank |
| 副 | Fù | Deputy-; vice- |
| 若干 | Ruògān | Several |
| 人选 | Rénxuǎn | Selection of a person |
| 总理 | Zǒnglǐ | Premier |
| 提名 | Tímíng | Nominate |
| 闭会 | Bìhuì | Not in session |
| 期间 | Qījiān | Period of time; when |
| 主席 | Zhǔxí | Chairman |
| 任免 | Rènmiǎn | Appoint and remove (or dismiss) someone |
| 设立 | Shèlì | Establish; set up |
| 组成 | Zǔchéng | Composition; form |
| 程序 | Chéngxù | Procedure; process |

| 应当 | Yīngdāng | Shall; must[5] |
| 宏观 | Hóngguān | Macro- |
| 调控 | Tiáokòng | Regulate and control |
| 调整 | Tiáozhěng | Adjust; regulate; revise |
| 发挥 | Fāhuī | Give free reign to; bring into play |
| 作用 | Zuòyòng | Function; use |
| 法定 | Fǎdìng | Legal |
| 以 | Yǐ | Same meaning as 把 and 用 |
| 境内 | Jìngnèi | Domestic (lit. within the borders) |
| 一切 | Yīqiè | All; every |
| 债务 | Zhàiwù | Debt; liability |
| 单位 | Dānwèi | Entity[6] |
| 不得 | Bùdé | Must not; may not |
| 拒 | Jù | Refuse; resist |
| 统一 | Tǒngyī | Unify |
| 印制 | Yìnzhì | Print |
| 版 | Bǎn | Edition; version |
| 将 | Jiāng | Literary Chinese for 把 |

---

5 Law Practice Tip: In legal English, there is a difference between "must" and "shall." "Shall" has several meanings including "must" and "will." In modern legal English the trend is to avoid using "shall." When "shall" is used in the mandatory sense, then the word "must" is used.

6 Law Practice Tip: Dānwèi is used to describe the organization to which you belong, e.g. your employer. In the past, when there was no private economy, the Dānwèi played a much more significant role in the lives of its workers. It provided housing, schools, hospitals, cafeterias, etc.

| | | |
|---|---|---|
| 面额 | Miàn'é | Denomination |
| 图案 | Tú'àn | Design |
| 式样 | Shìyàng | Style |
| 规格 | Guīgé | Norms; standards |
| 予以 | Yǔyǐ | 予以 and 加以 both mean "to do x." In English, we would not translate either |
| 公告 | Gōnggào | Public announcement |
| 发售 | Fāshòu | Sell; put on sale |
| 代 | Dài | Substitute |
| 币 | Bì | Money; currency |
| 票 | Piào | Bank note; bill |
| 券 | Quàn | Ticket; certificate |
| 以 | Yǐ | In order to |
| 代替 | Dàitì | Replace |
| 库 | Kù | Depository |
| 分支 | Fēnzhī | Branch |
| 调拨 | Diàobō | Allocate |
| 基金 | Jījīn | Funds |
| 按照 | Ànzhào | In accordance with |
| 上级 | Shàngjí | Higher, superior level |
| 办理 | Bànlǐ | Handle; take care of |

| | | |
|---|---|---|
| 违反 | Wéifǎn | Violate (a law) |
| 动用 | Dòngyòng | Draw on; use |
| 运用 | Yùnyòng | Utilize; apply |
| 工具 | Gōngjù | Means; tools; instruments |
| 要求 | Yāoqiú | Demands; requirements |
| 银行业 | Yínhángyè | Banking (industry/sector) |
| 比例 | Bǐlì | Ratio; proportion |
| 交存 | Jiāocún | Deposit |
| 存款 | Cúnkuǎn | Bank deposits (n.) |
| 准备金 | Zhǔnbèijīn | Reserves; depository reserves |
| 确定 | Quèdìng | Define; fix; determine |
| 基准 (基本标准) | Jīzhǔn (Jīběn biāozhǔn) | Benchmark (interest) rate |
| 开立 | Kāilì | Open |
| 账户 | Zhànghù | Bank accounts |
| 再贴现 | Zàitiēxiàn | Rediscount |
| 向 | Xiàng | 向 and 对 combine with a number of different verbs to generally mean "to" or "for" |
| 商业银行 | Shāngyè yínháng | Commercial banks |
| 提供 | Tígōng | Provide; offer |
| 贷款 | Dàikuǎn | (bank) Loan |
| 公开 | Gōngkāi | Open; public |

| 国债 | Guózhài | National debt |
|------|---------|---------------|
| 政府 | Zhèngfǔ | Government |
| 及 | Jí | And; as well as (literary Chinese meaning the same as 和 and 跟) |
| 所列 | Suǒliè | Listed (lit. which are listed in x) |
| 具体 | Jùtǐ | Concrete; specific |
| 条件 | Tiáojiàn | Requirements; conditions |
| 法律 | Fǎlǜ | Law |
| 行政 | Xíngzhèng | Administrative |
| 法规 | Fǎguī | Administrative laws and regulations[7] |
| 协助 | Xiézhù | Provide assistance |
| 相互 | Xiānghù | Mutually |
| 之间 | Zhījiān | Between; among |
| 协调 | Xiétiáo | Coordinate |
| 服务 | Fúwù | Service |
| 办法 | Bànfǎ | Rules; regulations |
| 会同 | Huìtóng | Handle jointly with |
| 结算 | Jiésuàn | Settlement |
| 规则 | Guīzé | Rule; regulation |

---

7 Law Practice Tip: "行政法规" are legislations adopted by the State Council. They are the third level of legislation in China, only lower than the Constitution and Laws passed by National People's Congress or its Standing Committee.

| | | |
|---|---|---|
| 对 | Duì | 向 and 对 combine with a number of different verbs to generally mean "to" or "for" |
| 数额 | Shù'é | Amount |
| 期限 | Qīxiàn | Time limit; term |
| 方式 | Fāngshì | Manner; method |
| 地方 | Dìfāng | Local |
| 各级 | Gèjí | All levels |
| 部门 | Bùmén | Department; branch; section |
| 非 | Fēi | Non-; not- |
| 以及 | Yǐjí | As well as; and; too |
| 但 x 除外 | Dàn x chúwài | With the exception of x |
| 特定 | Tèdìng | Specific; specified; specially designated |
| 担保 | Dānbǎo | Guarantee |
| 权 | Quán | Authority; power; right |
| 行为 | Xíngwéi | Act; conduct; behavior |
| 进行 | Jìnxíng | Carry out; conduct |
| 检查 | Jiǎnchá | Examine; inspect |
| 特种 | Tèzhǒng | Special type |
| 代理 | Dàilǐ | Represent; act as an agent |
| 所称 y 是指 z | Suǒchēng y shìzhǐ z | The term y means z |
| 发放 | Fāfàng | Provide; give; grant |

| 用于 | Yòngyú | Use for or in |
|---|---|---|
| 目的 | Mùdì | Purpose |
| 建议 | Jiànyì | Suggest |
| 自 x 起 | Zì x qǐ | Beginning from x |
| 收到 | Shōudào | Receive |
| 之 | Zhī | Literary Chinese. The modern charater would be 的 |
| 回复 | Huífù | Reply; response |
| 报送 | Bàosòng | Submit |
| 必要 | Bìyào | Necessary; essential; indispensible |
| 资产负债表 | Zīchǎn fùzhài biǎo | Balance sheet (lit. asset and debt statement) |
| 利润表 | Lìrùn biǎo | Income statement |
| 财务 | Cáiwù | Financial |
| 会计 | Kuàijì | Accounting |
| 报表 | Bàobiǎo | Forms (for reporting statistics); report forms |
| 资料 | Zīliào | Data; materials |
| 建立 | Jiànlì | Establish |
| 信息 | Xìnxí | Information |
| 共享 | Gòngxiǎng | Share |
| 机制 | Jīzhì | Mechanism |

| 收入 | Shōurù | Income; revenue |
| --- | --- | --- |
| 减除 | Jiǎnchú | Minus; deduct |
| 该 | Gāi | That[8] |
| 支出 | Zhīchū | Expenses; expenditures |
| 财政 | Cáizhèng | Financial; finance |
| 核定 | Hédìng | Checked and ratified; appraised and decided upon |
| 提取 | Tíqǔ | Withdraw (from a bank) |
| 总 | Zǒng | Total |
| 净利润 | Jìnglìrùn | Net profit |
| 上缴 | Shàngjiǎo | Turn in or hand over (money) to a higher body |
| 亏损 | Kuīsǔn | Deficit; financial loss |
| 拨款 | Bōkuǎn | Allocate funds |
| 弥补 | Míbǔ | Cover; make up for a deficiency |
| 责任 | Zérèn | Responsibility; liability |
| 处罚 | Chǔfá | Penalty |
| 的 | De | 的 is often used without the term it modifies. Here the missing term could be 时候 (time, i.e. "when") or 情况 (circumstance) |

---

8 Law Practice Tip: In modern legal English the term "that" is used. In older legal English, the term "said" is used.

| 给予 | Jǐyǔ | Give |
|---|---|---|
| 未 | Wèi | Literary Chinese for 还没 |
| 区别 | Qūbié | Distinguish |
| 情形 | Qíngxíng | Circumstances; situation |
| 警告 | Jǐnggào | Warn; admonish |
| 没收 | Mòshōu | Confiscate; expropriate |
| 违法 | Wéifǎ | Illegal |
| 所得 | Suǒdé | What you have obtained |
| 处 | Chǔ | Sentence to |
| 倍 | Bèi | Times (multiplier) |
| 罚款 | Fákuǎn | Penalty; fine |
| 不足 | Bùzú | Less than |
| 负有 | Fùyǒu | Bear; carry |
| 直接 | Zhíjiē | Direct |
| 董事 | Dǒngshì | Director |
| 人员 | Rényuán | Personnel |
| 构成 | Gòuchéng | Form; constitute |
| 犯罪 | Fànzuì | Commit a crime |
| 追究 | Zhuījiū | Investigate and affix (responsibility or liability) |
| 刑事 | Xíngshì | Criminal |

| | | |
|---|---|---|
| 当事人 | Dāngshìrén | Parties; party |
| 不服 | Bùfú | Refuse to obey; do not accept |
| 诉讼 | Sùsòng | Litigation |
| 提起 | Tíqǐ | Bring (an action) |
| 之一 | Zhīyī | 的一个 |
| 主管 | Zhǔguǎn | Responsible for; in charge of |
| 处分 | Chǔfèn | Sanction; punish |
| 擅自 | Shànzì | Do sth. without authorization |
| 造成 | Zàochéng | Cause; bring about |
| 损失 | Sǔnshī | Loss (financial, economic, etc.) |
| 承担 | Chéngdān | Assume; bear |
| 部分 | Bùfen | Partial |
| 赔偿 | Péicháng | Compensate |
| 社会团体 | Shèhuì tuántǐ | Social organizations (usually refers to NGOs) |
| 强令 | Qiánglìng | Forcibly or arbitrarily give orders |
| 及其 | Jíqí | And; as well as (literary Chinese) |
| 泄露 | Xièlòu | Leak (information); divulge |
| 秘密 | Mìmì | Secret |
| 知悉 | Zhīxī | Know; learn of |
| 尚 | Shàng | Literary Chinese for 还没 |

# D. Notice of the China Banking Regulatory Commission on Further Strengthening Mortgage Loan Risk Management (2009) Text[9]

## 银监会关于进一步 加强 按揭 贷款 风险 管理的 通知

各银监局，各政策性银行、国有 商业银行、股份制商业银行，中国邮政储蓄银行：

最近，部分地区 房地产 市场出现较大 波动，房地产信贷 尤其是按揭贷款业务中诸如"假按揭"、"假首付"、"假房价"、"二套房贷"标准放宽等问题也开始有所 暴露。为加强信贷管理，切实 防范按揭贷款风险，促进按揭贷款业务健康 有序发展，现 将有关事宜通知如下：

一、加强房地产行业 形势 研判。各银行业金融机构要进一步加强宏观经济 运行、相关行业产业状况、相关政策面的分析 研究，密切 关注房地产市场走势、行业运作 特征，密切关注经济周期、市场波动、资金 链 松紧、居民 预期

---

9 Source: Yin jian hui guan yu jin yi bu jia qiang an jie dai kuan feng xian guan li de tong zhi [Notice of the China Banking Regulatory Commission on Further Strengthening Mortgage Loan Risk Management] (issued by the China Banking Regulatory Commission, June 19, 2009) *available at* www.chinalawinfo.com or at http://www.romaway.com/finance/BShowNews-1170743.html (last visited May 30, 2011).

变化等可能给按揭贷款业务带来的风险。

二、严格 贷前 检查和按揭贷款发放 标准。各银行业金融机构要严格执行《国务院 办公厅关于促进房地产市场健康发展的若干 意见》(国办发(2008) 131号)、《中国人民银行 中国银行业监督管理委员会关于加强商业性房地产信贷管理的通知》(银发〔2007〕359号)、《中国银监会关于进一步加强房地产行业授信风险管理的通知》(银监发[2008]42号)规定，坚持贷款风险审慎指标 控制，严格借款人 资格 审查，注重 从 源头 上防范贷款风险。要坚持面测 面试和实 访 制，把做实每笔贷款的尽职 调查作为发放贷款的前提 条件。坚持落实 借款 合同 面签 制度，核实借款人首付款 真实情况，采取切实有效措施防范"假按揭"、"假首付"现象的发生。

坚持重点 支持借款人购买 首套 自住 住房的贷款需求，严格遵守第二套房贷的有关政策不动摇。要坚持贷款标准，严格借款人资格审查，审慎评估借款人风险，确定 合理的贷款利率。不得以 征信 系统未联网、异地 购房难调查等为 由 放弃"二套房贷"政策约束，不得自行 解释"二套房贷"认定标准，不得以任何手段 变相 降低首付款的比例 成数。

三、进一步完善按揭贷款风险防控制度。各银行业金融机构要根据外部市场环境的变化 以及 自身业务发展的需要，建立完善与自身

承受 能力和风险管理能力相适应的按揭贷款管理体制 机制，按照审慎经营 原则 细 化有关操作要求和业务流程，合理配置 资源，全面 提升对按揭贷款客户的风险识别、计量和管理能力。做好客户群识别与区分工作，改善 差别化服务水平，提高差别化管理与定价能力。进一步优化 业绩 考核体系，从制度上引导 分支 机构重视 内控机制建设和风险管理。

四、进一步加强按揭贷款风险状况动态防控。对已经发放的按揭贷款，要加强监测和分析，用好银监会客户风险监测预警 系统，重点做好对客户违约以及交叉违约情况的监测。加强对房地产抵押物的管理，定期对抵押物价值重估和动态监测，必须时采取追加担保或压缩贷款等动态风险控制措施。对于 违反 "二套房贷"规定发放的住房按揭贷款，即使贷款已分类为正常类或关注类，各银行业金融机构要重新对其分类，同时要严格追究相关违规责任人员的责任，并及时将拨备 补提情况和责任人追究查处情况上报 相应 监管 部门。银行业协会要充分 发挥 协调、维权 职能，进一步加强行业信息 共享机制、风险防控合作机制的建设，健全完善"黑名单"制度，必要时组织采取协调一致的风险处置措施。

五、加大 监督 力度和对违法 违规 行为的查处力度。各级银行业监管机构加大对按揭贷款业务的监管力度，认真梳理 存在的问题，开

展有针对性的调查、抽查、暗访和现场检查，加强窗口指导和风险提示，切实防范信贷风险。对检查中发现的违法违规问题，要督促进行整改，严肃追究责任，对问题比较严重、整改不到位、屡查屡犯、继续违规的机构和责任人员要加大处罚力度，可视情况依法采取包括准入限制在内的相关监管措施，如暂停相关机构(分支机构)房地产按揭贷款业务、暂停房地产贷款业务条线的高管准入、暂停境内外新设机构准入等。对因贷前、贷中、贷后管理不到位、制度执行不到位造成损失的机构和责任人，要落实责任，严肃处罚。对银行业金融机构内部工作人员和外部不法分子勾结、合伙骗贷的，一经查实，要严肃追究责任，涉嫌犯罪的依法送司法机构处理。查处中发现的重大事项，各银监局要及时上报。

中国银行业监督管理委员会

二〇〇九年六月十九日

# E. Vocabulary of Notice of the China Banking Regulatory Commission on Further Strengthening Mortgage Loan Risk Management (2009)

| Chinese | Pinyin | English |
| --- | --- | --- |
| 银监会 (中国银行业监督管理委员会) | Yínjiānhuì (Zhōngguó Yínháng Yè Jiāndū Guǎnlǐ Wěiyuánhuì) | China Banking Regulatory Commission |
| 进一步 | Jìnyībù | Further |
| 加强 | Jiāqiáng | Strengthen |
| 按揭 | Ànjiē | Mortgage |
| 贷款 | Dàikuǎn | Loan |
| 风险 | Fēngxiǎn | Risk |
| 管理 | Guǎnlǐ | Manage |
| 通知 | Tōngzhī | Notice |
| 银监局 | Yínjiān Jú | Banking authority |

| | | |
|---|---|---|
| 政策性银行 | Zhèngcèxìng yínháng | (Government) Policy/non-commercial bank[10] |
| 国有 | Guóyǒu | State-owned |
| 商业 | Shāngyè | Commercial |
| 股份制商业银行 | Gǔfènzhì shāngyè yínháng | Joint-stock commercial bank |
| 邮政储蓄银行 | Yóuzhèng chǔxù yínháng | Postal savings bank |
| 地区 | Dìqū | Region |
| 房地产 | Fángdìchǎn | Real estate |
| 市场 | Shìchǎng | Market |
| 较大 | Jiàodà | Comparatively large[11] |
| 波动 | Bōdòng | Fluctuation |
| 信贷 | Xìndài | (financial) Credit |
| 尤其 | Yóuqí | Especially; particularly |
| 业务 | Yèwù | Business |
| 诸如 | Zhūrú | Such as |
| 假按揭 | Jiǎ ànjiē | False mortgage[12] |

---

10 Background Tip: These are non-profit banks established and funded by the Central government to support government policy. There are only three such banks: the Export-Import Bank of China, China Development Bank, and Agricultural Development Bank of China.

11 Law Practice Tip: The term "relatively large" is often used in Chinese law. In the Law on Legislation, the term is defined later in the text of the law. In the Criminal Law, the term is typically defined by later interpretations by the Supreme People's Court.

12 Background Tip: When a real estate developer falsely "sells" property to employees or relatives in order to apply for a loan from a bank.

| 假首付 | Jiǎ shǒufù | False down payment |
|---|---|---|
| 假房价 | Jiǎ fángjià | False price |
| 二套房贷 | Èrtàofángdài | One mortgage for two residences[13] |
| 放宽 | Fàngkuān | Relax restrictions |
| 有所 | Yǒusuǒ | Somewhat; to some extent |
| 暴露 | Bàolù | Expose; reveal |
| 切实 | Qièshí | Feasible; realistic |
| 防范 | Fángfàn | Look out for; be on guard |
| 促进 | Cùjìn | Promote; advance |
| 健康 | Jiànkāng | Healthy |
| 有序 | Yǒuxù | To be orderly |
| 现 | Xiàn | 现在 |
| 将 | Jiāng | Literary Chinese for 把 |
| 事宜 | Shìyí | Relevant matters |
| 如下 | Rúxià | As set forth below |
| 行业 | Hángyè | Trade; profession; industry |
| 形势 | Xíngshì | Circumstances |
| 研判 (研究判断) | Yán pàn (Yánjiū pànduàn) | Look into and determine |

---

13 Background Tip: Part of the mortgage loan would initially be used to purchase the principal residence. The rest of the mortgage loan would be used to purchase a second (or more) residence.

| 金融机构 | Jīnróng jīgòu | Financial organization; structure |
|---|---|---|
| 宏观经济 | Hóngguān jīngjì | Macro-economy |
| 运行 | Yùnxíng | Operation; function |
| 相关 | Xiāngguān | Related |
| 产业 | Chǎnyè | Industry |
| 分析 | Fēnxī | Analysis |
| 研究 | Yánjiū | Look into; research the possibility of |
| 密切 | Mìqiè | Closely |
| 关注 | Guānzhù | Follow closely; pay close attention to |
| 走势 | Zǒushì | Trend |
| 运作 | Yùnzuò | Operation |
| 特征 | Tèzhēng | Characteristic |
| 周期 | Zhōuqī | Cycle |
| 资金 | Zījīn | Funds; funding |
| 链 | Liàn | Chain |
| 松紧 | Sōngjǐn | Tightness; elasticity (lit. loose/tight) |
| 居民 | Jūmín | Resident; inhabitant |
| 预期 | Yùqī | Anticipated; expected |
| 严格 | Yángé | Strict; rigorous |
| 贷前 | Dàiqián | Pre-loan |
| 检查 | Jiǎnchá | Examination; inspection |
| 发放 | Fāfàng | Provide; give; grant |

| | | |
|---|---|---|
| 标准 | Biāozhǔn | Standard |
| 执行 | Zhíxíng | Carry out; implement |
| 国务院 | Guówùyuàn | State Council |
| 办公厅 | Bàngōngtīng | General Office |
| 若干 | Ruògān | Several |
| 意见 | Yìjiàn | Opinion |
| 授信 | Shòuxìn | Credit |
| 规定 | Guīdìng | Stipulate; provide |
| 坚持 | Jiānchí | Unremitting; persistent |
| 审慎 | Shěnshèn | Cautious; careful |
| 指标 | Zhǐbiāo | Indicator |
| 控制 | Kòngzhì | Control |
| 借款人 | Jièkuǎnrén | Borrower |
| 资格 | Zīgé | Qualifications |
| 审查 | Shěnchá | Investigate; review |
| 注重 | Zhùzhòng | Pay attention to; emphasize |
| 从 x 上 | Cóng x shàng | From x |
| 源头 | Yuántóu | Source |
| 面测 | Miàncè | Investigate in person |
| 面试 | Miànshì | In-person interview |
| 实 | Shí | Actual; real |
| 访 (访问) | Fǎng (Fǎngwèn) | Visit; call on |

| | | |
|---|---|---|
| 制 (制度) | Zhì (Zhìdù) | System (administrative; political) |
| 笔 | Bǐ | Counter for sums of money, e.g. debts |
| 尽职 | Jìnzhí | Do or fulfill one's duty |
| 调查 | Diàochá | Investigate |
| 前提 | Qiántí | Premise |
| 条件 | Tiáojiàn | Requirement; condition |
| 落实 | Luòshí | Implement |
| 借款合同 | Jièkuǎn hétóng | Loan contract |
| 面签 | Miànqiān | Sign in person |
| 核实 | Héshí | Verify |
| 首付款 | Shǒufùkuǎn | Down payment |
| 真实 | Zhēnshí | True; real |
| 采取 | Cǎiqǔ | Adopt; take |
| 有效 | Yǒuxiào | Valid; effective |
| 措施 | Cuòshī | Measures; steps |
| 现象 | Xiànxiàng | Appearance; phenomenon |
| 发生 | Fāshēng | Occur; happen |
| 重点 | Zhòngdiǎn | Emphasis; focus |
| 支持 | Zhīchí | Support |
| 购买 | Gòumǎi | Purchase |
| 首套 | Shǒutào | First residence (套 is the measure word for 房) |

| 自住 | Zìzhù | Personal residence |
|------|-------|--------------------|
| 住房 | Zhùfáng | Housing |
| 需求 | Xūqiú | Needs |
| 遵守 | Zūnshǒu | Adhere to; abide by |
| 房贷 (住房贷款) | Fángdài (Zhùfáng dàikuǎn) | Residential mortgage |
| 动摇 | Dòngyáo | Waver; be indecisive |
| 评估 | Pínggū | Evaluate; evaluation |
| 确定 | Quèdìng | Define; fix; determine |
| 合理 | Hélǐ | Reasonable |
| 利率 | Lìlǜ | Interest rate |
| 以 x 为 y | Yǐ x wéi y | Take x as y |
| 征信 | Zhēngxìn | Credit information or financial statement for an individual or group |
| 系统 | Xìtǒng | System |
| 联网 | Liánwǎng | Network |
| 异地 | Yìdì | In another place |
| 购房 | Gòufáng | Purchase of a house |
| 由 (理由) | Yóu (Lǐyóu) | Reason; grounds |
| 放弃 | Fàngqì | Abandon; give up |
| 约束 | Yuèshù | Binding |
| 自行 | Zìxíng | By oneself |

| | | |
|---|---|---|
| 解释 | Jiěshì | Interpret; interpretation |
| 认定 | Rèndìng | Determine; establish |
| 手段 | Shǒuduàn | Method |
| 变相 | Biànxiàng | Covert; in disguised form |
| 降低 | Jiàngdī | Reduce; lower |
| 比例 | Bǐlì | Proportion |
| 成数 | Chéngshù | Percentage |
| 完善 | Wánshàn | Improve; perfect |
| 防控 | Fángkòng | Prevention and control |
| 银行业 | Yínhángyè | Banking (industry/sector) |
| 外部 | Wàibù | External |
| 变化 | Biànhuà | Change |
| 以及 | Yǐjí | As well as; and (literary Chinese meaning the same as 跟 and 和) |
| 自身 | Zìshēn | Self; oneself |
| 建立 | Jiànlì | Establish |
| 与 | Yǔ | And; together with |
| 承受 | Chéngshòu | Bear; accept |
| 能力 | Nénglì | Ability; capability; capacity |
| 适应 | Shìyìng | Suit; fit |
| 体制 | Tǐzhì | System |
| 机制 | Jīzhì | Mechanism |

| 按照 | Ànzhào | In accordance with |
|------|--------|---------------------|
| 经营 | Jīngyíng | Engage in or run a business |
| 原则 | Yuánzé | Principle |
| 细 | Xì | Detail |
| 化 | Huà | -ize (lit. change to x) |
| 操作 | Cāozuò | Operations |
| 流程 | Liúchéng | Procedure |
| 配置 | Pèizhì | Deploy |
| 资源 | Zīyuán | Natural resources |
| 全面 | Quánmiàn | All around; comprehensive; total; overall |
| 提升 | Tíshēng | Promote; raise |
| 客户 | Kèhù | Client; customer |
| 识别 | Shíbié | Discern; identify |
| 计量 | Jìliàng | Measure; quantify |
| 群 | Qún | Group; grouping |
| 区分 | Qūfēn | Separate; delineate |
| 改善 | Gǎishàn | Improve |
| 差别 | Chābié | Differentiation |
| 定价 | Dìngjià | Fixed or set price |
| 优化 | Yōuhuà | Optimize |
| 业绩 | Yèjì | Achievement |
| 考核体系 | Kǎohétǐxì | Evaluation system |

| 引导 | Yǐndǎo | Guide; lead |
|------|--------|-------------|
| 分支 | Fēnzhī | Branch |
| 机构 | Jīgòu | Organization; organ |
| 重视 | Zhòngshì | Treat as important |
| 内控 | Nèikòng | Internal controls |
| 建设 | Jiànshè | Construction |
| 动态 | Dòngtài | Dynamic |
| 监测 | Jiāncè | Monitor |
| 预警 | Yùjǐng | Early warning |
| 系统 | Xìtǒng | System |
| 违约 | Wéiyuē | Breach; violate (a contract) |
| 交叉 | Jiāochā | Cross; simultaneous |
| 抵押物 | Dǐyáwù | Collateral (the estate under mortgage) |
| 定期 | Dìngqī | Regularly |
| 价值 | Jiàzhí | Value; worth |
| 重估 | Chónggū | Re-calculate; re-evaluate |
| 追加 | Zhuījiā | Supplement |
| 压缩 | Yāsuō | Compress; reduce |
| 对于 | Duìyú | As for; toward |
| 违反 | Wéifǎn | Violate (a law) |
| 即使 | Jíshǐ | Even if |
| 分类 | Fēnlèi | Classify |

| | | |
|---|---|---|
| 正常 | Zhèngcháng | Regular; normal |
| 其 | Qí | Literary Chinese for 他 or 它 |
| 追究 | Zhuījiū | Investigate and affix (responsibility or liability) |
| 拨备 | Bōbèi | Loss reserves |
| 补提 | Bǔtí | Raise; increase |
| 查处 | Cháchǔ | Investigate and handle |
| 上报 | Shàngbào | Report upward |
| 相应 | Xiāngyìng | Corresponding |
| 监管 | Jiānguǎn | Oversee; supervise |
| 部门 | Bùmén | Department; branch; section |
| 银行业协会 | Yínhángyè xiéhuì | Banking association |
| 充分 | Chōngfèn | Fully |
| 发挥 | Fāhuī | Give free reign to; bring into play |
| 协调 | Xiétiáo | Coordinate |
| 维权 (维护权力) | Wéiquán (Wéihù quánlì) | Protection of rights |
| 职能 | Zhínéng | Function; role |
| 信息 | Xìnxī | Information |
| 共享 | Gòngxiǎng | Share |
| 健全 | Jiànquán | Perfect; strengthen |
| 黑名单 | Hēimíngdān | Blacklist |
| 组织 | Zǔzhī | Organization |

| | | |
|---|---|---|
| 一致 | Yīzhì | Identical (views or opinions) |
| 处置 | Chǔzhì | Handle; dispose of |
| 加大 | Jiādà | Increase; intensify |
| 监督 | Jiāndū | Control; supervise |
| 力度 | Lìdù | Strength |
| 违法违规 | Wéifǎ wéiguī | Illegal (lit. violate laws and/or regulations) |
| 行为 | Xíngwéi | Act; conduct; behavior |
| 梳理 | Shūlǐ | Put in order |
| 存在 | Cúnzài | Existing |
| 开展 | Kāizhǎn | Develop; launch; unfold |
| 针对 | Zhēnduì | Aimed or directed at |
| 抽查 | Chōuchá | Spot-check; carry out selective examinations |
| 暗访 | Ànfǎng | Conduct a secret investigation |
| 现场 | Xiànchǎng | Site |
| 指导 | Zhǐdǎo | Guide; direct |
| 提示 | Tíshì | Point out; call attention to |
| 督促 (监督促进) | Dūcù (Jiāndū cùjìn) | Supervise and urge |
| 进行 | Jìnxíng | Carry out; conduct |
| 整改 | Zhěnggǎi | Rectify |
| 严肃 | Yánsù | Strictly |
| 到位 | Dàowèi | Reach goal; meet standard |

| | | |
|---|---|---|
| 屡查屡犯 | Lǚchá lǚfàn | Repeat investigation or repeat offenders |
| 处罚 | Chǔfá | Penalize; punish |
| 可视情况 | KěShìqíngkuàng | Depending on the circumstances |
| 依法 | Yīfǎ | Legally; in accordance with the law |
| 准入 | Zhǔnrù | Permit to enter |
| 限制 | Xiànzhì | Restrict; limit |
| 暂停 | Zàntíng | Suspend |
| 条线 | Tiáoxiàn | Line (of business) |
| 高管 (高级管理) | Gāoguǎn (Gāojíguǎnlǐ) | Executive or senior management |
| 境内外 | Jìngnèiwài | Domestic and foreign |
| 新设 | Xìnshè | Newly established |
| 造成 | Zàochéng | Cause; bring about |
| 损失 | Sǔnshī | Loss (financial or economic, etc.) |
| 不法 | Bùfǎ | Lawless |
| 分子 | Fènzǐ | Elements |
| 勾结 | Gōujié | Collude with |
| 合伙 | Héhuǒ | Partner |
| 骗贷 | Piàndài | To get a loan by cheating |
| 的 | De | 的 is often used without the term it modifies. Here, the omitted term is probably 时候 (when) or 情况 (circumstances) |

| 经 (经过) | Jīng (Jīngguò) | Go through; be x'd |
|---|---|---|
| 查实 | Cháshí | Check and verify (lit. check the truthfulness or accuracy) |
| 涉嫌 | Shèxián | Suspected of a crime |
| 犯罪 | Fànzuì | Commit a crime |
| 司法 | Sīfǎ | Judicial |
| 处理 | Chǔlǐ | Handle; deal with |

# Chapter 10
# Company Law

# 公 司 法

Gōng　Sī　Fǎ

# A. Introduction to Company Law in the People's Republic of China

By *Wang Zhizhou*, LLM

The company is a fundamental form of business organization. People incorporate their capital, assets, and intellectual property or even management skills, to conduct massive production and resist unexpected, but potentially huge, commercial risks. Therefore, the company is vital for a modern economic system. The history of company law in China is quite short compared with that of the western world, but the oftentimes politically-charged nature of its development in China is an interesting phenomenon.

In the West, companies were part of the industrial revolution. In China, companies did not emerge until the early development of capitalism and the demands of industrial production near the end of the Qing dynasty. The Qing commercial code was part of the basis for the 1929 Corporate Regulations of Republic of China ("ROC"), which was then replaced by the 1946 Corporate Law. In 1949, with the founding of the People's Republic of China, this law was abolished, but a problem arose as how to deal with those companies already established under the old legal system.

A provisional regulation on privately-owned enterprises was promulgated in 1950 and, during the process of socialist transformation from 1956 to 1966, private corporations were phased out. Officials appointed by the government were to control enterprises to ensure the government's economic plans would be strictly implemented.

Following the 1978 reform and opening up, fundamental change occurred to the political and economic system. As Deng Xiaoping then pointed out, China's focus should turn to the development of the national economy, and accordingly, capital, advanced technology, and new ideas for economic development from foreign countries should be examined.

In order to attract and encourage foreign investment, China enacted the 1979 Law of the PRC on Equity Joint Ventures which expressly stipulated that the form of an equity joint venture ("EJV") must be a limited liability company ("LLC"). In 1986, the Law of the PRC on Wholly Foreign-owned Enterprises also set the LLC as the standard form for wholly owned foreign investment enterprises.

Legislation regulating purely domestic enterprises was also enacted. These laws and regulations, however, were made based on a system of classifying business organizations by their ownership which caused unnecessary different and unfair treatment. Another problem with this system was that the internal governance structure was ignored by both the NPC and the government-appointed management of the enterprises. Huge business failures resulted, together with a flood of fraud and corruption cases.

Decades after they were abolished by the socialist transformation in the 1960s, the concepts of shareholders and equity were recognized again by the government in the early 1990s. The first true company law of the PRC took effect in 1994. It was the product of lengthy discussions and was designed to help the failing SOEs get rid of their operational difficulties by transplanting a modern, internal corporate structure.

The 1993 law introduced concepts which were important for the modern management and healthy operation of corporations, e.g. issuance of shares and bonds, account books and a financial system, merger, bankruptcy, as well as dissolution and liquidation. The 1993 law also paved the way for corporations to seek financing in the capital markets.

The most recent stage in the evolution of company law in China took place in 2005 when the Standing Committee of the NPC enacted the current company law. Although on the surface the 2005 law looks similar to the 1993 law in terms of their basic structure, there are important conceptual changes. The new law makes incorporation easier and encourages corporate autonomy.

The law also allows establishment of a company with a sole shareholder and improves the internal governance structure. Shareholders play a much more important and active role in running a corporation, e.g. shareholders may ask the court to intervene if they believe that the act of an officer or director threatens the interests of the company. An independent director system was introduced and minority shareholders' interests are better protected. In addition, the doctrine of piercing the corporate veil is now recognized for the first time.

The Supreme People's Court issued two judicial interpretations of the 2005 law, first in 2006 and again in 2008.

# B. Text of Company Law (2006)[1]

# 中华人民共和国公司法

第一章 总则

第一条 为了规范公司的组织和行为，保护公司、股东和债权人的合法权益，维护社会经济 秩序，促进社会主义市场经济的发展，*制定*本法。

第二条 本法*所称*公司*是指* 依照本法在中国境内 设立的有限 责任公司和股份有限公司。

第三条 公司是企业 法人，有独立的法人财产，享有法人财产权。公司以 其全部财产*对*公司的债务 承担责任。

有限责任公司的股东*以*其认缴的出资 额为 限对公司承担责任；股份有限公司的股东以其认购的股份为限对公司承担责任。

第四条 公司股东依法享有资产收益、参与重大决策和选择 管理 者等权利。

第五条 公司从事 经营活动，必须遵守法

---

1 Source: Zhonghua Renmin Gongheguo Zhongguo gong si fa [Company Law (P.R.C.)] (promulgated by the Nat'l People's Cong., Oct. 27, 2005, effective Jan. 1, 2006) *available at* http://www.gov.cn/flfg/2005-10/28/content_85478.htm (last visited May 30, 2011).

律、**行政法规**, 遵守社会公德、**商业 道德**, **诚实 守信**, **接受**政府和社会公众的监督, 承担社会责任。

公司的合法权益受法律保护, 不受**侵犯**。

**第六条** 设立公司, 应当依*法向*公司登记 机关 申请设立登记。**符合**本法规定的设立**条件**的, 由公司登记机关分别登记为有限责任公司或者股份有限公司; 不符合本法规定的设立条件的, 不得登记为有限责任公司或者股份有限公司。

法律、行政法规规定设立公司**必须** *报经批准*的, 应当在公司登记前**依法** **办理**批准手续。

公众可以向公司登记机关申请**查询**公司登记事项, 公司登记机关应当提供查询**服务**。

**第七条** 依法设立的公司, 由公司登记机关**发给**公司**营业** 执照。公司营业执照签发日期为公司成立日期。

公司营业执照应当**载明**公司的**名称**、住所、**注册** 资本、**实收**资本、经营范围、**法定 代表**人姓名等事项。

公司营业执照记载的事项发生**变更**的, 公司应当依法办理变更登记, 由公司登记机关**换发**营业执照。

**第八条** 依照本法设立的有限责任公司, 必须在公司名称中**标明**有限责任公司或者有限公司**字样**。

依照本法设立的股份有限公司, 必须在公司名称中标明股份有限公司或者股份公司字样。

**第九条** 有限责任公司变更为股份有限公司, 应当符合本法规定的股份有限公司的条件。股份有限公司变更为有限责任公司, 应当符合本法规定的有限责任公司的条件。

有限责任公司变更为股份有限公司的, 或者股份有限公司变更为有限责任公司的, 公司变更前的**债权**、债务由变更后的公司**承继**。

**第十条** 公司以其**主要**办事**机构** 所在地为住所。

**第十一条** 设立公司必须依法制定公司**章程**。公司章程对公司、股东、**董事**、**监事**、**高级**管理人员具有 约束 力。

**第十二条** 公司的经营范围由公司章程规定, 并依法登记。公司可以**修改**公司章程, 改变经营范围, 但是应当办理变更登记。

公司的经营范围中属于法律、行政法规规定须经批准的项目, 应当依法经过批准。

**第十三条** 公司法定代表人依照公司章程的规定, 由董事长、**执行董事**或者经理**担任**, 并依法登记。公司法定代表人变更, 应当办理变更登记。

**第十四条** 公司可以设立**分公司**。设立分公司, 应当向公司登记机关申请登记, **领取**营业执照。分公司不具有法人**资格**, 其**民事**责任由公司承担。

公司可以设立子公司,子公司具有法人资格,依法独立承担民事责任。

第十五条 公司可以向**其他**企业**投资**;但是,除法律另有规定外,**不得**成为对所投资企业的债务承担**连带**责任的出资人。

第十六条 公司向其他企业投资或者为他人**提供 担保**,依照公司章程的规定,由董事会或者股东会、股东大会**决议**;公司章程对投资或者担保的**总额**及单项投资或者担保的**数额**有**限额**规定的,不得**超过**规定的限额。

公司为公司股东或者实际**控制**人提供担保的,必须经股东会或者股东大会决议。

**前款**规定的股东或者受前款规定的实际控制人**支配**的股东,不得参加前款规定事项的**表决**。**该**项表决由**出席**会议的其他股东所持表决权的**过半数 通过**。

第十七条 公司必须保护**职工**的合法**权益**,依法与职工**签订 劳动 合同**,参加社会保险,**加强**劳动保护,**实现 安全 生产**。

公司应当采用多种**形式**,加强公司职工的**职业 教育**和**岗位 培训**,提高职工**素质**。

第十八条 公司职工依照《中华人民共和国**工会法**》组织工会,**开展**工会活动,维护职工合法权益。公司应当为本公司工会提供必要的活动条件。公司工会代表职工**就**职工的劳动**报酬**、工作时间、**福利**、保险和劳动安全**卫生**等事项依法与公司签订**集体**合同。

公司依照**宪法**和**有关**法律的规定,通过职工代表大会或者其他形式,实行**民主**管理。

公司**研究**决定**改制**以及经营方面的重大问题、制定重要的**规章**制度时,应当听取公司工会的意见,并**通过**职工代表大会或者其他形式听取职工的意见和**建议**。

# C. Vocabulary of Company Law (2006)

| Chinese | Pinyin | English |
| --- | --- | --- |
| 公司 | Gōngsī | Company |
| 章 | Zhāng | Chapter[2] |
| 总则 | Zǒngzé | General principles |
| 规范 | Gūifàn | Standardize; normalize |
| 组织 | Zǔzhī | Organization |
| 行为 | Xíngwéi | Act; conduct; behavior |
| 股东 | Gǔdōng | Shareholder |
| 债权人 | Zhàiquánrén | Creditor |
| 合法 | Héfǎ | Legal |
| 权益 | Quányì | Rights and interests |
| 维护 | Wéihù | Protect |
| 经济 | Jīngjì | Economy |

---

2 Law Practice Tip: There is no standard English translation for this term and related terms such as 条 tiáo (Article). In part, this is because their usage in Chinese is not standardized.

| | | |
|---|---|---|
| 秩序 | Zhìxù | Order |
| 促进 | Cùjìn | Promote; advance |
| 市场 | Shìchǎng | Market |
| 发展 | Fāzhǎn | Development |
| 制定 | Zhìdìng | Formulate; enact |
| 所称 y 是指 z | Suǒchēng y shìzhǐ z | The term y means z |
| 依照 | Yīzhào | In accordance with |
| 境内 | Jìngnèi | Domestic (lit. within the borders) |
| 设立 | Shèlì | Establish; set up |
| 有限 | Yǒuxiàn | Limited |
| 责任 | Zérèn | Responsibility; liability |
| 股份 | Gǔfèn | Shares; stock |
| 企业 | Qǐyè | Enterprise |
| 法人 | Fǎrén | Legal person (i.e. legally established entity)[3] |
| 独立 | Dúlì | Independent |
| 财产 | Cáichǎn | Property |
| 享有 | Xiǎngyǒu | Have; enjoy (rights, benefits, prestige, etc.) |
| 以 | Yǐ | Same meaning as 把 and 用 |
| 其 | Qí | Literary Chinese for 他的 |

3 Law Practice Tip: This is a legal term of art. Natural persons are individuals. Legal persons are entities created by law (e.g. a corporation).

| 对 | Duì | 对 and 向 combine with a number of different verbs to generally mean "to" or "for" |
|---|---|---|
| 债务 | Zhàiwù | Debt; liabilities |
| 承担 | Chéngdān | Assume; bear |
| 以 x 为 y | Yǐ x wéi y | Take x as y |
| 认缴 | Rènjiǎo | Paid in[4] |
| 出资 | Chūzī | Capital |
| 额 | É | Amount |
| 限 | Xiàn | Limit; restrict |
| 认购 | Rèngòu | Subscribe (to purchase shares or bonds) |
| 收益 | Shōuyì | Income; profit; earnings |
| 参与 | Cānyǔ | Participate in |
| 决策 | Júecè | Policy decision |
| 选择 | Xuánzé | Select; choose |
| 管理 | Guǎnlǐ | Manage |
| 者 | Zhě | 者 is literary Chinese and is used after an adjective or verb as a substitute for a person, entity, or thing |

---

4 Law Practice Tip: When doing due diligence on this kind of company when it is being purchased, it is critical to confirm (by an independent accounting firm) that the capital has, in fact, been paid in.

| | | |
|---|---|---|
| 从事 | Cóngshì | Engage in |
| 经营 | Jīngyíng | Engage in or run a business |
| 遵守 | Zūnshǒu | Adhere to; abide by |
| 行政法规 | Xíngzhèng fǎguī | Administrative laws and regulations[5] |
| 公德 | Gōngdé | Social ethics; morality |
| 商业 | Shāngyè | Commercial |
| 道德 | Dàodé | Ethics |
| 诚实 | Chéngshí | Honest |
| 守信 | Shǒuxìn | Trustworthy |
| 接受 | Jiēshòu | Receive |
| 公众 | Gōngzhòng | Public |
| 监督 | Jiāndū | Control; supervision |
| 侵犯 | Qīnfàn | Violate; infringe upon (a right) |
| 向 | Xiàng | 对 and 向 combine with a number of different verbs to generally mean "to" or "for" |
| 登记 | Dēngjì | Register |
| 机关 | Jīguān | Organ (administrative or government) |
| 申请 | Shēnqǐng | Apply for |

5 Law Practice Tip: "行政法规" are legislations adopted by the State Council. They are the third level of legislation in China, only lower than the Constitution and Laws passed by National People's Congress or its Standing Committee.

| | | |
|---|---|---|
| 符合 | Fúhé | Conform to; comply with |
| 条件 | Tiáojiàn | Requirement; condition |
| 的 | De | 的 is often used without the term it modifies. Here the missing term could be 时候 (time, i.e. "when") or 情况 (circumstance) |
| 由 x | Yóu x | By x; it is up to x to… |
| 分别 | Fēnbié | Distinguish |
| 为 | Wéi | Take; treat as |
| 必须 | Bìxū | Shall; must |
| 报 | Bào | Report to |
| 经 (经过) | Jīng (Jīngguò) | Go through; be x'd |
| 批准 | Pīzhǔn | Approval |
| 依法 | Yīfǎ | Legally; in accordance with the law |
| 办理 | Bànlǐ | Handle; take care of |
| 手续 | Shǒuxù | Process; procedure |
| 查询 | Cháxún | Search; look for |
| 事项 | Shìxiàng | Item; matter |
| 服务 | Fúwù | Service |
| 发给 | Fāgěi | Issue |
| 营业 | Yíngyè | Business |
| 执照 | Zhízhào | License |

| | | |
|---|---|---|
| 签发 | Qiānfā | Sign and issue |
| 载明 | Zǎimíng | Record |
| 名称 | Míngchēng | Name (of an entity) |
| 注册 | Zhùcè | Registered |
| 资本 | Zīběn | Capital[6] |
| 实收 | Shíshōu | Paid in (actually received) |
| 范围 | Fànwéi | Scope[7] |
| 法定 | Fǎdìng | Legal |
| 代表人 | Dàibiǎorén | Representative[8] |
| 变更 | Biàngēng | Change; amend |
| 换发 | Huànfā | Reissue |
| 标明 | Biāomíng | Mark; indicate |
| 字样 | Zìyàng | Model words; "the words x" |
| 债权 | Zhàiquán | Creditor's claim |
| 承继 | Chéngjì | Take on; assume |
| 主要 | Zhǔyào | Principal |
| 机构 | Jīgòu | Organization; structure |

6 Law Practice Tip: In China, registered capital refers to the amount of capital the investors have pledged to pay. This is to be distinguished from paid in capital, the amount actually paid. Paid in capital typically must be verified by an accounting firm. Various rules and regulations set minimum thresholds for registered capital required for entities depending upon the kind of activity the entity will engage in.

7 Law Practice Tip: In the U.S., scope of business is not a critical issue. In China, the government strictly enforces a company's declared scope of business.

8 Law Practice Tip: The Legal Representative is an important person. They are the official representative of the company.

| 所在地 | Suǒzàidì | Local (lit. the place where it is located) |
|---|---|---|
| 章程 | Zhāngchéng | Articles of Association (incorporation)[9] |
| 董事 | Dǒngshì | Director |
| 监事 | Jiānshì | Supervisor |
| 高级 | Gāojí | Senior |
| 具有 | Jùyǒu | Fully possess; have |
| 约束 | Yuèshù | Binding |
| 力 | Lì | Force |
| 修改 | Xiūgǎi | Revise; modify; amend |
| 项目 | Xiàngmù | Project |
| 董事长 | Dǒngshìzhǎng | Chair of the Board of Directors |
| 执行 | Zhíxíng | Carry out; implement |
| 担任 | Dānrèn | Hold post of; take on the task of |
| 分 | Fēn | Branch |
| 领取 | Lǐngqǔ | Receive |
| 资格 | Zīgé | Qualifications |
| 民事 | Mínshì | Civil[10] |
| 子 | Zǐ | Subsidiary |
| 其他 | Qítā | Other |

---

9 Law Practice Tip: In the U.S., the term Articles of Incorporation would be used. The practice in China is to say Articles of Association. The latter term is often used in the U.S. for unincorporated entities.

10 Law Practice Tip: The word "civil" here is a Civil Law concept.

| | | |
|---|---|---|
| 投资 | Tóuzī | Invest |
| 不得 | Bùdé | Must not; may not |
| 连带 | Liándài | Joint |
| 提供 | Tígōng | Provide; offer |
| 担保 | Dānbǎo | Guarantee |
| 决议 | Juéyì | Resolution |
| 总额 | Zǒng'é | Total amount |
| 单项 | Dānxiàng | Individual; discrete |
| 数额 | Shù'é | Amount |
| 限额 | Xiàn'é | Limit (lit. the limiting amount) |
| 超过 | Chāoguò | Exceed |
| 控制 | Kòngzhì | Control |
| 前款 | Qiánkuǎn | Preceding clause; above provision |
| 支配 | Zhīpèi | Control; dominate |
| 表决 | Biǎojué | Vote on; vote |
| 该 | Gāi | That[11] |
| 出席 | Chūxí | Attend |
| 过半数 | Guòbànshù | Majority (simple) |
| 通过 | Tōngguò | Enact; pass |
| 职工 | Zhígōng | Staff and workers |

11 Law Practice Tip: In modern legal English the term "that" is used. In older legal English, the term "said" is used.

| | | |
|---|---|---|
| 权益 | Quányì | Rights and interests |
| 签订 | Qiāndìng | Sign (a contract or agreement) |
| 劳动 | Láodòng | Labor |
| 合同 | Hétóng | Contract |
| 社会保险 | Shèhuì bǎoxiǎn | Social insurance[12] |
| 加强 | Jiāqiáng | Strengthen |
| 实现 | Shíxiàn | Realize; achieve; bring about |
| 安全 | Ānquán | Safe; secure |
| 生产 | Shēngchǎn | Production; manufacture |
| 采用 | Cǎiyòng | Select; use; adopt |
| 形式 | Xíngshì | Form |
| 职业 | Zhíyè | Occupational; professional |
| 教育 | Jiāoyù | Education |
| 岗位 | Gǎngwèi | Post; station |
| 培训 | Péixùn | Training |
| 素质 | Sùzhì | Quality |
| 工会 | Gōnghuì | Union |
| 开展 | Kāizhǎn | Develop; launch; unfold |
| 就 | Jiù | With regards to; as for |
| 报酬 | Bàochóu | Compensation; pay |

---

12 Law Practice Tip: Social Security in China includes: pensions, unemployment, medical, disability, maternity, and childcare.

| | | |
|---|---|---|
| 福利 | Fúlì | Benefits; welfare |
| 卫生 | Wèishēng | Health; hygiene; sanitation |
| 集体 | Jítǐ | Collective |
| 宪法 | Xiànfǎ | Constitution |
| 有关 | Yǒuguān | Relevant |
| 民主 | Mínzhǔ | Democratic |
| 研究 | Yánjiū | Look into; research the possibility of |
| 改制 | Gǎizhì | Change the structure[13] |
| 规章 | Guīzhāng | Rules; regulations |
| 听取 | Tīngqǔ | Listen to (listen and take in) |
| 通过 | Tōngguò | Pass through |
| 建议 | Jiànyì | Suggestions |

---

13 Background Tip: This actually refers to a change of ownership from state ownership to private ownership.

# Chapter 11
# Court Decisions

# 法院的判决

Fǎ　Yuàn　De　Pàn　Jué

# A. Introduction to Case Law

By *Mana Moriarty*, Esq.

There is no comprehensive system of case reporting in China. Over the years, a variety of court decisions have been made available in print form and electronically by the courts and various publishers in an attempt to make the system more transparent.

In 2005, the Supreme People's Court introduced the 《案例指导制度》 (Ànlì zhǐdǎo zhìdù Case Guidance System). The goals of this system, as described by the Supreme People's Court, include uniform application of judicial standards, guidance for lower courts, and enriching and developing legal theory.

The Court selects and edits decisions from courts around the country that demonstrate exemplary judicial reasoning, especially in difficult or complex cases. Although these cases are not binding, the Supreme People's Court has hinted courts' failure to refer to and apply the reasoning of

decisions similar to those they face could lead to reversal on appeal. These cases are posted on the Supreme People's Court web page. In November 2010, the Supreme People's Court issued a document to formally establish the case guidance system.

Much like the debate surrounding the Federal Sentencing Guidelines in the U.S., some see the uniform application of judicial standards as a euphemism for restricting judicial discretion, while others see it as a good step in the right direction of addressing the problem of large court systems around the world of courts in different parts of the country reaching different results under the same law in cases with similar facts. Some scholars have called for more detailed selection criteria for model cases, believing that more cases, and more carefully selected cases, subjected to an open selection and editorial process, would better help achieve the three goals.

# B. Determining Foreign Elements in Economic Disputes Involving Enterprises Text[1]

## 企业 经济 纠纷中涉外 因素的认定

山东东营 中院 裁定 横店 公司 申请 不予 执行 仲裁 裁决 案

### 裁判 要旨

对于 国内企业法人之间的民事纠纷, 部分 法律 事实发生在国外的, 应认定案件具有涉外 因素。对申请不予执行涉外仲裁裁决的司法 审查, 仅 限于对仲裁程序方面的审查。

### 案情

2002年2月11日, 山东横店草业畜牧 有限公司 (以下简称横店公司) 与 约翰迪尔（天津） 国际 贸易有限公司(以下简称约翰迪尔公司) 签订 农机设备 买卖 合同。横店公司支付部分 货款后, 对约定 应 于2004年3月31日、2005年 3月31日各支付975854.61美元的货款未予支付。 约翰迪尔公司于2007年3月29日将 争议 提交 中

---

1 Source: Qi ye jing ji jiu fen zhong she wai yin su de ren ding [Determining Foreign Elements in Economic Disputes Involving Enterprises] (promulgated by the Shandong Intermediate People's Ct., Apr. 24, 2009) *available at* http://oldfyb2009.chinacourt.org/public/detail. php?id=127807 (last visited October 26, 2011).

国国际经济贸易仲裁委员会（以下简称仲裁委员会），请求裁决横店公司支付本案合同项下应于2005年3月31日支付的合同款975854.61美元及利息，并承担仲裁费用。仲裁委员会认为，本案合同合法有效，本案所涉货物的交付始于国外，具有涉外因素，合同争议的处理适用中华人民共和国法律。约翰迪尔公司依约交付了合同项下货物。故裁决横店公司向约翰迪尔公司支付本案合同项下合同款应于2005年3月31日支付的欠款975854.61美元及利息，仲裁费184907元由横店公司承担。山东省东营市中级人民法院根据约翰迪尔公司的执行仲裁裁决申请立案执行后，横店公司向法院提出不予执行仲裁裁决申请。

### 裁判

东营市中级人民法院认为，中国国际经济贸易仲裁委员会受理本案符合法定程序。由于对涉外仲裁裁决的司法审查，仅限于仲裁程序方面的审查，故申请人对仲裁裁决实体内容的异议，不属本案的审查范围，法院对此不予审查。依照《中华人民共和国民事诉讼法》第二百五十八条第一款的规定，裁定驳回申请人横店公司申请不予执行（2008）中国贸仲京裁字第0130号裁决书的申请。

### 解析

本案属涉外民事案件还是国内争议案件，是当事人双方在仲裁审理程序和法院审查申请不予执行仲裁裁决中都有争议的一个焦点问题。该问题的认定直接涉及仲裁规则的适用及司法审查的范围问题。

《最高人民法院关于适用〈中华人民共和国民事诉讼法〉若干问题的意见》第三百零四条规定：当事人一方或双方是外国人、无国籍人、外国企业或组织，或者当事人之间的民事法律关系的设立、变更、终止的法律事实发生在国外，或者诉讼标的物在外国的民事案件，为涉外民事案件。对于本案的性质，约翰迪尔公司主张，涉案合同货物由美国和欧洲厂商生产，合同约定的装运港为美国和西欧港口，产生、变更或消灭民事权利义务关系的法律事实部分发生在国外，本案具有涉外因素。横店公司则认为，本案争议双方的主体都是中国企业法人，且双方在中国境内订立合同，仲裁标的物是设备款，其交付也在中国境内，本案应属国内争议案件而非涉外案件。

笔者认为，本案应认定为涉外案件，理由有三：一、虽然争议双方的主体都是中国企业法人，双方订立合同的行为发生在我国境内，但是，合同约定本案所涉交易货物的装运港为美国和西欧港口，货物的交付始于国外，也就是说，部分法律事实发生在国外。二、约翰迪尔公司是依据中国法律在保税区设立的外资企业，根据《保税区监管办法》的规定，保税区是境内关外由海关实施**特殊**监管的区域，保税区内的企业与境内保税区外企业之间的货物或**服务 贸易**属**跨关境**贸易，**视同 进出口**贸易**予以**管理。三、本案争议标的物是设备款，合同约定**定金**的支付方式是以**信用证**方式支付，横店公司支付的部分设备款也是**通过**信用证的形式支付。依照《**最高人民法院关于涉外民商事案件诉讼管辖若干问题的规定**》第三条的规定，信用证纠纷案件属涉外民商事案件，**尽管**本案的**案由**不是信用证纠纷，但根据该条内容，本案合同**款项**的支付方式**无疑**具有涉外因素的性质。因此，仲裁委员会与法院认定本案属涉外民事案件符合**上述**司法解释的规定。

本案案号为：（2008）东民三初字 第56号

**案例 编写人**：山东省东营市中级人民法院**梅雪芳**

# C. Vocabulary of Determining Foreign Elements in Economic Disputes Involving Enterprises

| Chinese | Pinyin | English |
| --- | --- | --- |
| 企业 | Qǐyè | Enterprise |
| 经济 | Jīngjì | Economic |
| 纠纷 | Jiūfēn | Dispute |
| 涉外 | Shèwài | Foreign |
| 因素 | Yīnsù | Factors; elements |
| 认定 | Rèndìng | Determine; establish |
| 东营 | Dōngyíng | Dongying City |
| 中院 (中级人民法院) | Zhōngyuàn (Zhōngjí Rénmín Fǎyuàn) | Intermediate People's Court |
| 裁定 | Cáidìng | Decision |
| 横店 | Héngdiàn | Hengdian |
| 公司 | Gōngsī | Company |

| 申请 | Shēnqǐng | Apply for |
|---|---|---|
| 不予 | Bùyú | Not grant or give; decline (literary Chinese) |
| 执行 | Zhíxíng | Carry out; implement |
| 仲裁 | Zhòngcái | Arbitration |
| 裁决 | Cáijué | Decision |
| 案 (案件) | Àn (Ànjiàn) | Case |
| 裁判 | Cáipàn | Judgment |
| 要旨 | Yàozhǐ | Main idea; gist |
| 对于 | Duìyú | As for |
| 国内 | Guónèi | Domestic |
| 法人 | Fǎrén | Legal person (i.e. legally established entity)[2] |
| 民事 | Mínshì | Civil |
| 法律 | Fǎlǜ | Law |
| 事实 | Shìshí | Facts |
| 的 | De | 的 is often used without the term it modifies. Here the missing term could be 时候 (time, i.e. when) or 情况 (circumstance) |
| 具有 | Jùyǒu | Fully possess; have |

2 Law Practice Tip: This is a legal term of art. Natural persons are individuals. Legal persons are entities created by law (e.g. a corporation).

| | | |
|---|---|---|
| 对 | Duì | 对 and 向 combine with a number of different verbs to generally mean "to" or "for" |
| 司法 | Sīfǎ | Judicial |
| 审查 | Shěnchá | Investigate |
| 仅 | Jǐn | Only |
| 限于 | Xiànyú | Limited to |
| 程序 | Chéngxù | Procedure; process |
| 案情 | Ànqíng | Details of a case; facts of a case |
| 畜牧 | Xùmù | Animal husbandry |
| 有限公司 | Yǒuxiàn gōngsī | Ltd. |
| 以下简称 x | Yǐxìa jiǎnchēng x | Abbreviated below as x[3] |
| 与 | Yǔ | And; together with |
| 约翰迪尔 | Yuēhàn Dí'ér | John Deere |
| 天津 | Tiānjīn | Tianjin |
| 国际 | Guójì | International |
| 贸易 | Màoyì | Trade |
| 签订 | Qiāndìng | Sign (a document) |
| 农机 | Nóngjī | Farm machinery |
| 设备 | Shèbèi | Equipment |

---

3 Law Practice Tip: In modern legal English, the term would be "below." In older legal English, the term would be "hereinafter."

| 买卖 | Mǎimài | Sales |
|---|---|---|
| 合同 | Hétóng | Contract |
| 支付 | Zhīfù | Pay (money) |
| 货款 | Huòkuǎn | Payment for goods |
| 约定 | Yuēdìng | Agree upon |
| 应 (应当) | Yīng (Yīngdāng) | Shall; must[4] |
| 于 | Yú | In; on (literary Chinese) |
| 未 | Wèi | Literary Chinese for 还没 |
| 将 | Jiāng | Literary Chinese for 把 |
| 争议 | Zhēngyì | Dispute |
| 提交 | Tíjiāo | Submit; refer |
| 中国国际经济贸易仲裁委员会 | Zhōngguó Guójì Jīngjì Màoyì Zhòngcái Wěiyuánhuì | China International Economic and Trade Arbitration Commission (CIETAC) |
| 本 | Běn | Literary Chinese for 这个 |
| 项下 | Xiàngxià | Under the terms of which |
| 及 | Jí | And; as well as (literary Chinese meaning the same as 跟 and 和) |
| 利息 | Lìxí | Interest |
| 并 | Bìng | And; moreover |

---

4 Law Practice Tip: In legal English, there is a difference between "must" and "shall." "Shall" has several meanings including "must" and "will." In modern legal English the trend is to avoid using "shall." When "shall" is used in the mandatory sense, then the word "must" is used.

| 承担 | Chéngdān | Assume; bear |
|---|---|---|
| 费用 | Fèiyòng | Expenses |
| 合法 | Héfǎ | Legal |
| 有效 | Yǒuxiào | Valid; effective |
| 货物 | Huòwù | Goods |
| 交付 | Jiāofù | Handover; deliver |
| 始于 | Shǐyú | Began in |
| 处理 | Chǔlǐ | Handle; deal with |
| 适用 | Shìyòng | Apply |
| 依约 | Yīyuē | In accordance with the agreement |
| 故 | Gù | Literary Chinese for 所以 |
| 向 | Xiàng | 对 and 向 combine with a number of different verbs to generally mean "to" or "for" |
| 根据 | Gēnjù | Based on; according to |
| 立案 | Lì'àn | Place a case on file; lit. set up a case file[5] |
| 提出 | Tíchū | Raise; propose (an idea) |
| 受理 | Shòulǐ | Accept (a case) |
| 符合 | Fúhé | Conform to; comply with |

---

5 Law Practice Tip: In the filing of law suits and some kinds of applications, the first step taken by the receiving court/agency is to have the court/agency decide if it will accept the filing. This acceptance is called 立案.

| 法定 | Fǎdìng | Legally mandated |
|---|---|---|
| 由于 | Yóuyú | Due to; as a result of |
| 对 (对于) | Duì (Duìyú) | As for; toward |
| 实体 | Shítǐ | Substance |
| 异议 | Yìyì | Objection; opposition |
| 不属 | Bùshǔ | Does not belong to or fall under |
| 范围 | Fànwéi | Scope |
| 依照 | Yīzhào | In accordance with |
| 诉讼法 | Sùsòngfǎ | Procedure Law |
| 条 | Tiáo | Article[6] |
| 款 | Kuǎn | Clause |
| 规定 | Guīdìng | Stipulation; provision |
| 驳回 | Bóhuí | Reject; dismiss |
| 解析 | Jiěxī | Analysis |
| 当事人 | Dāngshìrén | Party |
| 双方 | Shuāngfāng | Both parties |
| 焦点 | Jiāodiǎn | Focal |
| 该 | Gāi | That[7] |
| 直接 | Zhíjiē | Direct |

---

6 Law Practice Tip: Chinese laws and regulations typically consist of: parts (编), chapters (章), sections (节), and articles (条). There is no definitive English translation for these terms.

7 Law Practice Tip: In modern legal English the term "that" is used. In older legal English, the term "said" is used.

| 规则 | Guīzé | Rule; regulation |
|---|---|---|
| 若干 | Ruògān | Several |
| 无国籍人 | Wúguójírén | Stateless person |
| 组织 | Zǔzhī | Organization |
| 设立 | Shèlì | Establish; set up |
| 变更 | Biàngēng | Change; amend |
| 终止 | Zhōngzhǐ | Termination (at end of contract term) |
| 标的物 | Biāodìwù | Subject matter |
| 性质 | Xìngzhì | Nature; character |
| 主张 | Zhǔzhāng | Claim; assertion |
| 涉案 | Shè'àn | Involved in the case |
| 由 x | Yóu x | By x |
| 厂商 | Chǎngshāng | Firm; company |
| 生产 | Shēngchǎn | Produce; manufacture |
| 装运 | Zhuāngyùn | Load and transport |
| 港 | Gǎng | Port |
| 为 | Wéi | Take; treat as |
| 港口 | Gǎngkǒu | Ports |
| 消灭 | Xiāomiè | Eliminate; expire; abolish; extinguish |
| 权利 | Quánlì | Rights |
| 义务 | Yìwù | Duty; obligation |
| 关系 | Guānxi | Guanxi; relationship |

| 认为 | Rènwéi | Think or believe that |
|---|---|---|
| 双方 | Shuāngfāng | Both sides |
| 主体 | Zhǔtǐ | Subject |
| 且 | Qiě | Moreover |
| 境内 | Jìngnèi | Domestic (lit. within the borders) |
| 订立 | Dìnglì | Enter into (a contract) |
| 设备款 | Shèbèikuǎn | Money for equipment |
| 交付 | Jiāofù | Handover; deliver |
| 属 | Shǔ | Belong to |
| 而 | Ér | And; and yet |
| 非 | Fēi | 不是 |
| 笔者 | Bǐzhe | Author (of this piece) |
| 理由 | Lǐyóu | Reason |
| 行为 | Xíngwéi | Act; conduct; behavior |
| 依据 | Yījù | Follow; act in accordance with |
| 保税区 | Bǎoshuìqū | Free trade zone (protected from tax) |
| 外资 | Wàizī | Foreign invested |
| 监管 | Jiānguǎn | Oversee; supervise |
| 办法 | Bànfǎ | Methods |
| 规定 | Guīdìng | Stipulation; provision |
| 关外 | Guānwài | Outside of customs |
| 海关 | Hǎiguān | Customs |

| 特殊 | Tèshū | Special |
|---|---|---|
| 服务 | Fúwù | Service |
| 贸易 | Màoyì | Trade |
| 跨关境 | Kuàguānjìng | Cross border |
| 视同 | Shìtóng | Regard as |
| 进出口 | Jìnchūkǒu | Import-export |
| 予以 | Yǔyǐ | 予以 and 加以 both mean "to do x." In English, we would not translate either |
| 定金 | Dìngjīn | Down payment; deposit |
| 方式 | Fāngshì | Way; manner; method |
| 信用证 | Xìnyòngzhèng | Letter of credit |
| 通过 | Tōngguò | Go through |
| 管辖 | Guǎnxiá | Jurisdiction |
| 尽管 | Jǐn'guǎn | Even though |
| 案由 | Ànyóu | Issue in the case |
| 款项 | Kuǎnxiàng | Section/item in a legal document |
| 无疑 | Wúyí | No doubt |
| 上述 | Shàngshù | Above mentioned |
| 案例 | Ànlì | Case |
| 编写人 | Biānxiěrén | Author |
| 梅雪芳 | Méi Xuěfāng | Mei Xuefang |

# D. Web Pages That are Creative are Copy-rightable Works Text[8]

## 具有 独创性 的网站 页面 属于 作品

西安中院 判决 乔哲 诉西安西部国际 旅行社 侵犯 著作权 纠纷 案

发布时间：2009－04－10 08:04:01

### 裁判 要旨

网站的页面设计 不 属于简单的对 事实的 排列，*而是* 作者 独特 构思的体现和智慧的结晶，具有独创性、可复制性，符合作品的构成要件，属于作品的范畴，应受著作权法 保护。

### 案情

2006年11月25日西安光大国际旅行社与乔哲签订的网站建设 合同 约定：西安光大国际旅行社委托乔哲在互联网上建设网站，乔哲为西安光大国际旅行社提供网站制作 栏目、网站页面设计、数据库、程序 开发。

2007年3月15日西安光大国际旅行社开通 www.xaeits.com网站，为 维护网站网页的版权，与乔哲签订的补充 协议约定：www.xaeits.com

---

8 Source: Ju you du chuang xing de wang zhan ye mian shu yu zuo pin [Web Pages that are Creative are Copyrightable Works] (promulgated by the Xi'an Intermediate People's Ct., Apr. 10, 2009) *available at* http://oldfyb2009.chinacourt.org/public/detail.php?id=127420 (last visited May 30, 2011).

网站的**域名** 归西安光大国际旅行社**所有 并 管理** 使用，网页的版权**由** 双方 共同 行使；如果发现本网站版权被**盗用 链接**、盗用版权、盗用网站**后台**，双方有权单独或联合 **采取 法律途径**共同维护双方的**合法 利益**，乔哲对www.xaeits.com网站上的网页内容**享有**著作权，有权对侵犯该网页著作权的**行为** *提出* 诉讼。

2007年3月24日西部旅行社**就** 其开立的网站www.xaxbgl.com进行了备案。

www.xaeits.com网页**载明**了西安光大旅行社**优惠 酒店的价格**、机票价格、汽车**租赁价格、公司 简介**、**招聘** 信息、国际、**国内游 线路**等内容；www.xaxbgl.com的页面也**显示**了酒店的价格、机票价格、汽车租赁价格、公司简介、招聘信息、国际、国内游线路等内容。

**经** 比对，二者页面内容、**结构**、排列位置、文件名、部分文字和图片、**滚动** 文字栏 基本相同。

**此外**，www.xaxbgl.com网站页面上显示了西安光大国际旅行社的**名称和来访客户的**详细信息。

乔哲**起诉 认为**，西部旅行社未 经同意，使用 其为西安光大国际旅行社创作的网页，侵犯了其著作权，**故 诉至** 西安市中级人民法院，**请求 判令**：西部旅行社立即 停止侵犯www.xaeits.com网站全部网页著作权的行为；赔礼道歉；赔偿 原告 损失 及 合理 开支4.6万元。

**裁判**

西安市中级人民法院**审理**后认为，本案**所涉**网站页面是作者独特构思的体现和智慧的结晶，具有独创性、可复制性，符合作品的构成要件，应受著作权法保护。

西安光大国际旅行社与乔哲约定了**争讼 之**网站网页的版权由双方共同行使，乔哲对网页享有著作权，因此乔哲作为本案原告起诉，诉讼**主体 适格**。

西部旅行社的网站页面**实质**上**采用了**与乔哲设计的网站页面相同的表现形式，构成对争讼之著作权的侵犯。

判决：西部旅行社立即停止侵犯争讼之www.xaeits.com网站全部网页著作权的行为；赔偿乔哲损失1.5万元；驳回乔哲**其他**诉讼请求。宣判后，**当事人** 均未上诉，判决已**生效**。

**评析**

一、网页**是否能构成作品**

作品**是指**文学、**艺术**和科学 领域内具有独创性并能以**某种**有形式复制的**智力 成果**。

这种智力创造成果**应当 包括**能够在一定的时间内以**数字代码**形式固定在**磁盘或光盘**等有形**载体**上并保持**稳定的状态**，为社会**公众 直接或借助 机器**所感知、复制。

著作权法**所称**创作**是指**直接产生文学、艺术和科学作品的智力活动。

作为我国著作权法保护的作品首先**必须**是作者独立创作的,具有独创性;**其次**必须表现了作者的构思,具有**表达性**;最后必须可以以某种形式固定在一定的物质载体上,**加以**复制,并**被人**感知,具有可复制性。

**汇编**若干作品、作品的**片断**或者不构成作品的数据或者其他**材料**,对其内容的**选择**或**编排**体现独创性的作品,为汇编作品,其著作权由汇编人享有,**但行使著作权时,不得**侵犯原作品的著作权。

**可见**,如果网站设计人员**通过**自己的选择和编排,**将特定**类别的作品**放到**网站或网站的某一栏目中,并将它们通过一定的链接关系组织起来,方便**访问者查询**,或者将不同的信息放置到数据库中,只要设计者对所汇编的作品或作品部分享有**正当的使用权**,则其汇编后产生的著作权也应得到保护。

本案所涉网站页面虽然所使用的颜色、文字、信息等**处于公知**领域,但设计者将该页面的颜色、文字、**图标以数字化**的方式加以特定的**组合**,并以数字化形式**发表**并固定在计算机硬盘上,可为社会公众借助**联网主机所接触**,给人以**视觉**上的美感,**此**不属于简单的对事实的排列,而是作者独特构思的体现和智慧的结晶,具有独创性、可复制性。

根据最高人民法院《关于审理**涉及**计算机网络著作权纠纷案件**适用**法律若干问题的**解释**》第二条"受著作权法保护的作品,包括著作权法第三条规定的各类作品的数字化形式。在**网络环境下无法**归于著作权法第三条列举的作品**范围**,但在文学、艺术和科学领域内具有独创性并能以某种有形形式复制的其他智力创作成果,人民法院应当**予以保护**"之规定,争讼之网页符合作品的构成要件,应受著作权法保护。

二、委托设计作品著作权的**归属**

委托作品是指受**他人**委托创作的作品。委托人与**受托人**双方约定,受托人为委托人完成某项**事务**。

《中华人民共和国著作权法》第十一条、第十七条规定:著作权属于作者,本法**另有**规定**的除外**。创作作品的**公民**是作者。如无**相反证明**,在作品上**署名**的公民、**法人**或者其他组织为作者。受委托创作的作品,著作权的归属由委托人和受托人通过合同约定。合同未**明确**约定或者没有**订立合同的**,著作权属于受托人。

**结合本案**,西安光大国际旅行社就其开立的网站网页的**版权虽**约定了由双方共同行使,但对网页著作权的归属约定不明确,之后西安光大国际旅行社**出具**证明称乔哲对网站网页内容享有著作权,乔哲有权对侵犯网站网页著作权的行为提出诉讼;

**因此**西部旅行社在没有**充分证据**证明乔哲不是争讼之作品著作权人的情形下,涉案网站www.xaeits.com的网页作品著作权属于乔哲所有, 乔哲作为本案原告起诉, 其诉讼主体是适格的。

三、对侵犯著作权行为的认定

侵犯著作权行为是指未经著作权人同意, 又无法律上的**依据, 擅自**对享有著作权作品的使用以**及以**其他**非法 手段**行使著作权的行为。

**剽窃**属于侵犯著作权行为的一种形式, 它与**抄袭 系 同义语**, 是指将他人作品全部或部分作为自己的作品予以发表, 包括**原封不动的照抄照搬**和**改头换面**的抄袭。

其构成要件**为**: 有剽窃他人作品的事实或行为**违法性**; **侵害**了作者的**人格权**和**财产权**或有**损害**事实的发生; 违法行为与损害后果有**因果关系**; 剽窃主体**主观**上**存在 过错**。

本案中, 西部旅行社网站页面在**整体 版式**、色彩、图案、栏目**设置**、数据、**下拉 菜单的运用**等方面, 与乔哲设计的网页基本相同; 西部旅行社网站页面上显示了西安光大国际旅行社的名称和来访客户的详细信息; 乔哲为西安光大国际旅行社设计网站的页面使用时间**先于**西部旅行社网站使用页面的时间; **且**西部旅行社也

未能**提供**证据证明其使用的网站页面由其独立完成或来自公有领域。

**由此**事实可以证明, 西部旅行社有机会从互联网上接触过乔哲设计的网站页面, 西部旅行社的网站页面实质上采用了与乔哲设计的网站页面相同的表现形式, 其主要特征构成实质性**相似**, 符合剽窃行为的构成要件。根据《中华人民共和国著作权法》第四十七条的规定: 未经著作权人许可, 复制其作品属侵权行为之规定, 西部旅行社未经乔哲许可, 也未**向**乔哲支付**报酬**, 以**经营**为**目的**, 擅自使用乔哲依法享有著作权的网页内容, 并将该页面上载到互联网上, 已构成对争讼之著作权的侵犯。

**综上**, 法院考虑到网站设计**费用**、争讼之作品的类型、西部旅行社的主观过错**程度**、侵权**情节**、造成的后果**等 因素, 酌情 确定**了包括合理的**调查费用**及**律师**费用在内的赔偿**数额**。

本案案号: (2008)西民四初字第119号

**案例 编写人**: 重庆市**高级人民法院 孙海龙**陕西省西安市中级人民法院**姚建军**。

# E. Vocabulary of Web Pages That are Creative are Copyrightable Works

| Chinese | Pinyin | English |
|---------|--------|---------|
| 具有 | Jùyǒu | Fully possess; have |
| 独创性 | Dúchuàngxìng | Creativity |
| 网站 | Wǎngzhàn | Website |
| 页面 | Yèmiàn | Page layout |
| 属于 | Shǔyú | Is; fall within |
| 作品 | Zuòpǐn | Works |
| 中院 (中级人民法院) | Zhōngyuàn (Zhōngjí Rénmín Fǎyuàn) | Intermediate People's Court |
| 判决 | Pànjué | Judgment |
| 乔哲 | Qiáozhé | Qiaozhe (Plaintiff's name) |
| 诉 | Sù | Sue; vs. |
| 国际 | Guójì | International |
| 旅行社 | Lǚxíngshè | Travel agency |

| | | |
|---|---|---|
| 侵犯 | Qīnfàn | Violate; infringe upon (a right) |
| 著作权 | Zhùzuòquán | Copyright (lit. right to a work) |
| 纠纷 | Jiūfēn | Dispute |
| 案 (案件) | Àn (Ànjiàn) | Case |
| 发布 | Fābù | Issue (a ruling, regulation, etc.) |
| 裁判 | Cáipàn | Judgment |
| 要旨 | Yàozhǐ | Main idea; holding |
| 设计 | Shèjì | Design |
| 不 x 而是 y | Bù x érshì y | It is not x, but rather y |
| 对 | Duì | 对 and 向 combine with a number of different verbs to generally mean "to" or "for" |
| 事实 | Shìshí | Facts |
| 排列 | Páiliè | Arrange; put in order |
| 作者 | Zuòzhe | Author |
| 独特 | Dútè | Unique; distinctive |
| 构思 | Gòusī | Work out the plot of a literary work or the composition of a painting |
| 体现 | Tǐxiàn | Embodiment |
| 智慧 | Zhìhuì | Wisdom; intelligence |
| 结晶 | Jiéjīng | Crystallization |
| 可复制 | Kěfùzhì | Reproducible |

| | | |
|---|---|---|
| 符合 | Fúhé | Conform to; comply with |
| 构成要件 | Gòuchéng yàojiàn | Necessary elements |
| 范畴 | Fànchóu | Category |
| 应 (应当) | Yīng (Yīngdāng) | Shall; must |
| 法 | Fǎ | Law[9] |
| 保护 | Bǎohù | Protect |
| 案情 | Ànqíng | Details of the case; facts |
| 签订 | Qiāndìng | Sign (a document) |
| 建设 | Jiànshè | Construction |
| 合同 | Hétóng | Contract |
| 约定 | Yuēdìng | Agree upon |
| 委托 | Wěituō | Entrust; delegate; consign |
| 互联网 | Hùliánwǎng | Internet |
| 提供 | Tígōng | Provide; offer |
| 制作 | Zhìzuò | Make |
| 栏目 | Lánmù | Headings |
| 数据库 | Shùjùkù | Database |
| 程序 | Chéngxù | Program; arrangement of links |
| 开发 | Kāifā | Development |
| 开通 | Kāitōng | Launch; inaugurate |

---

9 Background Tip: China's Copyright Law (受著作权法) was enacted in 2001.

| 为 (为了) | Wèi (Wèile) | For the sake of; in order to |
|---|---|---|
| 维护 | Wéihù | Protect |
| 版权 | Bǎnquán | Copyright |
| 与 | Yǔ | And; together with |
| 补充 | Bǔchōng | Supplemental |
| 协议 | Xiéyì | Agreement |
| 域名 | Yùmíng | Domain name |
| 归 x 所有 | Guī x suǒyǒu | Belong to x |
| 并 | Bìng | And; moreover |
| 管理 | Guǎnlǐ | Manage |
| 使用 | Shǐyòng | Use |
| 由 x | Yóu x | By x |
| 双方 | Shuāngfāng | Both sides |
| 共同 | Gòngtóng | Together; jointly |
| 行使 | Xíngshǐ | Exercise (a right) |
| 本 | Běn | Literary Chinese for 这个 |
| 盗用 | Dàoyòng | Misappropriate |
| 链接 | Liànjiē | Link |
| 后台 | Hòutái | Background |
| 单独 | Dāndú | Alone; on its own |
| 联合 | Liánhé | Jointly |
| 采取 | Cǎiqǔ | Take; adopt |

| | | |
|---|---|---|
| 法律 | Fǎlǜ | Legal |
| 途径 | Tújìng | Means; ways |
| 合法 | Héfǎ | Legal |
| 利益 | Lìyì | Interest; benefit |
| 享有 | Xiǎngyǒu | Have; enjoy (rights, benefits, prestige, etc.) |
| 该 | Gāi | That[10] |
| 行为 | Xíngwéi | Act; conduct; behavior |
| 提出 | Tíchū | Raise; propose (an idea) |
| 诉讼 | Sùsòng | Litigation |
| 就 | Jiù | With regard to; as for |
| 其 | Qí | Literary Chinese for 他 |
| 备案 | Bèi'àn | Put on record; file |
| 载明 | Zǎimíng | Record |
| 优惠 | Yōuhuì | Preferential |
| 酒店 | Jiǔdiàn | Hotel |
| 价格 | Jiàgé | Price |
| 机票 | Jīpiào | Airline ticket |
| 租赁 | Zūlìn | Rent |
| 公司 | Gōngsī | Company |
| 简介 | Jiǎnjiè | Brief introduction; synopsis |

---

10 Law Practice Tip: In modern legal English the term "that" is used. In older legal English, the term "said" is used.

| | | |
|---|---|---|
| 招聘 | Zhāopìn | Invite applicants for a job; recruiting |
| 信息 | Xìnxí | Information |
| 国内游 | Guónèiyóu | Domestic trip |
| 线路 | Xiànlù | Routes |
| 显示 | Xiǎnshì | Display |
| 经 (经过) | Jīng (Jīngguò) | Go through; be x'd |
| 比对 | Bǐduì | Compare |
| 二者 | Èrzhě | Both |
| 结构 | Jiégòu | Structure |
| 位置 | Wèizhì | Position; location |
| 文件 | Wénjiàn | Document |
| 部分 | Bùfèn | Some |
| 图片 | Túpiàn | Pictures |
| 滚动 | Gǔndòng | Scrolling |
| 文字栏 | Wénzìlán | Text box |
| 基本 | Jīběn | Basically |
| 相同 | Xiāngtóng | Identical |
| 此外 | Cǐwài | In addition; moreover |
| 名称 | Míngchēng | Name (of an entity) |
| 来访 | Láifǎng | Visiting |
| 客户 | Kèhù | Client; customer |
| 详细 | Xiángxì | Detailed |

| 起诉 | Qǐsù | Sue; start a lawsuit |
|---|---|---|
| 认为 | Rènwéi | Think, believe that |
| 未 | Wèi | Literary Chinese for 还没 |
| 其 | Qí | Literary Chinese for 它 |
| 故 | Gù | Literary Chinese for 所以 |
| 诉至 x | Sùzhì x | File a law suit at x |
| 请求 | Qǐngqiú | Request; ask |
| 判令 | Pànlìng | Verdict |
| 立即 | Lìjí | Immediately |
| 停止 | Tíngzhǐ | Stop |
| 赔礼道歉 | Péilǐ dàoqiàn | Apologize |
| 赔偿 | Péicháng | Compensate |
| 原告 | Yuángào | Plaintiff |
| 损失 | Sǔnshī | Loss (financial; economic; etc.) |
| 及 | Jí | And; as well as (literary Chinese meaning the same as 和 and 跟) |
| 合理 | Hélǐ | Reasonable |
| 开支 | Kāizhī | Expenses |
| 审理 | Shěnlǐ | Try; hear (a case) |
| 所 | Suǒ | Which |
| 涉 | Shè | Involved |
| 争讼 | Zhēngsòng | Contested; disputed |

| 之 | Zhī | Literary Chinese for 的 |
|---|---|---|
| 主体 | Zhǔtǐ | Subject |
| 适格 | Shìgé | Eligible; having standing |
| 实质 | Shízhì | Substantively |
| 采用 | Cǎiyòng | Select; use; adopt |
| 驳回 | Bóhuí | Reject; dismiss |
| 其他 | Qítā | Other |
| 宣判 | Xuānpàn | Pronounce judgment |
| 当事人 | Dāngshìrén | Parties |
| 均 | Jūn | All; completely; 都 |
| 上诉 | Shàngsù | Appeal |
| 生效 | Shēngxiào | Go into effect; become effective |
| 评析 | Píngxī | Analysis |
| 是否 | Shìfǒu | Whether |
| 构成 | Gòuchéng | Form; constitute |
| 是指 | Shìzhǐ | This refers to; means |
| 艺术 | Yīshù | Art |
| 科学 | Kēxué | Science |
| 领域 | Lǐngyù | Area; field |
| 某种 | Mǒuzhǒng | Some kind of |
| 智力 | Zhìlì | Intelligent; intellectual |
| 成果 | Chéngguǒ | Result; achievement |

| | | |
|---|---|---|
| 应当 | Yīngdāng | Shall; must[11] |
| 包括 | Bāokuò | Include |
| 数字代码 | Shùzìdàimǎ | Digital code |
| 固定 | Gùdìng | Fixed; set |
| 磁盘 | Cípán | Computer disk |
| 光盘 | Guāngpán | CD-ROM |
| 载体 | Zàitǐ | Carrier |
| 稳定 | Wěndìng | Stable |
| 状态 | Zhuàngtài | State; status |
| 公众 | Gōngzhòng | Public |
| 直接 | Zhíjiē | Directly |
| 借助 | Jièzhù | Get help from |
| 机器 | Jīqì | Machine; machinery |
| 感知 | Gǎnzhī | Sense; perceive |
| 所称 x 是指 y | Suǒchēng x shìzhǐ y | The term x refers to y |
| 必须 | Bìxū | Shall; must |
| 其次 | Qícì | Next |
| 表达性 | Biǎodáxìng | Expressive |
| 加以 | Jiāyǐ | 予以 and 加以 both mean "to do x." In English, we would not translate either |

---

11 Law Practice Tip: In legal English, there is a difference between "must" and "shall." "Shall" has several meanings including "must" and "will." In modern legal English the trend is to avoid using "shall." When "shall" is used in the mandatory sense, then the word "must" is used.

| 被人 | Bèirén | Cause someone to x |
|------|--------|--------------------|
| 汇编 | Huìbiān | Compile; collect |
| 若干 | Ruògān | Several |
| 片断 | Piànduàn | Segment |
| 材料 | Cáiliào | Materials |
| 选择 | Xuánzé | Select; choose |
| 编排 | Biānpái | Programming |
| 但 (但是) | Dàn (Dànshì) | However |
| 不得 | Bùdé | Must not; may not |
| 可见 | Kějiàn | It can be seen that |
| 通过 | Tōngguò | Go through |
| 将 | Jiāng | Literary Chinese for 把 |
| 特定 | Tèdìng | Specific; specified; specifically designated |
| 类别 | Lèibié | Category |
| 放到 | Fàngdào | Put to |
| 某一 | Mǒuyī | A certain |
| 关系 | Guānxì | Relationship |
| 访问者 | Fǎngwènzhě | Visitors (者 is literary Chinese and is used after an adjective or verb as a substitute for a person, entity, or thing. Here, it literally means people who visit) |

| 查询 | Cháxún | Searches |
|------|--------|----------|
| 正当 | Zhèngdàng | Proper; legitimate |
| 使用权 | Shǐyòngquán | Right of use; right to use |
| 则 | Zé | Then |
| 处于 | Chǔyú | Located in; is in |
| 公知 | Gōngzhī | Public knowledge |
| 图标 | Túbiāo | Icon (computer) |
| 以 | Yǐ | Same meaning as 把 and 用 |
| 数字化 | Shùzìhuà | Digitalized; coded |
| 组合 | Zǔhé | Combination |
| 发表 | Fābiǎo | Publish; issue |
| 硬盘 | Yìngpán | Hard drive |
| 联网 | Liánwǎng | Connected |
| 主机 | Zhǔjī | Host computer |
| 接触 | Jiēchù | Contact |
| 视觉 | Shìjué | Visual sense |
| 此 | Cǐ | Literary Chinese for 这个 |
| 涉及 | Shèjí | Involved; concern |
| 适用 | Shìyòng | Apply |
| 解释 | Jiěshì | Interpretation |
| 环境 | Huánjìng | Environment |
| 无法 | Wúfǎ | Unable to; cannot |

| 归于 | Guīyú | Belong to |
|------|-------|-----------|
| 列举 | Lièjǔ | Set forth; list |
| 范围 | Fànwéi | Scope |
| 予以 | Yǔyǐ | 予以 and 加以 both mean "to do x." In English, we would not translate either |
| 规定 | Guīdìng | Stipulation; provision |
| 归属 | Guīshǔ | Ownership |
| 他人 | Tārén | Another person |
| 受托人 | Shòutuōrén | Agent (as opposed to principal) |
| 项 | Xiàng | Counter for 事务 |
| 事务 | Shìwù | Affairs; matters (political or economic) |
| 另有 x 的除外 | Lìngyǒu x de chúwài | Except as provided in x |
| 公民 | Gōngmín | Citizen |
| 无 | Wú | Literary Chinese for 没有 |
| 相反 | Xiāngfǎn | Opposite; to the contrary |
| 证明 | Zhèngmíng | Proof; evidence |
| 署名 | Shǔmíng | Sign one's name; signed |
| 法人 | Fǎrén | Legal person (i.e. legally established entity)[12] |
| 明确 | Míngquè | Definitely; clearly |
| 订立 | Dìnglì | Enter into (a contract) |

12 Law Practice Tip: This is a legal term of art. Natural persons are individuals. Legal persons are entities created by law (e.g. a corporation).

| 的 | De | 的 is often used without the term it modifies. Here the missing term could be 时候 (time, i.e. "when") or 情况 (circumstance) |
|---|---|---|
| 结合 | Jiéhé | Integrate; combine |
| 虽 (虽然) | Suí (Suírán) | Although |
| 之后 | Zhīhòu | 以后 |
| 出具 | Chūjù | Provide (evidence) |
| 因此 | Yīncǐ | Because of this (literary Chinese) |
| 充分 | Chōngfèn | Sufficient |
| 证据 | Zhèngjù | Evidence; proof |
| 依据 | Yījù | Basis |
| 擅自 | Shànzì | Do something without authorization |
| 以及 | Yǐjí | As well as; and; too (literary Chinese meaning the same as 跟 and 和) |
| 非法 | Fēifǎ | Illegal |
| 手段 | Shǒuduàn | Method |
| 剽窃 | Piāoqiè | Pirate; plagiarize |
| 抄袭 | Chāoxí | Plagiarize |
| 系 | Xì | Belong to; is |
| 同义语 | Tóngyìyǔ | Synonym |
| 原封不动 | Yuánfēngbùdòng | Intact (lit. the original seal has not been |

broken); word for word

| | | |
|---|---|---|
| 照抄照搬 | Zhàochāozhàobān | Plagiarism |
| 改头换面 | Gǎitóuhuànmiàn | Superficial changes |
| 为 | Wéi | Take; treat as |
| 违法性 | Wéifǎxìng | Illegality |
| 侵害 | Qīnhài | Infringe on |
| 人格权 | Réngéquán | Right of personality |
| 财产权 | Cáichǎnquán | Property rights |
| 损害 | Sǔnhài | Harm; damage |
| 因果关系 | Yīnguǒguānxì | Causal relationship |
| 主观 | Zhǔguān | Subjective |
| 存在 | Cúnzài | Exist |
| 过错 | Guòcuò | Fault; wrong |
| 整体 | Zhěngtǐ | Whole; entirety |
| 版式 | Bǎnshì | Page format |
| 设置 | Shèzhì | Set up; install |
| 下拉 | Xiàlā | Pull down |
| 菜单 | Càidān | Menu |
| 运用 | Yùnyòng | Utilization; application |
| 先于 | Xiānyú | Earlier than |
| 且 | Qiě | Moreover |
| 提供 | Tígōng | Provide; present |

| 由此 | Yóucǐ | From this |
|------|--------|-----------|
| 相似 | Xiāngsì | Resemble; similar |
| 向 | Xiàng | 对 and 向 combine with a number of different verbs to generally mean "to" or "for" |
| 报酬 | Bàochóu | Compensation; pay |
| 经营 | Jīngyíng | Engage in or run a business |
| 目的 | Mùdì | Purpose |
| 综上 | Zōngshàng | To sum up |
| 考虑 | Kǎolǜ | Think over; consider |
| 费用 | Fèiyòng | Expenses |
| 程度 | Chéngdù | Degree (level or extent) |
| 情节 | Qíngjié | Circumstance; situation |
| 等 | Děng | Etc. |
| 因素 | Yīnsù | Factors; elements |
| 酌情 | Zhuóqíng | Take the circumstances into consideration |
| 确定 | Quèdìng | Define; fix; determine |
| 调查 | Diàochá | Investigation |
| 律师 | Lǜshī | Lawyer |
| 数额 | Shù'é | Amount |
| 案例 | Ànlì | Case |
| 编写人 | Biānxiěrén | Author |

| 高级人民法院 | Gāojí Rénmín Fǎyuàn | High People's Court |
| 孙海龙 | Sūn Hǎilóng | Sun Hailong |
| 姚建军 | Yáo Jiànjūn | Yao Jianjun |

# Chapter 12
# Lawyer's Work
# 律 师 的 工 作
Lǜ　　Shī　　De　　Gōng　Zuò

# A. Release of Letter of Guarantee Text

# 保证责任免除函

公司（*下称* "债权人"或"本公司"）与B公司（下称"保证人"）经友好**协商**，债权人于2007年3月　日签署本保证责任免除函（下称"本函"），同意**无条件地**、**不可撤销地**、永久地免除保证人对保证债务（定义见下文）所可能**承担**的一切保证责任。**具体 内容 如下**：

一、保证**债务**

本函*所称*保证债务*是指* 根据1995年6月16日C公司（"债务人"）与中国**工商银行**南京分行签署之《**技术 改造 贷款 合同**》（下称"贷款合同"）项下债务人尚未 归还的贷款本金、利息、债务人**逾期 还款 违约金**、以及可能**发生**的债务人对债权人的损害 赔偿金和债权人**实现** 债权的费用（**包括担不限于 诉讼费和律师费**）。

二、债权**转移**

贷款合同项下之债权已 *由* 中国工商银行南京分行转让给本公司。本公司在本函签署之日为债务人在贷款合同项下所有合同债务的债权人。

三、保证责任免除

*自*本函签署之日*起*，债权人无条件地、不可撤销免除保证人*对*本函第一条定义的保证债务所可能**承担** 任何责任。 在本函签署后，债权人**永久 放弃** 就保证债务可能向保证人**提出**任何**请求**或主张的权利。

四、债权人承诺与声明

1、债权人是本函第一条定义的保证债务的**真实债权人**；

2、债务人是债权人的**下属 企业**；

3、本函对保证人保证责任的免除是无条件、不可撤销和永久的；**及**

4、本函内容已经债权人仔细 **审阅 并 理**

解,债权人签署本函完全出于**自愿**,没有任何**误解**或受到任何**误导**。

五、本函约**束力**

本函由债权人**为**债务人和保证人的**利益** *而* 特别签署。 本函*经*债权人签署*后*,*对*其自身及其可能的权利**受让方**或**继承方***均有*不可撤销的约束力。

债权人:

**注册**地址:

**授权** **代表**签署:

姓名:

职务:

公司**盖章**:

债务人及**见证方**:

注册地址:

授权代表签署:

姓名:

职务:

公司盖章:

# B. Vocabulary of Release of Letter of Guarantee

| Chinese | Pinyin | English |
| --- | --- | --- |
| 保证 | Bǎozhèng | Guarantee; ensure |
| 责任 | Zérèn | Responsibility; liability |
| 免除 | Miǎnchú | Relieve; release |
| 函 | Hán | Letter; document |
| 公司 | Gōngsī | Company |
| 下称 x | Xiàchēng | Below referred to as x |
| 债权人 | Zhàiquánrén | Creditor |
| 本 | Běn | Literary Chinese for 这个 |
| 与 | Yǔ | And; together with |
| 经 (经过) | Jīng (Jīngguò) | Go through; be x'd |
| 协商 | Xiéshāng | Bargain; consult |
| 于 | Yú | In; on |
| 签署 | Qiānshǔ | Sign |
| 无条件地 | Wútiáojiànde | Unconditionally |
| 不可撤销地 | Bùkě chèxiāode | Irrevocably |

| 定义 | Dìngyì | Definition |
|---|---|---|
| 承担 | Chéngdān | Assume; bear |
| 一切 | Yīqiè | All |
| 具体 | Jùtǐ | Concrete; specific |
| 内容 | Nèiróng | Content |
| 如下 | Rúxià | As set forth below |
| 债务 | Zhàiwù | Debt; liabilities |
| 所称 x 是指 y | Suǒchēng x shìzhǐ y | The term x refers to y |
| 根据 | Gēnjù | Based on; according to |
| 工商银行 | Gōngshāng Yínháng | Bank of Industry and Commerce |
| 技术 | Jìshù | Technology |
| 改造 | Gǎizào | Transform; reform |
| 贷款 | Dàikuǎn | Loan |
| 合同 | Hétōng | Contract |
| 项下 | Xiàngxià | Under the terms of which |
| 尚未 | Shàngwèi | Literary Chinese for 还没 |
| 归还 | Guīhuán | Return |
| 本金 | Běnjīn | Principal |
| 利息 | Lìxī | Interest |
| 逾期 | Yúqī | Exceed time limit; overdue |
| 还款 | Huánkuǎn | Pay back money |
| 违约金 | Wéiyuējīn | Damages (for breach) |

| | | |
|---|---|---|
| 以及 | Yǐjí | As well as; and; too (literary Chinese meaning the same as 跟 and 和) |
| 发生 | Fāshēng | Occur; happen |
| 损害 | Sǔnhài | Harm; damages |
| 赔偿金 | Péichángjīn | Compensation |
| 实现 | Shíxiàn | Realize; achieve; bring about |
| 费用 | Fèiyòng | Expenses |
| 包括但不限于 | Bāokuò dàn bùxiànyú | Including, but not limited to |
| 诉讼 | Sùsòng | Litigation |
| 律师 | Lùshī | Lawyer |
| 转移 | Zhuǎnyí | Shift; transfer; divert |
| 已 | Yǐ | 已经 |
| 由 x | Yóu x | By x |
| 之 | Zhī | Literary Chinese for 的 |
| 自 x 起 | Zì x qǐ | Beginning from x |
| 对 x 承担 y | Duì x chéngdān y | Bear y for x |
| 任何 | Rènhé | Any |
| 永久 | Yǒngjiǔ | Permanently |
| 放弃 | Fàngqì | Abandon; give up |
| 就 | Jiù | With regards to; as for |
| 提出 | Tíchū | Raise; propose (an idea) |
| 请求 | Qǐngqiú | Request; ask |

| 主张 | Zhǔzhāng | Claim |
|---|---|---|
| 承诺 | Chéngnuò | Acknowledge; promise |
| 声明 | Shēngmíng | Announcement |
| 真实 | Zhēnshí | True; real |
| 下属 | Xiàshǔ | Subsidiary |
| 企业 | Qǐyè | Enterprise |
| 及 | Jí | And; as well as (literary Chinese meaning the same as 跟 and 和) |
| 仔细 | Zǐxì | Carefully; attentively |
| 审阅 | Shěnyuè | Go over; review |
| 并 | Bìng | And |
| 理解 | Lǐjiě | Understand |
| 自愿 | Zìyuàn | Voluntary |
| 误解 | Wùjiě | Misunderstanding |
| 误导 | Wùdǎo | Misleading |
| 约束力 | Yuēshùlì | Binding force |
| 为 x 而 y | Wèi x ér y | Do y for the sake of x |
| 利益 | Lìyì | Interests; benefits |
| 经 x 后 | Jīng x hòu | After x |
| 对 x 均有 y | Duì x jūnyǒu y | Have full y with regards to x |
| 自身 | Zìshēn | Self; oneself |
| 受让方 | Shòuràngfāng | Assignee |

| 继承方 | Jìchéngfāng | Successor |
|---|---|---|
| 注册 | Zhùcè | Registered |
| 授权 | Shòuquán | Authorized |
| 代表 | Dàibiǎo | Representative[1] |
| 盖章 | Gàizhāng | Chop; affix seal; stamp (v.)[2] |
| 见证方 | Jiànzhēngfāng | Witness |

---

1 Law Practice Tip: In China, these kinds of documents are often notarized. The notary would verify that the person signing is, in fact, an authorized representative by reviewing relevant documents from the company.

2 Law Practice Tip: In China, companies have a single official chop (stamp) which is used to "sign" documents and authorize bank transactions. They use a red ink pad. A common tactic in a partnership dispute is to abscond with the company chop. This chop has the same effect as a corporate seal in the U.S., but is used to "sign" all manner of official documents. The English word "chop" is used in China as both a noun and a verb, e.g. "take the chop and chop the invoice."

# C. Law Office E-mail Text

# Seeking Legal Advice from Colleagues

From: 林彦

To: All Lawyers

Subject: RE: 问题请教_建设 工程 分包人 的资质对分包合同 效力的影响

各位同事:

我们在工作中遇到 如下问题, 特向各位请教:

1. 背景:

某 建筑工程总承包 方A与分包人B签订了一份分包合同( "分包合同" ), 将某些工作( "分包工程" )分包给B完成。该分包工程中包含了若干 项资质才能开展的工作, 而B仅 具有其中某一项工作所需资质。

2. 相关 法律 规定:

(1)《合同法》第272条第3款的规定: "禁止承包人将工程分包给不具备相应资质条件的单位……"

(2)《最高人民法院关于审理建设工程施工合同纠纷 案件 适用法律问题的解释 》(法释(2004)14号,自2005年1月1日起施行)第一条规定:

"建设工程施工合同具有下列情形之一的, 应当根据合同法第五十二条第 ( 五 ) 项的规定, 认定无效:

一 承包人未 取得建筑施工企业资质或者超越资质等级 的……"

(3) 根据《合同法》第52条第5项的规定: 违反法律、行政法规的强制性规定的, 合同无效。

3. 问题:

(1) 该分包合同是否会因分包人B不具备开展全部分包工程所需资质而全部成为无效? 或者, 分包合同不会因此全部无效, 而仅仅是其中分包人B不具备资质的那部分无效?

(2) 如该分包合同**实际上**已经**履行**了一段时间，那么: 如在**实践**中该分包合同被法院认定为无效(全部无效或部分无效)，那么法院会如何处理该分包合同中已经履行的部分(比如已经向分包人B**支付**的**价款**；分包人B已经完成的工程等)? 该分包合同的各缔约方是否会**因此 遭到 处罚**?

如各位同事在实践中遇到过**上述**问题或类似问题，还请**在 百忙 之中 不吝 赐教**。十分感谢!

上海**分所** 傅思德

# Conflict of Interest Check

From: 陆 XX

To: All Lawyers

Subject: **冲突 检索**

各位同事:

我们**拟 代表**一个**客户**对 "北京**XXX有限公司**" 和 "YYY（上海）有限公司" **进行 尽职调查**，而且之后我们的客户拟**收购**上述两家公司。因此，**现**需要进行**利益**冲突检索。如果哪位同事现在正在**代理**上述两家公司或其**股东**的**业务**，烦请 **告知**我们。

**由于 事务 紧急**，烦请大家在今天之内**给予 答复**，谢谢!

北京分所 陆xx

# D. Vocabulary of Law Office E-mail

| Chinese | Pinyin | English |
| --- | --- | --- |
| 建设 | Jiànshè | Construction |
| 工程 | Gōngchéng | Engineering |
| 分包人 | Fēnbāorén | Sub-contractor |
| 资质 | Zīzhì | Capability |
| 合同 | Hétóng | Contract |
| 效力 | Xiàolì | Effectiveness; validity |
| 影响 | Yǐngxiǎng | Affect; influence |
| 遇到 | Yùdào | Encounter |
| 如下 | Rúxià | As set forth below |
| 背景 | Bèijǐng | Background |
| 某 | Mǒu | Some; a certain |
| 建筑 | Jiànzhù | Build; construction; architecture |
| 总承包 | Zǒngchéngbāo | General contractor |
| 方 | Fāng | Party |
| 签订 | Qiāndìng | Sign (a contract or agreement) |

| 将 | Jiāng | Literary Chinese for 把 |
| 该 | Gāi | That[3] |
| 包含 | Bāohán | Include; contain |
| 若干 | Ruògān | Several |
| 项 | Xiàng | Counter for 资质 |
| 开展 | Kāizhǎn | Develop; launch; begin |
| 仅 | Jǐn | Only |
| 具有 | Jùyǒu | Fully possess; have |
| 相关 | Xiāngguān | Relevant |
| 法律 | Fǎlù | Law; legal |
| 规定 | Guīdìng | Provision |
| 条 | Tiáo | Article[4] |
| 款 | Kuǎn | Clause |
| 禁止 | Jìnzhǐ | Prohibit |
| 具备 | Jùbèi | Possess; have |
| 相应 | Xiāngyìng | Corresponding |
| 单位 | Dānwèi | Entity[5] |

3 Law Practice Tip: In modern legal English the term "that" is used. In older legal English, the term "said" is used.

4 Law Practice Tip: Chinese laws and regulations typically consist of: parts (编), chapters (章), sections (节), and articles (条). There is no definitive English translation for these terms.

5 Law Practice Tip: Dān wèi is used to describe the organization to which you belong, e.g. your employer. In the past, when there was no private economy, the Dān wèi played a much more significant role in the lives of its workers. It provided housing, schools, hospitals, cafeterias, etc. In modern Chinese is it often best translated as "entity."

| 法院 | Fǎyuàn | Court |
|---|---|---|
| 审理 | Shěnlǐ | Try, hear a case |
| 施工 | Shīgōng | Work on (construction) |
| 纠纷 | Jiūfēn | Dispute |
| 案件 | Ànjiàn | Case |
| 适用 | Shìyòng | Apply |
| 解释 | Jiěshì | Interpretation |
| 法释 | Fǎshì | Legal Interpretations |
| 施行 | Shīxíng | Come into force |
| 根据 | Gēnjù | Based on; according to |
| 认定 | Rèndìng | Determine; establish |
| 未 | Wèi | Literary Chinese for 还没 |
| 取得 | Qǔdé | Obtain; acquire |
| 超越 | Chāoyuè | Exceed; surpass |
| 等级 | Děngjí | Grade; rank; level |
| 的 | De | 的 is often used without the term it modifies. Here the missing term could be 时候 (time, i.e. "when") or 情况 (circumstance) |
| 违反 | Wéifǎn | Violate (a law) |
| 强制性 | Qiángzhìxìng | Mandatory; compulsory |
| 因 x 而 y | Yīn x ér y | To y because of x |
| 仅仅 | Jǐnjǐn | Only; merely; barely |

| | | |
|---|---|---|
| 实际上 | Shíjìshàng | Actual; realistic; in practice |
| 履行 | Lǚxíng | Perform; fulfill; carry out |
| 实践 | Shíjiàn | Put into practice |
| 支付 | Zhīfù | Pay (money) |
| 价款 | Jiàkuǎn | Price |
| 缔约 | Dìyuē | Conclude (contract, agreement, treaty) |
| 因此 | Yīncǐ | Because of this (literary Chinese) |
| 遭到 | Zāodào | Meet with; encounter |
| 处罚 | Chǔfá | Penalize; punish |
| 上述 | Shàngshù | Above mentioned |
| 类似 | Lèisì | Similar |
| 在 x 之中 | Zài x zhīzhōng | When x |
| 百忙 | Bǎimáng | "You are so busy" |
| 不吝 | Bùlìn | Generous (lit. not stingy) |
| 赐教 | Cìjiào | Enlighten |
| 分所 | Fēnsuǒ | Branch office of a law firm |
| 冲突 | Chòngtù | Conflict |
| 检索 | Jiǎnsuǒ | Check |
| 拟 | Nǐ | Intend; plan to |
| 代表 | Dàibiǎo | Represent |
| 客户 | Kèhù | Client |
| 有限公司 | Yǒuxiàn gōngsī | Ltd. |

| 进行 | Jìnxíng | Carry out; conduct |
|---|---|---|
| 尽职调查 | Jìnzhí diàochá | Due diligence (lit. investigation to fulfill one's duty) |
| 收购 | Shōugòu | Purchase; buy |
| 现 | Xiàn | 现在 |
| 利益 | Lìyì | Interest |
| 代理 | Dàilǐ | Represent (as a lawyer) |
| 股东 | Gǔdōng | Shareholder |
| 业务 | Yèwù | Business |
| 烦请 | Fánqǐng | Please be so kind as to |
| 告知 | Gàozhī | Inform; notify |
| 由于 x | Yóuyú x | Because of x |
| 事务 | Shìwù | Matter |
| 紧急 | Jǐnjí | Urgent |
| 给予 | Jǐyǔ | Give |
| 答复 | Dáfù | Reply |

# Chapter 13
# Researching Chinese Law

# 中国法律研究

Zhōng　Guó　　Fǎ　　Lǜ　Yán　Jiū

# Introduction to Chinese Legal Research

By *Keiko Okuhara*, Bibliographic Services/Systems Librarian, University of Hawaii

Chinese legal research can be difficult for a number of reasons. There is no indigenous equivalent of the commonly used legal search engines such as *LEXIS* or *Westlaw* for Chinese language sources and, while increasingly less of a problem, it is often difficult to find Chinese laws (particularly local laws) on the Internet. However, both *Westlaw China* and *Bei Da Fa Bao* (北大法宝) are becoming more and more sophisticated and useful for legal research on Chinese law.

In the past, many local and national rules and regulations were not public information. Research on *Chinese law* in English has its own difficulties. For example, if you are searching English language sources, there is no official, much less standard, translation of the titles of the laws, rules, and regulations.

## I.    Sources and Hierarchy of Chinese Law

In China, there are two types of organs empowered to make legislative enactments: state-power organs (国家权力机关 guójiā quánlì jīguān) and administrative organs (行政机关 xíngzhèng jīguān). The National People's Congress (全国人民代表大会 Quánguó Rénmín Dàibiǎodàhuì) (NPC) and its Standing Committee (常务委员会 Chángwù Wěiyuánhuì) as well as local peoples' congresses are types of state-power organs. Only the NPC may amend the Constitution, and only the NPC and its Standing Committee may enact laws (法 fǎ), rules (条例 tiáolì), and resolutions (决议 juéyì). The NPC only meets two weeks a year, so most laws come from its Standing Committee.

The State Council (国务院 Guówùyuàn) and its departments formulate administrative rules and regulations (行政法规 xíngzhèng fǎguī). Local administrative rules (地方政府规章) are enacted by Provincial and some municipal governments, namely the executive branches at certain levels. Local regulations (地方性法规) are enacted by Provincial and some municipal people's congress and their standing committees.

A.    Interpretation of Laws

The Constitution only authorizes the NPC Standing Committee to interpret both the Constitution and the laws, although some scholars believe that NPC can exercise that kind of power. As a practical matter, however, the NPC and its Standing Committee seldom exercise their power to interpret laws.

B.    Judicial and Administrative Interpretations:

Most statutory interpretation is done by the Supreme People's Court (SPC) (最高人民法院 Zuìgāo Rénmín Fǎyuàn). However, an important difference from the common law system is that the concept of *stare decisis* does not apply nor does the concept of "case in controversy." As noted in the General Introduction to the CLR as well as the introduction to Chapter 11 on court decisions, specific decisions issued by the SPC in individual cases are not binding. However, in recent years, these court decisions are increasingly influential on lower courts. The interpretations issued by the SPC, are however, binding. These interpretations are not based on a specific case, but rather are issued by the court's Adjudication Committee (审判委员会 Shěnpàn Wěiyuánhuì), typically in response to interpretation issues which have arisen at the trial court level across the country. Several such interpretations are included in the CLR.

The SPC and the Supreme People's Procuratorate (SPP) (最高人民检察院 Zuìgāo Rénmín Jiāncháyuàn) are both authorized to interpret laws and regulations. If the two interpretations differ, they must be submitted to the Standing Committee of the NPC for final interpretation. The SPC issues its judicial interpretations in three forms: interpretations (解释 jǐeshì), stipulations (规定 guīdìng), and replies (批复 pīfu). There are five forms of SPP interpretations: interpretations (解释 jǐeshì), stipulations (规定 guīdìng), opinions (意见 yìjiàn), circulars (通知 tōngzhī), and replies (批复 pīfù). It is not uncommon for the Supreme People's Court and the Supreme People's Procuratorate to jointly issue interpretations.

II.    Research Strategies

When you initiate your legal research, a set of research methods has to be developed based on your research goals and needs. Your research strategy will vary depending on 1) your Chinese language skills and your knowledge of the Chinese legal system, 2) the language of the text you need, and 3) the availability of resources. Obviously, it is best to be able to use both Chinese and English resources. However, if your research outcome has to be written in English, an English resource might save time by providing a translation of relevant laws and regulations. As noted in the General Introduction to the CLR, there is a wide range in the quality of available translations.

Knowledge of the Chinese legal system and structure will help you organize your research, especially relating to where and how to find the information. Therefore, if you do not possess background information on the Chinese legal system, you may want to begin there.

A.  Statutory Search:

The primary sources of law in the PRC are statues, administrative rules and regulations, as well as judicial interpretations issued by the SPC and the SPP. Although few laws and regulations were enacted prior to 1978, they have proliferated in the PRC since the 1980s. However, adequate quality control on legal publishing has not been established, thus less qualified publications undermine the reliability and authenticity of Chinese legal publications, especially online legal resources. Moreover, because systematic updating services are not available, the currency of the information should be verified. Internet-based secondary sources such as treatises, law reviews, restatements, online journals or news are also few because secondary sources are not targeted by Chinese legal publishers.

B.  Case Law:

As noted above, the precedential authority of cases is not formally recognized. The SPC publishes its monthly Gazette of the Supreme People's Court (《中华人民共和国最高人民法院公报》 Zhōnghuá Rénmín Gōnghéguó Zuìgāo Rénmín Fǎyuàn Gōngzuò Gōngbào) and annual Work Report (《工作报告》 Gōngzuò Bàogaò) that include important cases selected by the Adjudication Committee of the SPC. In addition, since 1992, the China Practicing Law Institute (中国应用法学研究所 Zhōngguó Yīngyòng Fǎxué Yánjiūsuó), a research organ of the SPC, has published a series entitled Selective Compilation of the People's Courts Cases. The judgments (裁判文书 cáipàn wénshū) in the compilations only include facts and holdings of the courts without much legal reasoning. On the other hand, cases (案例 ànlì) reported in the Gazette include the legal reasoning by the judges who adjudicated the cases.

In 2005, the Supreme People's Court introduced the 案例指导制度 (ànlì zhǐdǎo zhìdù Case Guidance System). The goals of this system, as described by the Supreme People's Court, include uniform application of judicial standards, guidance for lower courts, and enriching and developing legal theory.

The Court selects and edits decisions from courts around the country that demonstrate exemplary judicial reasoning, especially in difficult or complex cases. Although these cases are not binding, the Supreme People's Court has hinted courts' failure to refer to and apply the reasoning of decisions similar to those they face could lead to reversal on appeal. These cases are posted on the Supreme People's Court web page.

Very recently, the State Intellectual Property Office (SIPO) (国家知识产权局 Guójiā Zhīshìquán Jú) started to publish on its web page cases SIPO felt were helpful for the courts and lawyers to better understand the application of the intellectual property law in China.

Although an increasing number of judgments are being published, a comprehensive official or even unofficial reporting system and editorial enhancements are not available. Moreover, case locators such as an index, digest, supplement, cross-reference and other finding tools, are rarely published.

C.   Chinese Legal Resources:

Chinese laws are not codified in one place as we find in the *United State Code*. If you are looking for a translation of a primary source, *Chinalawinfo* or *Isinolaw* provide the most comprehensive English translations of laws and administrative rules and regulations as well as cases. In November 2008, Thomson Reuters Legal launched *Westlaw China* which covers more than 300,000 laws and regulations and contains digests of laws for thirty-two topics in Chinese and nine topics in English. All this information is easily accessible with search tools familiar to any *Westlaw* user.

**Another resource is a Chinese government website**中国法院网 (ZhōngguóFǎyuànwǎng) *Chinese Court Net*[1]. Chinese Court Net is a free and comprehensive searchable database. World News Connection[2] also provides English translations of new PRC legislation. An on-line and print publication, *China Law and Practice*, lists new laws and regulations with their titles, issuing and effective dates, applicability, and main contents. With your subscription to *China Law and Practice*, the publisher provides up to three free full texts of laws per month. *China Law and Practice* also lists new laws and regulations with their titles and promulgation and implementation dates.

It is also worthwhile to try more general Internet search engines such as google.com for English and www.baidu.com, www.sohu.com, or www.sina.com for Chinese materials. In addition, you may be able to get help from Chinese law experts around the world by posting your inquiry to the Chinese law e-mail listserv such as China Law[3] or Chinese Law Prof Blog[4].

Journal literature as a secondary source is a good way to obtain background information and to locate the text of a foreign law and a citation. The Chinese Academic Journals Database can locate law review articles on your topics written in Chinese. Last, but not least, law libraries which hold Chinese legal materials, including the Library of Congress, provide access to collections on Chinese law in both English and Chinese language through their online catalog.

III.   Research Guides

A.   Research Methods & Guides

1.   *Guides to Research* <http://ls.wustl.edu/Chinalaw>

---

1 http://www.chinacourt.org (Chinese) or http://en.chinacourt.org/ (English)
2 http://wnc.fedworld.gov
3 http://hermes.gwu.edu/archives/chinalaw.html
4 http://lawprofessors.typepad.com/china_law_prof_blog/

This is an Internet Chinese Legal Research Center for Mainland China, Taiwan, and Hong Kong.

2. *ChinaLaw* < http://www.washlaw.edu/forint/asia/china.html>

Links to information on China's constitution, government, Chinese law firms, laws, China bar association, China dispute resolution, Chinese legal research, China's prime minister, legislature, and a China law guide.

3. *Chinese Legal Research Guide* <http://www.loc.gov/law/help/guide/nations/china.html>

4. *A Complete Research Guide to the Laws of the People's Republic of China* <http://www.llrx.com/features/prc.htm>

5. *Globalex Finding Chinese Law on the Internet* <http://www.nyulawglobal.org/globalex/China.htm>

6. Luo, Wei. *Chinese Law and Legal Research*. Buffalo, N.Y. W.S. Hein 2005.

7. *Chinese Area Studies Guide* < http://gort.ucsd.edu/ceal/>

8. *Law and Technology Resources for Legal Professionals* <http://www.llrx.com> Search by "China." This offers research guides on many different aspects of international law.

B. Useful Websites on Chinese Legal Research

1. *Web Resources for Chinese Law* <http://www.library.ubc.ca/law/chineselaw.html> Selected Internet resources for Chinese law. All sites are free and in English.

2. *China Law Reporter* < http://www.abanet.org/dch/committee.cfm?com=IC860000> Created by the American Bar Association International Law China Committee.

3. *Internet Law Library China* <http://www.lawmoose.com/internetlawlib/57.htm>

4. *China Law Databases* <http://florasapio.blogspot.com/2008/06/legal-databases.html>

5. *China Today: Law and Justice* < http://www.chinatoday.com/law/a.htm >

6. *China Law Digest* <http://www.chinalaw-digest.com/> Bilingual, monthly web digest. Covers the latest legal news, legislative developments, and important cases - free, but requires registration.

7. *Chinese Law* <http://ls.wustl.edu/Chinalaw/intersou.html>

8. *Martindale-Hubbell International Law Digest* <http://www.lexis.com/research/xlink?ORIGINATION_CODE=00188&source=MARHUB;INTDIG&search=&autosubmit=yes&searchtype=bool>

C. Finding Laws

Bilingual resources include:

1. 北大法律信息网 *LawInfoChina* <http://www.chinalawinfo.com/index.asp> (Chinese) or <http://www.lawinfochina.com/index.asp> (English). Houses a full text database of English translations of primary law and selected cases of the PRC.

2. *Isinolaw*. <http://www.isinolaw.com>. It provides legal information on the PRC in simplified and traditional Chinese and English.

3. 公报目录 *The People's Republic of China*

*Official Gazettes Tables of Contents* <http://china-lawinfo.com/Gazette/> (Chinese) or <http://china-lawinfo.com/Gazette/e_index.asp> (English)

4. *China Index* <http://www.oefre.unibe.ch/law/icl/ch_indx.html> China's constitution and declaration of human rights.

5. *NovexCn.com* <http://www.novexcn.com/> Translations of Chinese laws and regulations, as well as political, social, and economic news about China in English.

6. *Database of Laws and Regulations* <http://www.npc.gov.cn/englishnpc/Law/Integrated_index.html> On-line database hosting a collection of the laws enacted by the NPC and NPCSC and administrative regulations by the State Council.

7. *Ministry of Commerce of the People's Republic of China (MOFCOM)* <http://www.mofcom.gov.cn> (Chinese) or <http://english.mofcom.gov.cn> (English)

8. *Lexadin* < http://www.lexadin.nl/wlg/legis/nofr/oeur/lxwechi.htm> All inclusive comprehensive website with links to most Chinese laws.

Chinese language resources include:

1. 法律图书馆 *Law-lib* < www.law-lib.com> Offers a simple searchable database on Chinese laws and regulations.

2. 新法规速递 *New Chinese Laws and Regulations* <http://www.law-lib.com/law/>

3. 国家知识产权局 *State Intellectual Property Office* <http://www.sipo.gov.cn/sipo2008/> (Chinese) or <http://www.sipo.gov.cn/sipo_English/> (English)

4. 国信中国法律网<http://chinalaw.net/>

5. 中央政府门户网站 *PRC Government Homepage* <http://www.gov.cn/flfg/index.htm> (Chinese)

D. Finding Cases

Chinese or bilingual resources include:

1. 中国法院网 *Supreme People's Court website* <http://www.chinacourt.org> (Chinese) or <http://en.chinacourt.org/> (English)

2. 北大法律信息网 *LawInfoChina* <http://www.chinalawinfo.com/index.asp> (Chinese) or <http://www.lawinfochina.com/index.asp> (English)

3. 中国知识产权司法保护 *Judicial Protection of IPR in China* (Provides laws and case summaries on intellectual property rights in China) <http://www.chinaiprlaw.cn> (Chinese) or <http://www.chinaiprlaw.com/english/default.htm> (English)

4. 中国法律年鉴 *China Law Year Book*. Contains selected cases. An abridged English translation is available for the 1987 edition only.

English resources include:

1. *China's Foreign Trade (Online business magazines)* <http://www.cbw.com/cft/>

2. China Law Reports. Singapore: Butterworths Asia, in co-operation with China Law and Cultural Publications, 1995

E. Encyclopedias and Yearbooks

English or bilingual resources include:

1. *Encyclopedia Britannica Online Chinese law* <http://www.britannica.com/EBchecked/

topic/112592/Chineselaw#tab=active~checked%2 Citems~checked&title=Chinese%20law%20--%20 Britannica%20Online%20Encyclopedia>

2. Encyclopedia of Chinese Law. Hong Kong: Asia Law & Practice,1993-

3. Law Yearbook of China. Beijing: Press of Law Yearbook of China, 2002-

F. Bibliographic Databases / Library Catalogs Chinese or bilingual resources include:

1. 中国国家图书馆 *China National Library* <http://www5.nlc.gov.cn/> (Chinese) or <http://www.nlc.gov.cn/old/old/english.htm> (English) or <http://www.nlc.gov.cn/en/indexen.htm>

2. 北京大学图书馆 *Peking University Library* <http://www.lib.pku.edu.cn/>

3. 清华大学图书馆 *Tsinghua University Library* <http://innopac.lib.tsinghua.edu.cn/screens/opacmenu.html>

4. 中国法律图书馆在线 *China Law Library Online* <http://www.chinalawlib.org.cn/>

English resources include:

1. *WorldCat OCLC FirstSearch* <http://www.worldcat.org/> A major database of books and other materials

2. *Asian Law Online* < http://www.law.unimelb.edu.au/alc/bibliography/> A collection of English language materials on Asian laws. Includes books, chapters in books, journal articles and theses.

G. Listservs & Blogs

1. *China Law* <http://hermes.gwu.edu/archives/chinalaw.html>

2. *Chinese Law Prof Blog* <http://lawprofessors.typepad.com/china_law_prof_blog/>

3. *ChinaLawBlog* <Chinalawblog.com>

# Index

# China Law Reader Co-Author CVs

*Lawrence Foster*

Lawrence C. Foster first learned Chinese in the mid-1960s and his first trip to Asia (Japan, Taiwan and Hong Kong) was in 1968. Since then, he has made countless trips to Asia. His education includes a Ph.D. in Chinese language and literature (1974) and a law degree (1981). Larry's professional career began as a professor of Chinese language and literature. After obtaining his law degree, he worked as a lawyer in Hawaii for six years before joining the University of Hawaii's School of Law as Associate Dean. He later served as Dean of the School of Law and is currently a Professor of Law. He teaches Securities Regulation, legal writing, and Readings in Chinese Law.

Larry moved to Shanghai in 2005. He still teaches law part-time at the University of Hawaii, but most of the year he lives and works in Shanghai. For two and one-half years he was a Senior Consultant at the Zhong Lun law firm in Shanghai. Now he focuses on providing legal writing and reasoning training programs for young Chinese lawyers in Shanghai and teaching at Peking University's School of Transnational Law located in Shenzhen.

In addition to his professional work, Larry is an elected member of the governing council of the Inter-Pacific Bar Association (a regional business lawyers organization with over 1,000 members), immediate past-President of the international alumni association of the East-West Center, and an a member of Law Asia and the American Bar Association.

*Tiffany Yajima*

Tiffany Yajima has lived and worked in Shanghai for more than a decade. She previously served as Senior Researcher at a major international law firm in Shanghai and as Managing Editor of Communications & Publications at the American Chamber of Commerce in Shanghai where her work has been published extensively in the Chamber's Insight magazine. She now resides in Honolulu where she consults for think tanks and organizations focused on Asia-pacific-related issues. She also currently serves as Communications Executive focusing on issues management at a public relations firm in Honolulu.

Ms. Yajima is a graduate of Vassar College in Poughkeepsie, New York where she majored in Asian studies and Chinese and minored in Japanese and economics. She has studied at Beijing University and Capital Normal University in Beijing, China and at Kansai Gaidai University in Osaka, Japan.

She earned her juris doctor degree from the William S. Richardson School of Law at the University of Hawaii at Manoa in 2007, during which time she served as extern to a federal judge in the U.S. District Court for the District of Hawaii, was elected President of the law school's Pacific-Asian Legal Studies Organization, and served as Editor and Managing Editor of the Asian Pacific Law & Policy Journal.

Ms. Yajima is a U.S. licensed attorney and is a member of the Hawaii State Bar Association.

*Lin Yan*

Lin Yan is Assistant Professor of Law at Shanghai Jiao Tong University's Ko Guan Law School. He received a LLB and LLM at the East China University of Political Sciences and Law in 2003, and graduated from the University of Wisconsin Law School in 2006 where he earned a M.L.I. and S.J.D.

Yan currently resides in Shanghai where he teaches constitutional law, comparative constitutionalism and legislation at Ko Guan Law School. His professional research interests include constitutional review, the NPC's oversight power, property rights and constitution, and legislation.